The Virginia Venture

THE EARLY MODERN AMERICAS

Peter C. Mancall, Series Editor

Volumes in the series explore neglected aspects of early modern history in the western hemisphere. Interdisciplinary in character, and with a special emphasis on the Atlantic World from 1450 to 1850, the series is published in partnership with the USC-Huntington Early Modern Studies Institute.

THE VIRGINIA VENTURE

American Colonization and English Society, 1580–1660

Misha Ewen

PENN

UNIVERSITY OF PENNSYLVANIA PRESS

PHILADELPHIA

Published by
University of Pennsylvania Press
Philadelphia, Pennsylvania 19104-4112
www.upenn.edu/pennpress

Printed in the United States of America on acid-free paper
10 9 8 7 6 5 4 3 2 1

Hardcover ISBN 9781512822991
Ebook ISBN 9781512823004

A catalog record for this book is available from the Library of Congress.

CONTENTS

INTRODUCTION

In seventeenth-century England, news swirled about ventures across the globe. Stories of English conquest and catastrophe made their way into ports, alehouses, and parliament, and some landed in the laps of people, like Katherine Conway, in their homes. On 3 April 1626, Henry Smyth, a servant, wrote to Katherine about a thirty-year-old chambermaid that he had "procured for her," who "can write, and is a very good needlewoman . . . one of few words, and a good demeanor." The maid had twelve years' experience serving "with very curious gentlewomen," including, "for some time . . . Mrs Tracy who went into Virginia." He wrote that Mrs. Tracy would have taken the woman with her "out of the good opinion which she had of her," but it seems the maid decided to stay behind.[1] When Katherine, who was a Virginia Company investor, read Henry's letter, it had been almost twenty years since the establishment of England's first permanent colony in America, at Jamestown, Virginia. In that time, thousands of English women, men, and children had voyaged across the Atlantic Ocean and planted further colonies in North America and the Caribbean.

Henry's letter conveyed how, in the intervening years, from the perspective of people at home, English overseas expansion had become commonplace, everyday even. Katherine's first thought when she read this letter was probably that the unnamed woman had been lucky to escape the fate that befell her former employers. The maid had been employed in the Gloucestershire household of Mary Tracy and her husband William, a local gentleman and one of the founders of the Berkeley Hundred plantation in Virginia. William, Mary, and their children Thomas and Joyce sailed for the colony in September 1620. Within two years, two of family were dead. William died in April 1621 and Joyce was killed, with her new husband Nathaniel Powle, during the violence that swept through the English plantations on the morning of 22 March 1622. A third of colonists, totaling 350 individuals, including many from Berkeley Hundred, were killed by local Algonquians. Against the odds, Mary and Thomas apparently survived and were able to return to England. Despite the attempts of investors in England, the Berkeley plantation was never fully revived.[2]

Receiving Henry's letter would have been a sharp reminder for Katherine of the personal and financial risks associated with overseas colonization. She was one of the first women to invest in the Virginia Company, but like the other shareholders, she never received the riches that the company promised. The mention of Mary Tracy in Henry's letter would have struck another chord with Katherine, because Mary was the sister of Sir Edward Conway, Katherine's husband. The families had a further kinship connection, because William Tracy's sister Dorothy, who died in 1613, had been Edward's first wife.[3] This generation of English colonists and investors had suffered loss in more than one sense. Still, people in early modern England were not deterred, and neither was Katherine. She never voyaged to America herself, but woven throughout her life, there were similar threads that bound her, through personal attachments, to England's burgeoning overseas empire in the Atlantic world.[4] She was born Katherine Hueriblock to Dutch parents, Giles Hueriblock and Catharyne Hendriex, who settled in London during the reign of Edward VI, after fleeing civil and religious unrest in the Low Countries. Katherine came of age in Elizabethan London, where she witnessed an explosion in the consumption of luxury foreign goods, like silk, spices, and tobacco. This demand stimulated the expansion of English overseas trade and colonization, creating lucrative opportunities for merchant families such as her own. By the time that she died in 1639, aged seventy-four, Katherine had witnessed the development of England from a nation with little global influence, to an increasingly powerful one, with colonies in America and established trading factories in India and Indonesia. During the winter of 1627, not long after she received Henry's letter, from her home in London she started corresponding about investment in St. John's, Newfoundland. Ultimately, the Conways decided against the Newfoundland venture, but Edward did become a shareholder in the Guiana Company.[5] Katherine Conway is an illustrative example, then, of how people in Elizabethan and Stuart England encountered English colonization in the Atlantic world—as a series of uncertain, fitful, even disastrous, starts, which by 1660 had culminated in an empire.

English colonialism permeated many layers of domestic society, and individuals with the means to invest, like Katherine Conway, were not the only people who experienced colonization close to home. If we consider the unnamed maidservant in Henry Smyth's letter, her story is also indicative of how individuals gained intimate experience of English colonial enterprise. She would have been resident in the Tracy household in the months, maybe years, preceding their departure for Jamestown. She would have witnessed the feverish attempts of their associates to prepare local women and men for colonization in Virginia. This meant not only ensuring that their families were provided for, but also buying the items that they would need for plantation, and providing their food and lodging in the months, weeks, and then finally in the days leading up to their departure. Fitting out the *Margaret* in the summer of 1619, the Berkley Hundred investors accrued expenses that included 4s. to "the boatman that brought the cider," 8s. 6d. "for the lodging of the servants and washing their clothes," and 15s. for "lodging and diet to Eliz[abeth] Hibbert of Gatscomb."[6] There are hundreds, if not thousands, of "micro-narratives" like these that suggest how, in the first half of the seventeenth century, colonial enterprise in England became ubiquitous.[7]

The Virginia Venture draws upon this web of evidence to examine how ordinary English women, men, and children encountered and engaged with colonial activity in myriad ways that contributed to the development of England's first permanent colony in America. There was significant "social depth" to the domestic colonial project in the period before 1660, meaning that colonization in Virginia responded to demands from below as well as above, and galvanized support across English society. It required the cooperation and collaboration of a broad range of actors, from wealthy investors like Katherine Conway to the unnamed maid of the Tracy family. The early seventeenth century also marked a defining era of colonial development and its relationship with English society at home. By mid-century, English empire-builders had tried and tested approaches to colonization that were intimately connected to practices in the domestic sphere. Colonization weighed heavily on local concerns and national debates, and the result was that English societal issues, including charity and poor relief, customary rights and moral economy, were all inflected by expansion in America.

Decades of scholarship have presented early English attempts to establish colonies in the Atlantic world as amounting to little more than "trial-and-error efforts," which received scant attention from the state or wider population until the decades following the Restoration.[8] More recently, historians have pushed back against this analysis and demonstrated that colonization in America was an important issue of state that preoccupied Jacobean policymakers and gentlemen.[9] Yet, the argument that the public, in its broadest sense, lacked interest in American colonization remains untested. My aim is to challenge this claim, by exploring how English citizens across the social spectrum both supported and resisted the practices associated with colonization. Writing this book required venturing much more deeply into the archive in order to reveal that across English society, whether it was through investment, charitable collections, or political debate, by writing letters, transporting vagrant children, or cultivating tobacco, women and men actively engaged with colonization in Virginia. These various encounters and experiences suggest that, contrary to the established view, there *was* significant social depth to English colonial enterprise as it emerged in the early seventeenth century.

The Virginia Venture provides a vantage point on how the activities of a cross section of English society made colonization in Jamestown possible and, in turn, the impact that colonization had on their lives. This includes an examination of how colonialism intertwined with the domestic sphere more broadly, determining that colonization in Virginia was intimately connected with English society through the shaping of behaviors and practices. Focusing on this significant reciprocal component of English colonialism reconfigures our understanding of the relationship between the Atlantic world and the metropole, showing that colonization in Virginia did more than occupy idle space in the English imperial imaginary. Rather, society at home was infused by the colonial project in various and contrasting ways: it crept into constitutional debates in parliament and colored everyday experiences in English towns and villages.

In 1626, when Katherine Conway received Henry Smyth's letter, many of the defining moments of early English attempts at colonization in the Atlantic world had already passed. The failed Roanoke venture was fading from memory and there was little hope of finding any of the surviving colonists left behind in 1587, who it was supposed had found refuge with local Carolina Algonquians.[10] In 1604, King James signed the Treaty of London, which brought to an end two decades of conflict with Spain and unencumbered raids on Spanish ships. James's reign marked a new phase of plantation and exploration in Ireland and the Americas, in places that were, importantly, not already claimed by other European empires.[11] There was no clean break with Elizabethan ventures, however, and many of the individuals who had promoted colonization in Virginia during Elizabeth's reign, including Sir Walter Ralegh and the polymath Richard Hakluyt, supported renewed efforts to colonize in the Jacobean era.[12] The Virginia Company received its charter from the king in 1606 and initially consisted of a council of elite merchants and nobles. While the London company directed colonization in the south of Virginia, the Plymouth company, founded by West Country interests, in Bristol, Exeter, and Plymouth, sent its colonists to the north in Sagadahoc, Maine. But the men and boys who set sail for Sagadahoc in 1606 hardly survived their first winter. The colonists succumbed to faction and failed to establish friendly trading relations with the local Indigenous population and were forced to abandon their project after little over a year.[13]

The Jamestown colonists hardly fared better. In the first few years, colonists suffered the impact of disease, starvation, and war with the Powhatans. John Rolfe's successful experiments with tobacco cultivation and his marriage to Pocahontas in 1614, ending the First Powhatan War, signaled a new phase of peace and prosperity. Between 1619 and 1622 alone, a further 3,570 colonists arrived in Virginia, including greater numbers of women. These advances bolstered the colonial economy and population, and they coincided with the arrival of the first enslaved Africans in English North America, at Point Comfort, Virginia, in August 1619. Only one month earlier, the Virginia Assembly, which gave property-owning male colonists a hand in governing themselves, met for the first time.[14] But this hard-won progress—as the Virginia Company and colonists saw it—was almost wiped out by the violence of 1622 and the Second Powhatan War that followed.[15] The English seized upon the attack as a "massacre," using it to justify an even more violent policy against the Algonquian people.[16] This event, alongside faction within the company, and the accusation that colonists had built an economy completely dependent upon tobacco, contributed to the dissolution of the Virginia Company in 1624. Charles I subsequently brought the colony under Crown authority in 1625. For Katherine Conway, and other company shareholders who were observing events from England, it was a disappointing outcome. But the colony was not, in all eyes, a failed experiment. Instead, in Jamestown the English had realized their ambition of permanent colonization in America, and the colony would influence the progression of English colonialism elsewhere, not least by establishing a commitment to plantation slavery.[17] As Katherine Conway reminds us, Virginia was never the only potential option for colonization in the Atlantic world: Ireland, Guiana, and Newfoundland were also within the orbit of her family. But Virginia is a distinct example of how English domestic colonial enterprise developed in this period. The Virginia Company stirred new interest in American colonization, galvanized an unprecedented amount of wider public support, and uniquely influenced and responded to issues in the domestic sphere. Virginia determined the shape of colonial enterprise elsewhere in the Atlantic world, and it is an example for which the surviving archival material is also incredibly rich.

Ensuring the permanence of the colony depended upon the Virginia Company's success at rallying local support across England. Weaving together these imperial stories reveals a rich tapestry of efforts that stretched across the whole of English society. This is not to deny that there was also resistance to the Virginia Company's efforts. In 1619, when a woman named Ruthe Pittman, from Wells, Somerset, appeared before the Justices of the Peace, she reported how she had been violently robbed of 6s. won playing at the Virginia Company's lottery.[18] It was stories such as these that helped to bring about the early termination of the lotteries, which had done so much to bolster the company's coffers. Johanna Howell, who was a persistent offender, succeeded in avoiding criminal transportation to Virginia when she "pleaded the belly" in court and was found to be pregnant.[19] Even when facing powerful colonial pressures, then, women could reassert their agency. Local people, in orchards and gardens in southwest England, cultivated crops of American tobacco from seeds their friends had sent home—tobacco that made its way into smokers' pipes in London. In 1658, thirty-six Commonwealth officers traveled to Cheltenham, Gloucestershire, on horseback to stamp out domestic tobacco growing. The Virginia Company, and later merchants trading to Virginia too, continuously petitioned the government to see it eradicated in favor of colonial produce. Nonetheless, the officers reported their surprise at being met by a "street full" of protesting "men and women," English tobacco growers.[20] These vignettes demonstrate just how local the colonial project could be. But they do more than reveal the ways in which ordinary folk, in their local settings, became entangled with the colonial enterprise far overseas: drawing out these stories emphasizes how the domestic priorities and actions of a diverse range of women and men actively shaped colonization.

Consider also Elizabeth Waters, who acted as the executrix of her husband John Waters, a biscuit maker. In 1623, she petitioned the Virginia Company for £13 10s., money it owed to her husband for ship biscuit he had supplied to the company. Although it was not explicitly recorded, it is likely that she worked alongside her husband in this trade and knew the business well. However, the company refused to reimburse her, unless she could provide a witness to the transaction. This led to her appearing in the Court of Chancery to compel Nicholas Dorling to confirm the truth of her claim.[21] This crumb of evidence speaks to the ways in which women were enmeshed in the domestic economies that supported empire-building, the pressure they put on trading companies, and how their work and agency is regularly concealed in archival records. It is only due to the company's reticence that Elizabeth's endeavors came to light. Including metropolitan women like Elizabeth in this book, in multiple and varied roles, forces us to recalibrate *what* constituted early modern empire-building and *who* was involved in it. *The Virginia Venture* illuminates what a broader public of empire-makers looked like, and how their everyday activity—the small tasks they performed—shaped the colonial project.[22] Individuals and events that might have been considered peripheral, parochial, or unimportant by previous generations of scholars actually reveal the extent to which everyday life in England strengthened the ties between colonization in America and society at home.

Of course, it is important to recognize that there was a spectrum of participation in domestic colonial enterprise, from what could be considered more passive or fleeting, to active, deeper, engagement. Often, this also means that the archival footprint is heavier for individuals who were more tightly involved with the colonial project, making it difficult to determine the exact motivations of those who contributed at the periphery: parishioners who donated money, or players at the company lotteries, for instance. Their imprint on the archive is lighter, as their interaction with the colonial project was short-lived. We cannot be certain that they understood the handing over of their wages as an act that would facilitate overseas expansion, by outfitting ships, clothing indentured servants, or fortifying Jamestown. But it would also be naive to assume that people made no plausible connection, when sermons in church and a ballad written for the lotteries explicitly promoted those associations. Equally, just because ordinary English women and men donated money in church, this does not mean that they were wholehearted supporters of colonization. From the very beginning, colonization had its detractors.

Still, whether they fully supported it or not, individuals' decision-making made colonization possible. *The Virginia Venture* explores this complex spectrum of engagement with English colonial enterprise, focusing on how broad swathes of English citizens experienced and contributed to colonization. In their roles as investors, donors, and migrants, or in positions of authority, like churchwardens, Justices of the Peace, and governors of houses of correction, women and men smoothed the way for practices in England that enabled overseas colonization to advance. It makes sense to examine this much more expansive experience of colonization, as most ordinary people in England would have encountered it and understood its implications. This means writing about individuals and events even when the evidence is more limited, instead working to "stretch archival fragments" in the words of scholar Marisa Fuentes.[23]

The following chapters explore key aspects of colonial enterprise as it emerged in English society. While each chapter focuses on a different theme, this varied approach is, nonetheless, purposeful. It allows us to get at the more discreet, and harder-to-reach, corners of English society in this period, towards an understanding of how ordinary citizens as well as the Crown and company responded to colonization. The chapters also follow an important stage of the early colonial project, from generating interest and raising investment, to mobilizing a labor force and producing commodities—in this case, tobacco. Chapter 1 is a study of how information about English colonization in America circulated through various forms, from print and manuscript, to material samples and eyewitness testimony, raising awareness as well as shattering expectations. Focusing on Virginia Company investors, Chapter 2 elucidates the ways that elite women and men were drawn into investing, through the persuasion of friends and familial networks, and the kinds of economic and social behaviors that company investment prompted. Chapter 3 further nuances our understanding of how capital investment in colonial enterprise was mobilized, examining the Virginia Company lotteries and church and charitable collections. Especially for those that could not afford shares in the company, investing in this way was accessible and proved to be widespread, ensuring that ordinary women and men were also implicated in the financing of empire. Chapter 4 explores how debates on poverty and paternalism intersected, and were associated, with criminal transportation, efforts to persuade poor families to migrate, and the indenture of poor children. This chapter shows that the practices associated with colonial transportation also forced new debates on domestic welfare reform. Finally, the development of the tobacco industry in England is the focus of Chapter 5. Tobacco was crucial for the economic sustainability of the Virginia Company and colony, yet the "domestication" of tobacco reveals how the entanglement of domestic and colonial interests sparked contestations over customary rights and political and moral economy throughout the seventeenth century.

The chapters move forward chronologically, and the analytical focus of the chapters also shifts. Whereas the first chapters explore the perspective of elite women and men who engaged with colonization, as promoters and financial investors, later chapters examine how actors from across the social spectrum responded to colonization, through donating money and playing at lotteries, as well as through voluntary and forced migration, trade, and consumption. The final two chapters, for example, focus on how the laboring poor, vagrants, and pauper children reacted to the practices of, and debates on, transatlantic migration and trade. This approach illustrates how engagement with colonial enterprise cut across layers of society in England, mobilizing a much broader social base of participants who underpinned the first permanent English colony in America.

In 1631, Katherine Conway was widowed, and seems to have lived out the rest of her life in Acton, Middlesex, where she was buried in 1639. Shortly after her husband's demise, she bought new items for her home, furnishing it with "Turkey work chairs," and, for herself, new clothes including a camlet gown, velvet cloak, and beaver hat, made with fur from America. She had in her employ a maid named Mary, who could have been the woman recommended by Henry Smyth five years before.[24] In these final years, she lived comfortably, helped in no small part by an annuity of £200 from plantations in Ireland she inherited from her husband.[25] Her wealth and the very fabric of her surroundings, from the clothing she wore to the chairs she sat on, were directly derived from England's overseas colonial and commercial ventures. And she was, herself, directly involved in driving trade and colonization, in Virginia and elsewhere. This book explores how individuals in England, like Katherine, Elizabeth Waters, and the tobacco planters who rioted in Cheltenham, were made actors in seventeenth-century empire-building and how they responded to the significant changes it wrought upon the fabric of English society itself.

CHAPTER 1

Circulating Ideas

Print, Rumor, and Material Samples

In March 1582, Thomas Aldworth, the mayor of Bristol, and the city's leading merchants gathered together to discuss the possibilities of colonization in Virginia. In 1578 Elizabeth I granted Sir Humphrey Gilbert letters patent to establish a colony in North America, but now he needed the practical support and investment of the country's nobility and merchants. The geographer Richard Hakluyt published *Divers Voyages Touching the Discovery of America* in 1582, a practical and comprehensive guide to colonization in North America, to further Gilbert's project. From the Bristol mayor himself and also Sir George Peckham, a Catholic gentleman, word of *Divers Voyages* reached Sir Francis Walsingham, the queen's principal secretary. Walsingham described in a letter to Hakluyt how he had heard that he had "endeavoured, or given much lights for the discovery of the western parts yet unknown." Walsingham, together with Aldworth, then drew up a plan for Hakluyt to use his printed publication to persuade the city of Bristol to invest.[1] So it was that "an assembly of the merchants . . . gathered," probably in the city's common hall, on 27 March 1582. Letters privately sent by Walsingham to Aldworth were "read in public," but additionally, "some good light [was] given by Mr Hakluyt unto them that were ignorant of this country and enterprise." Hakluyt's speech and Walsingham's letters were so persuasive "that the motion grew generally so well liked that there was . . . set down by men's own hands . . . the sum of 2000 marks or upwards."[2] According to Peter Mancall, Hakluyt offered a "new kind of expertise: the knowledge of someone who knew the original manuscripts, had pored over the various editions of travel accounts, and whose own authority manifested itself in print." While Hakluyt's expertise was demonstrated by his mastery of manuscript sources, he also relied upon the tales of travelers. An early biographer noted that he kept "constant intelligence with the most noted Seamen at *Wapping* near *London*."[3] Hakluyt's successful endeavors in 1582 meant that Gilbert had sufficient investment to set sail for America in 1583, but he died at sea on his return from Newfoundland, never having achieved his purpose of planting a colony. Under the aegis of his half-brother, Sir Walter Ralegh, the venture continued, and in 1584 the first English colonists arrived at Roanoke, present-day North Carolina, marking a decisive shift in English colonial engagement with America.

During the first years of English colonization in the Atlantic world, when ships anchored home after returning from America, they spilled forth news and goods that were highly valued by observers in England. The episode in the Bristol common hall relays one of the ways that ideas about America were conveyed to audiences and how they were subsequently persuaded to invest in colonization. It is through such glimpses and fragmentary reporting that we can glean how a broader public interpreted the news, images, and ideas that came out of America. Previously, scholars including Catherine Armstrong have argued that a paucity of evidence means it is difficult to know how people responded to news from America.[4] But through a close reading of letters, manuscript, and print sources it is possible to challenge this perception. Instead, a picture builds of how ordinary citizens as well as elites gathered their knowledge from various sources, and how they determined what news should be heeded or dismissed. There was no single source of authentic knowledge about the "New World."

The tales of travelers and eyewitness accounts of ventures in Virginia, Sagadahoc, Guiana, Bermuda, and Newfoundland, and in search of the Northwest Passage, mingled in oral, epistolary, and print cultures. Indigenous captives in merchant households, talkative sailors, and material samples from America changed perspectives along with the sermons people heard in church or the pamphlets they read. As we will see, there was a vital connection between how people in parish churches, towns, and villages across England consumed information about, and readily participated in, a range of overseas projects. Understanding how people in England encountered ideas about America illuminates how domestic English society was transformed in this period, as individuals took up new identities, ways of thinking, and behaving.[5] But it also provides the essential backdrop for understanding how individuals' interest in Virginia was sparked. Only then can we appreciate how they were encouraged to promote, to invest, to migrate, or to demand colonial goods. An awareness of how ideas about Virginia, or America more broadly, spread throughout England clarifies the key theme of this book: how people responded to and participated in the domestic colonial project.

Promoting Virginia

Following attempts to settle English men at Roanoke in 1585, Thomas Harriot published *A Brief and True Report of the New Found Land of Virginia* in 1588, a work that "built up a substantial segment of western knowledge of the Americas."[6] Harriot's *True Report* described the appearance and habits of the Carolina Algonquians and raised hopes that colonists could engage in the production of valuable commodities like wine, oil, and sugar cane, woad, sassafras, pearls and silk, iron, copper, flax, and hemp.[7] Representations of the Indigenous peoples of America as well as investors' firsthand experience of Indigenous captives, visitors, and guests significantly shaped understandings of colonization in America. Harriot's *True Report* was co-authored by two Algonquian-speaking men, Manteo and Wanchese, who assisted him with the composition of the Algonquian dictionary and provided information about the people and geography of the Carolina coastline.[8] Also accompanying Harriot on the voyage to Roanoke was John White, who produced the first English images of the Algonquian people that inhabited the east coast of North America. White's watercolors, or limnings, captured the liveliness of his subjects. A medium associated with foreignness and strangeness, limnings also made observers feel that they were viewing subjects close-up, with their own eyes. These images carried the "visual-rhetorical effects of eyewitnessing" and could be just as persuasive as written accounts.[9] It is difficult to estimate how widely his watercolors circulated at the time, but no doubt leading patrons of the Virginia project including Queen Elizabeth, Sir Walter Ralegh, Thomas Harriot, and Richard Hakluyt would have received the first glimpses.

The publication of Harriot's *True Report* in 1588 came shortly after the discovery that the first garrison of men, left behind in 1586, had deserted. Supporters of colonization in Virginia were eager to bolster public support, making the publication of the third edition of Harriot's work in 1590, with Theodor de Bry's engravings based on John White's watercolors, very timely. Promoting Virginia gained new urgency in light of news of the "lost" Roanoke colonists. In 1587, John White had established around one hundred men, women, and children at Roanoke, including his own daughter and granddaughter, Eleanor and Virginia Dare. He returned to England in 1587 to gather new supplies but was prevented from returning to Roanoke as planned because of mounting tension between England and Spain. In anticipation of an assault, the Crown enforced a stay on English shipping, which continued after the failed Spanish Armada in 1588. By the time White was able to return in 1590, the colonists at Roanoke were gone. It was assumed they had been taken in by the nearby Croatan people, although this was never confirmed. Although there was no way to wholly manage this devastating news, the 1590 edition suggests that perceptions of Indigenous peoples, including their civility, was essential for underlining the viability of colonization in Virginia.[10]

The colonization of Jamestown in 1607 heralded a revival of publications on America.[11] The company itself published texts every year from 1609 to 1617 and in 1620, 1621, and 1624; in the first months of 1609 alone, eight sermons were delivered and several subsequently printed on its behalf.[12] "New World" promotional literature possessed significant rhetorical power, as Michael Drayton's poem "To the Virginian Voyage" suggests: "thy voyages attend / industrious Hakluyt / whose reading shall inflame / men to seek fame."[13] The Virginia Company's literary productions were particularly persuasive because they appealed to diverse groups in society, including those who were profit-driven, pious, or adventurous. The colonization of Virginia was presented as an endeavor that would return wealth of a material and non-material kind. Adventurers were promised that their pockets would be lined with gold, but of equal importance was the potential for the spiritual transformation of the Virginia Algonquians and the benefits that colonization would bring to the commonwealth at home.

There was, however, a more widespread contemporary preoccupation with literature that had a global flavor, including travel writing and representations of "otherness" in print and on the stage.[14] Inventories of bookshops and private and public libraries indicate that readers were interested in writings on America. The collected works of Anglican clergyman Samuel Purchas, *Purchas His Pilgrimage* (1613) and *Purchas His Pilgrims* (1625), were particularly popular.[15] Texts such as these were not just privately owned; instead public libraries in Norwich and Dorchester, both towns that the Virginia Company lotteries visited, also had copies.[16] *Purchas His Pilgrimage* was a composite work of various print and manuscript sources. Purchas drew his inspiration and evidence from Theodor de Bry's *America*, published in 1590, and the second edition of Richard Hakluyt's *The Principal*

Navigations, Voyages and Discoveries of the English Nation, published between 1598 and 1600. He also relied on more recent accounts from travelers like James Rosier and Virginia colonists Captain John Smith, Sir Thomas Dale, and Thomas West, Baron De la Warr, as well as Robert Gray's sermon for the Virginia Company.[17] The third edition of *Purchas His Pilgrimage* was printed in 1617, after John King, the Bishop of London and Purchas's patron, invited him to a dinner where he met Pocahontas, now baptized Rebecca, and her husband John Rolfe. In 1617, Purchas also met and spoke with Tomocomo, Pocahontas's kinsman.[18] We might wonder whether Purchas's encounters with Algonquians in England, including one who had converted to Christianity, renewed his enthusiasm for colonization in Virginia and spurred him to rush out a third edition. Either way, the interest that the second edition stimulated was probably good timing for the Virginia Company, which was using Pocahontas's visit to raise further public support and donations for the colony.[19]

First-hand experience of colonization may also have determined individual reading practices. Gentlewoman Anne Southwell did not invest in the Virginia Company, but she had connections to people and places that would have sparked her interest in English colonial enterprise. She lived in the Munster Plantation, Ireland, from 1603 until 1627, with her first husband, Thomas Southwell, who acquired land in Ireland from Walter Ralegh in 1598. Shortly following her return to England, she moved to Acton, Middlesex, in 1631, with her second husband Captain Henry Sibthorpe, where Virginia Company investor Lady Conway was her neighbor.[20] Southwell and Conway worshipped at St. Mary's Acton, where both have surviving church memorial tablets.[21] Southwell and Sibthorpe owned texts that would have quenched their interest in English colonial projects in Ireland and America, and more broadly European colonization in America, observations of non-European peoples, and Indigenous food and plants, including tobacco. This fascination is suggested by several books that were clustered in an inventory, including Samuel Purchas's *Purchas His Pilgrims* (1625) and John Gerard's *The Herbal or General History of Plants* (1597), which contained entries on tobacco. Women especially used herbals to influence design and embroidery. They also owned copies of Michel de Montaigne's *Essays* (1613), including "Of Cannibals," which was immediately followed by a copy of what might have been the work of French travel writer Fynes Moryson's *Itinerary* (1617).[22] The close personal proximity of men and women like Southwell and Sibthorpe to colonial projects, investors, and colonists no doubt influenced their consumption of literature.

In promoting colonization, the Virginia Company turned to a range of literary genres to entice readers and attract investors. The company's accounts provide some insight into how it produced and subsequently circulated printed books and sermons. Receipts for expenses in the period from May 1622 to May 1623 record sums that were paid to buy, copy, and translate print. These texts highlight the various issues that concerned colonists, as well as the different genres of promotional literature with which the company engaged. For instance, there were attempts in this period to diversify the colony's economy, moving away from a reliance on tobacco, signaled by the payment of 4s. 17d. "for a draught of the restraint of tobacco." Instead, money was spent to furnish colonists with books about silk production. The company paid 6s. "for writing out of a book on directions for feeding silkworms"; a further 2s. for copying out a sheet concerning silkworms; £1 10s. to the Frenchman and Keeper of Silkworms at Whitehall and Greenwich, John Bonoeil, for translating a French book on silkworms; and 7s. 6d. for copying nine sheets on "ordering" silkworms. Bonoeil's treatise on sericulture, written at the behest of Sir Edwin Sandys, was first published in 1620, and several copies were sent to Virginia to guide households in silk as an alternative to tobacco.[23] The accounts also record payments for the reproduction of promotional pamphlets and sermons. Robert Peasly was paid 4d. to "bear his charges to Graves-End" and for writing out four sheets of "the Present State of Virginia." He received a further 4s. for copying out six sheets of the "Declaration of the State of Virginia." Among these payments was a further 2s. 4d. for "four of Copeland's sermons," *Virginia's God Be Thanked*, printed in 1622.[24] The company was engaged in the production of a range of texts, including ones that bridged written and oral communication. It was through the genres of ballads and sermons that the company communicated with wider, illiterate audiences—who heard them in churches and in taverns—ensuring that they were informed about colonization in Virginia.[25]

Company sermons, alongside the distribution of company literature to booksellers around England, presented geographically dispersed opportunities for encounters with the promotion of Virginia.[26] When parishes across England collected donations for the colony and colonists, it is not difficult to imagine that ministers would have peppered their sermons with images of America and the evangelizing mission of colonists. Early writers of Virginia Company–sponsored sermons, like William Symonds, Robert Gray, and William Crashaw, who all published in 1609, found that most of their efforts were directed toward defending the project against criticism, including the right of the English to dispossess the Indigenous inhabitants of their land. Discussing the necessity of colonization to bring about civility, Symonds wrote: "One saith, England is a sweet country. True indeed . . . that whereas the country was as wild a forest, but nothing so fruitful, as Virginia, and the people in their nakedness did arm themselves in a coat armour of Woad, fetching their Curets and Polderns, from a painters shop: by the civil care of conquerors and planters it is now become a very paradise."[27] His sermon reflected the personal and familial concerns of potential colonists too, including the prospect of leaving loved ones behind and forfeiting their claims to inheritance.[28] Symonds also bemoaned the lack of enthusiasm shown by the ministry, whose "pretence of zeal, is clear discovered to be but hypocrisy, when we rather choose to mind unprofitable questions at home, then gaining souls abroad."[29] He entreated potential adventurers to "go on courageously, and notwithstanding the snorting idleness of the ministry, suspect not the blessing of God."[30]

Promoters of Virginia adopted the ballad genre with similar purpose, producing *Londons Lottery* (1612) and *Good News from Virginia* (1623) in order to appeal to the "common sort." The particular aim of the first ballad was to persuade individuals up and down English society to purchase tickets for the lottery, but the second ballad that was printed in the wake of the 1622 Powhatan attack on colonists encouraged continued migration to Virginia. The first part of *Good News* described how English colonists "slew those enemies / that massacred our men: / Took prisoners, corn and burnt their towns." After "shedding many Indians bloods," the author claimed "not one dares show a head."[31] What the English referred to as the "massacre" justified an immediate, bloody retaliation, and observers like Edward Waterhouse claimed it relieved English colonists from showing goodwill toward their Algonquian neighbors.[32] The ballad then turned toward the recovery of the colony following this disaster, and assured that "The Iron works and silk works both, / and vines shall be replanted." The ballad was concerned, then, with reassuring investors and potential settlers that the English had regained control in Virginia and were on a path to prosperity. It suggested that the survival of the colony only depended upon the transportation of more English men and women. The example of the gentlewoman Margaret Wyatt (née Sandys) was used to shame hesitant would-be settlers to "adventure": "The wife unto our Governor, / did safely here arrive: / With many gallants following her, / whom God preserve alive. / What man would stay when Ladies gay, / both lives and fortunes leaves."[33] The company's promotional literature, including ballads and sermons, was not just rehearsing godly arguments for colonization, but proffering news, persuading potential settlers, and shaping policy. Sermons and ballads are essential for understanding how ideas about America were disseminated in England, as their form allowed them to be consumed by audiences from various social backgrounds. Unlike with elite collections of Americana that were privately owned or could only be viewed after paying a fee, it is possible to imagine how through this media, ideas about America trickled down into wider society.[34]

Like the Virginia Company's "running lotteries," which traveled widely, print also brought colonization in Virginia closer to home for people across the country. Anthony Hilton, who had been employed by Gabriel Barbour to travel to Virginia and afterward the Hudson River in search of the Northwest Passage, wrote an excited letter to his mother Elizabeth Hilton on the first day of his voyage to Virginia. Hilton told his mother that he expected to return within two years, with "rich loading, a famous discovery, and much credit," and urged her to learn more about his destination. "Of all things concerning Virginia," he wrote, "you may fully understand by a book lately set forth in 1622." His recommendation suggests that company literature had played an important role in his decision to "adventure." He also instructed his mother that "the last edition" could be purchased "at Darlington, if not send to York for it." It is likely that Hilton had previously purchased Virginia Company print in these towns, which were 3 and 40 miles respectively from the village of Hurworth where his mother lived, and 216 and 173 miles from London.[35] Close proximity to London was not essential for access to print, and it seems neither was it necessary in order to consume literature about America.[36] Rather, readers could find relevant material in the vibrant provincial print market.

As Hilton's letter suggests, readers bought and circulated promotional literature, but they also actively engaged with it, developing their own ideas about colonization in the process. One reader in question, Nicholas Ferrar, had a significant personal and professional interest in Virginia.[37] In correspondence with his brother William, in January 1619, Nicholas revealed that he was following matters in the colony closely. He wrote, "I hear Mr Rolfe, hath made a particular book," *A True Relation of the State of Virginia* (1617).[38] John Rolfe directed his discourse to the king, urging for more "good and sufficient men" to "adventure" to the colony, so that "then might trial be made what lieth hidden in the womb of the ground."[39] Ferrar hoped Rolfe's text would "give good satisfaction here to curious demands," and suggested that the tract would affirm the "rights . . . of the Virginians." With the creation of the Virginia Assembly in 1619 and the ascendancy of Sir Edwin Sandys as leader of the company the previous year, colonists were eager to have their privileges as English subjects and rights as "ancient planters" confirmed. Ferrar felt that these issues were "but an ornament." Instead, he interpreted the real value of Rolfe's writing in the "knowledge . . . and full understanding" exhibited of "the real commodities" in Virginia. In response to *A True Relation*, he encouraged William to "employ your mind, and of all your observations pray you keep a perfect day book and let nothing escape you that you enquire not of" during his time in Virginia.[40] Nicholas Ferrar encouraged further textual production at a time when the success of the Virginia colony was increasingly important to his family.

In this same period, publications appeared that focused on the eyewitness testimony of those who had actually spent time at Jamestown. Early colonists like Captain John Smith, Sir George Percy, and Ralph Hamor all put pen to paper about their experiences. Smith's particular reverence of his status as an experienced eyewitness was reflected by one of the dedicatory verses in *The General History* (1624). Thomas Macarnesse wrote, "That thou might *read* and *know* and safely *see*, / What he by *practice*, thou by *Theory*."[41] Hamor was similarly compelled to offer his own account of the colony and the recent brokering of peaceable relations with Wahunsenacawh, the leader of the Powhatan, following Pocahontas's kidnapping and conversion.[42] Alluding to the material relations that had been established between Virginia and England, he wrote of tobacco that "Samples have been sent home, and no man disputeth the goodness," he had even tasted it himself.[43] It was not just Hamor's eye that could be relied upon, then, but his broader sensory perception.

Recording observations was not unique to the Virginia project. Similar journals were kept by Newfoundland's early settlers to assess whether long-term colonization was feasible.[44] The Sagadahoc colonists similarly recorded their progress, which Sir Ferdinando Gorges delivered to Robert Cecil, the Earl of Salisbury. In December 1607 he wrote, "I have sent unto your Lordship the journals that were taken by on of the ships, as I received it from their going out, until their return, by which the navigation will appear to be as easy as to Newfoundland but much more hopeful."[45] If William Ferrar did record his observations in Virginia, nothing has survived. Yet, anything that might have reached Nicholas in England may have provided him with important information, as shortly afterward he co-wrote, with Thomas Winston, *A Declaration of the State of the Colony and Affairs in Virginia*, published in 1620.[46]

Like Richard Hakluyt before, writers continued to rely upon the eyewitness accounts of sailors and travelers in order to produce texts that, they hoped, would encourage investors and guarantee the success of English colonization in America.

Despite the contemporary emphasis on writing and recording, the printed word was not necessarily valued or trusted more than that which was spoken. On the first page of the main text of Robert Johnson's *The New Life of Virginia* (1612), one reader scribbled "*Credite me vobis folium recitare sib(yllae),*" which translates as "Trust me to recite Sybil's leaf," or "I'm telling the gospel truth," a phrase borrowed from Juvenal's *Satires*, and, no doubt, meant to amuse other readers. The effect is that even before readers have devoured the whole text, they are confronted with its potential falsehoods.[47] Early modern print was certainly contested, but this did not prevent the Virginia Company or its supporters from seeking to overcome negative publicity through publications.[48] Printed literature was from the very beginning of English overseas expansion, and continued to be, a key device for developing knowledge about America and generating interest and investment in colonization.

Discoursing on Virginia

The physical distance between England and America was an obvious barrier to gathering reliable news. John Pory experienced this firsthand when he settled in Virginia. He described his position as "remote in place," and begged his patron to "have a little compassion upon me, and be pleased to send me, what pamphlets and relations of the Interim since I was with you."[49] For elite gentlemen whose livelihoods relied upon their ability to stay abreast of foreign affairs, including English diplomats posted in European cities, the challenges of geographic distance were also acute. Their letters reveal their anxiety to gather and verify sought-after news.[50] The veracity of printed reports about Virginia was often doubted, and news about colonial efforts that traveled through diplomatic correspondence on the Continent was received with similar hesitancy. For this reason, proximity to urban centers like London, Brussels, Paris, and The Hague provided individuals with a highly valued connection to wider news and print networks.[51]

Jacobean gentlemen's correspondence reveals an interconnected pan-European network of individuals who shared news about Virginia. First, there was Dudley Carleton, who was twenty-six years old when he was made ambassador to Venice in 1610, after which he was appointed to Savoy in 1615 and The Hague in 1616. During this time, he was supplied with anything newsworthy by John Chamberlain, a "man of letters," who spent his days news- and gossip-gathering in St. Paul's.[52] John Chamberlain was also a close friend of the diplomat Ralph Winwood, who was a promoter and director of the Virginia Company. Chamberlain and Winwood were members of a literary fellowship known as the Sireniacs, which included the diplomat Sir Thomas Edmondes, Jean Beaulieu, and Samuel Calvert, who was a clerk of the Virginia Company (as late as 1622). Winwood was also an associate of the ambassador Sir William Trumbull, who also received many letters from Beaulieu.[53]

Diplomats were keen observers of events in Virginia, and their letters are littered with news about the colony. Writing from Venice on 7 August 1608, where he was dispatched as an ambassador, Henry Wotton told Cecil, "There is here much discoursing of his Majesty's footings and foundations in Virginia, which I pray the God of Heaven to prosper."[54] It is also clear that supplying a patron with news was considered an obligation. Jean Beaulieu, John Searle, and Sir Thomas Edmondes all wrote to Trumbull of the departure of Thomas West, Baron De La Warr, for Virginia on 8 March 1610.[55] A few days earlier, Trumbull, who was posted in Brussels, received an apology from Sir John Wentworth (whose "letters have slept") for failing to keep him updated. Wentworth made up for this oversight now, writing that on his return to "town" he had found "every man's ears open to hear and hands full of news." Spencer, probably William Spencer, had died; John Brook and Sir Thomas Roe had sailed for Guiana; and the inaccurate news that Gates and Sir Thomas Dale were both "reputed dead with my Lord De La Warr for Virginia." "Thus," he wrote, "the world grows full of action, as is reported both from your parts France and Cleve."[56]

Correspondents closely followed and reported on events about the Virginia colony, but in their letters, they also offered observations on colonization. When, in May 1609, Sir Thomas Gates set out for Virginia with the Third Supply, there was much expectation: the company had been granted its Second Charter, which greatly expanded its powers and increased its number of shareholders.[57] Nine ships left, but only seven completed the Atlantic crossing. Under the command of Gates, Captain Christopher Newport, and Sir George Somers the vessels were scattered by a storm. In July, Gates's ship, the *Sea Venture*, landed in Bermuda where colonists survived for ten months.

On 9 November 1609, John More, who invested in the Virginia Company in 1609, wrote to Trumbull that "From Virginia we hear that the two best ships with Sir Thomas Gates are separated from the other five and are in danger to be lost."[58] Jean Beaulieu wrote to Trumbull on 30 November with a trustworthy report, as news had arrived with the returning vessels, "Some of the ships that are gone to Virginia are lately returned with word that their Admiral, wherein was Sir Thomas Gates, was so scattered by a tempest from the rest of the Company, that hereunto they could hear nothing of her, the rest having safely landed in Virginia." Beaulieu informed him that Thomas Dale's absence had led to disorder in the struggling colony. There were reports of "dissention" over the distribution of food, and news of a supposedly "Puritan" preacher had also reached him.[59] In a following letter, Beaulieu argued that the "unhappy beginning of the Plantation in Virginia" was due to "want of some man of authority (Sir Thomas Gates having been lost from the rest in the Admiral)."[60] His interpretation of the success of the colony was that men of better sort were needed.

Observers in Europe demanded and needed updates on foreign affairs, but they also received uncertain reports about Virginia. The tentative language used ("we hear" and "some say") communicated this uncertainty, too. On the shipwreck, for example, Beaulieu suggested that reports varied, as "some say the Admiral is now safely come to Virginia."[61] News from the colonists was similarly mistrusted. On 1 August 1613, Chamberlain sent a report to Carleton that was more optimistic about the colony's prospects, whereas one year before the very survival of colonists had been in question. He wrote, "There is a ship come from Virginia with news of their well doing, which puts some life into that action, that before was almost at the last cast." Nevertheless, the colonists had still failed to return goods of any material kind, and the veracity of their reports was doubted: "this ship brought no commodities from thence but only these fair tales and hopes."[62]

Not only were English audiences overseas interested in news about the colony, colonial promoters imagined support for the colony stretching beyond the English realm. In 1611, the Virginia Company council wrote to Sir Ralph Winwood at The Hague, asking him to garner support directly from "noble and worthy gents unto whom we have by our letters or others recommended it," including the colonels and chief commanders of the English in the Netherlands.[63] Letter writing and print were conjoined in a two-part process to promote the colony. John Beaulieu supplied Sir William Trumbull, who resided in Brussels, with the Virginia Company's latest work. He wrote, "Notwithstanding our unfortunate beginning in Virginia we do not faint in the work nor give it over," adding that "I send you a copy of a Proclamation lately made concerning that business."[64] The copy that Beaulieu sent could have been one of two broadsides printed by the company in 1609: *Considering There Is No Public Action,* or *For the Plantation in Virginia*. The second of these, *For the Plantation in Virginia,* focused upon the recruitment of colonists, wishing to "intimate and give notice to all Artificers, Smiths, Carpenters, Coopers, Shipwrights . . . Spinsters, and all other labouring men and women, that are willing to go to the said Plantation to inhabit there." Interested individuals were advised to visit the treasurer's house on Philpot Lane, where they could be registered as "adventurers." The broadside described how "their persons shall be esteemed a single share," and once in Virginia they would receive "houses to dwell in, with Gardens and Orchards, and also food and clothing." The proclamation was targeted at laborers, but a few short lines at the bottom were addressed to those that, "though they go not in their persons shall be accepted for Free-men of the Company." For this privilege, they were required to invest £25 "or more."[65] If he did send this broadside to Trumbull, it is likely that Beaulieu wanted him to communicate with those who were in a position to "adventure" their purses.

If Beaulieu's aim was to generate investment among English elites on the Continent, *Considering There Is No Public Action* is a more plausible candidate. It was a much longer rhetorical broadside, and although it was printed, it had a personal flavor, as it was addressed directly to the reader ("you"), had a blank space for the name of the investor, and was signed at the bottom by members of the Virginia council. The text offered details of "how many ways it hath pleased God to encourage us to go on, in that great work and enterprise of planting Colonies of our English Nation, in those parts of America." It also gave a historical account of the colony's development to date, including the king granting a charter to the company, the "stirring up of so many honorable minded Men, Lords, Knights, Merchants, and Gentlemen," the settlement of hundreds of colonists, and the recent departure of one thousand men and nine ships. After describing the religious and economic justifications for colonization, it requested, "if it shall seem good unto you," that the reader with their "friends and neighbours," townsmen and "Gentlemen and others of your County . . . raise such competent sums of money, as several men shall think good to adventure." The text tacitly requested the participation of readers, *if* they had been persuaded by the company's rhetoric. To further impress, there was enclosed "a Bill of Adventure, under the Seal of the Company; the Copy whereof we have sent you herein enclosed to peruse." Also enclosed were "some few of our Printed Books, which by reading and divulging the same among your friends, will further inform you of each particular." Signed by members of the Virginia council, including Sir Thomas Smythe, the Earl of Southampton, Sir Walter Cope, the Earl of Pembroke, Baron De La Warr, and Sir Thomas Roe, this proclamation clearly had an elite audience in mind—those who could afford a substantial investment and would appreciate the company's oratory on history, trade, and religion.[66] They did, however, also expect a wider audience. By asking their recipients to divulge what they read, their message and news of the colony was expected to reach a broader public.

Through the circulation of texts, individuals like Winwood and Trumbull, who were posted in diplomatic roles overseas, fulfilled their duty by staying abreast of the latest developments in foreign affairs. Only then could they effectively advise on and shape policy.[67] At The Hague, Dudley Carleton continued to receive news of the latest overseas developments from Chamberlain. On 8 July 1620, Chamberlain wrote to Carleton of the news that Henry Wriothesley, the Earl of Southampton, had been elected as treasurer of the Virginia Company. He reported that "there is hope matters will go forward there better than heretofore," and promised that, "if Harman call," to send "a book of all their orders and constitutions, with the names of all the adventurers and the sums."[68] *A Declaration of the State of the Colony and Affairs in Virginia: With the Names of the Adventurers, and Sums Adventured in that Action* (1620) described how through "directions, instructions, charters, and commissions" the colony was reformed and "beginneth now to have the face and fashion of an orderly state, and such as is likely to grow and prosper." The Virginia colony was, now, "a country too good for ill people." The text underlined the worthiness of the project by including the names of investors in the hope that more would be encouraged to "adventure" their purses.[69] What Chamberlain promised to send to Carleton would have furnished him with the latest news on the colony and also have presented a persuasive case for continued investment in the company.

Troubling News and Rumor

In February 1595, Lady Elizabeth Ralegh waved goodbye to her husband as he sailed from Plymouth harbor in search of the famed city of El Dorado.

Ralegh's expedition was a shattering failure in terms of public approval, and he failed to win back the support of the queen or convince her advisor and his patron, Robert Cecil, either. Having retired into Ireland, he wrote to Cecil, "What becomes of Guiana I much desire to hear whether it pass for history or a fable."[70] Ralegh reminds us of the interconnectedness between late-sixteenth- and early-seventeenth-century colonial ventures, and also the series of catastrophes that precluded permanent English colonization in America. Ralegh's Guiana venture, compounded by the tales of the "lost colonists" of Roanoke, had done little to encourage enthusiasm for colonial projects in America. But he hoped that he could sway opinion with the help of Thomas Harriot. Ralegh told Cecil that Harriot had drawn up a "plot," which he entreated Cecil to show to the queen. If she cast her eye on it, Ralegh was sure she would "bewail her negligence" of Guiana. "You may perceive by this relation that it is no dream which I have reported of Guiana," he wrote, and he bolstered his claim with material proofs of Guiana's riches. "I brought with me," he told Cecil, "a stone which being cut is very rare." What he had found was actually rose quartz, and while it did contain gold, he did not persuade experts in London of its value. But he persisted that the samples "bear witness of better," promising "there are not more diamonds in the East Indies than are to be found in Guiana."[71] The disbelief that characterized responses to Ralegh's ventures in Guiana would continue to color reactions to colonization in Virginia a decade later.

The apprehension that investors in England experienced as they awaited news from travelers returning from America was commonplace. In January 1596, Ralegh dispatched his associate Laurence Keymis with two ships, the *Darling* and *Discoverer*, for Guiana. Keymis sailed up the coast of Guiana and the Orinoco River but returned to England without El Dorado's fabled riches after escaping a skirmish with the Spanish. In July, Lady Ralegh anxiously awaited news. Writing to Cecil, she said "I understand that the *Darling* wherein Lemish [*sic*] went to Guiana is come into Yarmouth safely some eight days past," but "I have not heard one word from him or any of my men there." She continued, "as soon as I hear where they are: if it please you to send down a man to them . . . you may know what they have brought." Like her husband, Lady Ralegh despaired at the lack of enthusiasm shown more broadly by the English toward their venture in Guiana. She doubted that anything that Keymis had managed to bring back with him would be of much worth, "for that the Spaniards are already possessed in Guiana." She recognized herself the part that rumor had played in the difficulties she and her husband now faced as their prospects waned. She berated Cecil that "if he [Ralegh] had been as well credited in his reports and knowledges as it seemeth the Spaniards were: they had not now been possessed of that place."[72] Women like Lady Ralegh were not just passive spectators in their husband's exploits, they were active participants in colonial projects.

Proximity to maritime centers continued to shape how investors received information about colonial efforts in America. Beyond circulating promotional literature, manuscript reports, and letters, conversing at the side of ships and in nearby taverns helped observers make sense of events across the Atlantic. By the time that James VI of Scotland ascended to the English throne in 1603, hopes had, once again, turned toward Virginia. Although Ralegh no longer had a direct role in the venture, Robert Cecil, who was created the Earl of Salisbury in 1605, remained a key patron of colonial investors and promoters up until his death in 1612.[73] Shortly after the establishment of Jamestown, the publication of Captain John Smith's *A True Relation of . . . Virginia* (1608) provided some insight into how people learned of affairs in Virginia when ships with mariners aboard, who had witnessed events in the colony firsthand, returned to English ports. In its preface, the printer John Tappe conceded that "I can say nothing more then is here written, only what I have learned and gathered . . . as-well mariners as others, which have had employment that way."[74] People in seventeenth-century England relied upon various sites where they could acquire news in various media. In London, at the Royal Exchange, St. Paul's, and the nearby Blackfriars Theatre, you could browse the latest travel accounts, hear one of the company-sponsored sermons, or watch a play about America.[75] Like diplomats on the Continent, it was essential for statesmen and merchants to acquire the latest news in order to conduct business.[76] The publisher and letter writer Samuel Macham was located in St. Paul's, at the sign of the Bullhead, and so was well located to receive the latest tidings. Macham kept Sir Henry Hastings, the Earl of Huntingdon, who was a Virginia Company investor, informed of news from the colony and also supplied him with the newest print. But as well as conveying news from Virginia, he shared rumors from the royal court, concerning the escape of Lady Arabella and the imprisonment of the Earl of Northumberland and Sir Walter Ralegh.[77]

England's ports, which welcomed ships returning from transatlantic voyages, were the first nodes for receiving news about colonization in America. Here, letters and print, as well as the tales of travelers, fostered knowledge about overseas ventures. Individuals who had completed Atlantic voyages were witness to events in America, and along with the letters that their ships delivered they were the most important suppliers of news. Unlike letters, individuals were bearers of information that could be immediately consumed; unless the recipient of a letter was present at the portside, the letter first had to be delivered—which could take days—before its contents were revealed. The metropolis was, undoubtedly, an important setting for transnational and even transatlantic news sharing. But news sharing was an incredibly dynamic process, and the location of individuals in maritime centers and coastal areas meant that they had almost immediate access to the latest tidings. This did not mean, however, that news was received uncritically, or that it widely "raised hopes": in fact, the news gathered immediately from ships could have the opposite effect.[78]

Sir Ferdinando Gorges, who was a Virginia Company investor and one of the principal supporters of the company's venture in Maine, was ideally located to oversee the Sagadahoc colony. Gorges, who was also a distant relation of Ralegh and Gilbert, used his position in Plymouth, as the commander of its fort, to help keep his patron, the Earl of Salisbury, abreast of developments in Sagadahoc and Jamestown.[79] Discussing Captain Christopher Newport, who commanded the first fleet to Jamestown, Gorges wrote "I was not at home when he came first into the harbor, but I understood so much by him since, as I conceive a possibility of great good to be done in the place where they are."[80] His main focus, however, was on the fledging settlement in Maine. On 1 December 1607, he wrote to Salisbury about a ship that had arrived in Plymouth that very day "with great news of a fertile country, gallant rivers, stately harbors, and a people tractable . . . but no return to satisfy the expectation of the Adventurers." Gorges asked Salisbury to deliver "the enclosed" to Sir Francis Popham, writing that Popham would inform Salisbury of "what he receiveth, although I believe he will not hear of all, that hath passed." Gorges alluded to his position which gave him an advantage in gathering the most truthful reports. He emphasized the immediacy with which he received news upon the arrival of ships, "this present day," as well as his local standing and status as a military man, which no doubt afforded him some capital with the ship's crew. The information they were willing to impart to him could have been much more revealing than what colonists would write in a letter to Popham, and not without good reason. Popham had taken over his father Sir John Popham's interest in the colony since his death in June 1607. And what Gorges had learned of the colonists' progress was disheartening. He wrote that "those employed" lacked sufficient understanding of their task, resulting in "confusion . . . faction, and private resolution, as more at large your Lordship shall perceive, by my next."[81] Gorges's suggestion that "not all that has passed" would reach Popham is an intriguing insight into the economy of news in Plymouth, as he attempted to secure credit with Salisbury by suggesting that he was better placed to keep him informed of colonial matters. By early December, there were further worrying reports out of Maine. Gorges complained that "the childish factious ignorant timorous and ambitious persons, (for of that nature I find the composition to be) hath bred an unstable resolution, and a general confusion, in all their affairs." Gorges wrote "you may be pleased to send command to intercept all letters," in order to "better bring all to light."[82]

In another letter to Salisbury, dated 7 February 1608, Gorges suggested again that written reports from colonists were not wholly truthful, as they were trying to conceal their failures. It seems that he was relying upon the tidbits that he could gather from sailors. A ship had arrived "with advertisement of nothing more than we received at the first." Gorges had learned, though, of further troubling news of faction among the colonists. He did not discover this from the colonists themselves, whose reports he disparaged: "The President and his people, feeds us still with hopes of wonders, that will be had from thence in time."[83] Gorge's letters illuminate how ports acted as useful sites of information exchange and allude to the benefit to be had from learning news directly from ships. Moreover, his access to the news that sailors proffered provided Gorges with an important advantage as a supplicant in service to a patron. He secured information for Salisbury that was not in circulation elsewhere. Reports from returning colonists concerned promoters of Virginia not just because they could undermine the project, by dissuading investors and "adventurers," as discussed further below, but also because they undercut the rhetorical strategy of the Virginia Company itself.

The Virginia Company's promotional literature, including pamphlets, ballads, and sermons, presented colonization as the pursuit of the "common weal" and even the creation of a new commonwealth itself. Early seventeenth-century writers built upon a much older expansionist discourse that was shaped by civic humanism.[84] Discourses of commonwealth and civility provided gentlemen with the moral framework, tools, and justifications they needed to advance colonization.[85] But the practice of appealing to civic humanism in promotional literature served another important purpose too. Promoters of the colony wanted to appeal to individuals across the social spectrum, and their use of commonwealth discourse helped to achieve this.[86]

Just as the boundary between elite and largely illiterate popular culture in the early modern period was porous and indefinite, humanist thought was similarly permeable in English society.[87] The term "common weal," in particular, was a keyword that was employed up and down the social scale.[88] It was this term, which scholars have described as a "keyword of unusual importance in the early modern period" and "over-brimming with tensions and complexity," that the company used in its letters and publications.[89] The company preferred it over other cognate terms too, despite that, according to Phil Withington, in the 1610s, 1620s, and 1630s, "public good" tended to replace commonwealth.[90] Even in the absence of the term in the company's lottery ballad, the idea of shared responsibility was quietly invoked. The ballad offered a reworking of Cicero's retort "we are not borne for our selves, is a saying no less ancient then true":[91]

> We ought not live here, for ourselves,
> but for our country's good:
> and country's good, it is well known,
> long hath this purpose stood[92]

In the letters of investors, the ideals of civic humanism clearly influenced reflections on the colonies too, framing how promoters thought about the practices involved in colonization as well as the progress of colonists.

Writing to the Earl of Salisbury about Sagadahoc, Gorges complained that colonists failed to work toward the common good. Rather, he berated their idleness, concluding that "there must go other manner of spirits, to settle those business, before it will be brought to pass for I find the continuance of their idle proceedings, to have much prejudicialled [*sic*] the public good, dividing themselves into factions, each disgracing the other, even to the Savages, the one emulating the other's reputation amongst those brutish people."[93]

Success in America was reliant upon every colonist working toward the public good and not their private ends. Like the well-functioning body politic, the colony needed to operate as an organic whole. The reported factionalism and idleness of the Sagadahoc colonists proved that this was not the case, as not only were they failing to fulfill the ideals of the *vita activa*, but their disorder was actually dividing the body politic.[94] On 9 July 1612, John Chamberlain similarly disparaged the "extreme beastly idleness" of settlers in Jamestown.[95] These reports fostered the Virginia Company's fears that ill-suited men were voyaging to Virginia. In response, the company requested in 1610 that only "men of most use and necessity" should voyage to Jamestown for "the foundation of a common-wealth."[96]

The failure of the Sagadahoc venture meant that all eyes, and investors' hopes, were now turned to the company's fledging venture in Jamestown. But the Virginia Company struggled to control popular reports that threatened public approval and investors' goodwill. If supporters of the colony hoped for better and more truthful news, they also hoped that rumors would be suppressed. In the face of the horrors of the "starving time" during the winter of 1609 to 1610, when three-quarters of Jamestown colonists died from hunger, colonists escaped and returned to England by requisitioning several small boats. The company described how upon their arrival they began "giving out in all places where they come, (to color their own misbehavior, and the cause of their return with some pretense) most vile and scandalous reports."[97] There was an obvious verbal dimension to how the returning colonists supposedly spread news of the colony's troubles; it is also evident that the company could not act quickly enough to control or censor their speech. The Virginia Company and its supporters worried about the impact that unfettered news sharing could have on its efforts, warning its readers that only the unwise "hawk after the winged report of a vagabond rumor."[98] Similarly, company investor Robert Johnson strongly condemned the "incorrigible looseness of such untamed tongues."[99]

Rumor worried contemporaries more broadly because of the potential to create disorder and even spark rebellions. This threat stemmed, in part, from the association made between the "vulgar sort" and gossip: it was "a mode of political discourse that even the poorest members of society could freely engage in."[100] But gossip and rumor were not the preserve of the commons, and the Virginia Company poured scorn on "men that seem of better sort" who had "devised and given out" "sundry false rumors and despiteful speeches."[101] Gossip-mongering had some merits. Most people embraced rumor as indicative of public mood, and it was also considered somewhere on the spectrum of truth-telling, meaning that people, including the Sir William Trumbull, would not "condemn them altogether," because rumors often hinted at the truth.[102] The Virginia Company tried to mediate this difficulty, by asserting the authority and accuracy of its own printed accounts and by censoring letters from colonists.[103] However, the reliability of printed accounts was, as we have seen, not uncontested, even if the company attempted to present its own literature as a stable alternative to news acquired through conversing in port towns and city streets.

In a letter to Dudley Carleton, John Chamberlain complained of the hurt that colonists were doing to the reputation and prospects of the colony, writing "it is to be feared that that action will fall to the ground of it self, by the extreme beastly idleness of our nation." He explained that they were totally unprepared and unwilling to work and "will rather die and starve then be brought to any labour or industry to maintain themselves." More troubling, however, was a different matter, concerning news that "not past five days since here arrived a ship with ten men who (being sent forth to fish for their relief and having taken great store), have given them the ship and run away, and fill the town with ill reports, which will hinder that business."[104] Reflecting the concern shared by the Virginia Company and promoters of the colony that "ill reports" would damage the colony, Chamberlain's letter reveals the status that ships and port towns had acquired as troubling arenas of oral news sharing. Despite admonitions, observers continued to rely upon multiple sources to get their news, including print, letters, and the rumors that leaked from returning ships.[105]

Material Samples and Eyewitnesses

Some of the letters sent by colonists in Jamestown, during the first years of settlement, relayed a more successful beginning, emphasizing Virginia's promise to provide riches and treasure. The colonist William Brewster told Dudley Carleton of his first impressions: "This is all I will say to you, that such a Bay, a River and a land did never the eye of man behold: and at the head of the River, which is 160 miles long, are Rocks and mountains, that promise infinite treasure; but our forces be yet too weak, to make further discovery: now is the king's majesty offered, the most Stately, Rich kingdom in the world, never possessed by any Christian prince." Brewster wrote that he would have related more in his letter "had not this our ever renowned captain, Captain Newport, have come himself unto you, who will so justly and truly declare, better than I can, all this his discovery."[106] Brewster suggested that by conversing with Newport, Carleton would receive a more accurate report than his letter could provide. At around the same time, the Earl of Salisbury also received news about Jamestown from his close friend Sir Walter Cope, who was a director of the Virginia Company. Cope's letter gave a similar impression of discoveries in Virginia. Ore that had been brought back from the colony was said to contain gold, promising "*aureos pollicere montes*" or "golden mountains." But like Gorges, Cope's letter also suggested that news received should be treated with caution. He wrote, "If we may believe either in words or letters, we are fallen upon a land that promises more, than the land of promise: instead of milk we find pearl, and gold instead of honey. Thus they say, thus they write, but experience the wisest Schoolmistress must lead your Lordship, whose wisdom teaches to be of Slow belief."[107] Incoming news from colonists was fraught with uncertainty and here Cope advised the suspension of belief until "experience" could settle matters. It was only time that would tell if the colony would prove to be a "rich kingdom." Conflicting reports from Jamestown made receivers of news understandably wary. Like Gorges, they had to decide where to place their faith: in words or letters.

As suggested by Brewster's and Cope's letters, the feelings of uncertainty that overseas colonization instilled in English observers fomented a climate in which eyewitness accounts and samples of materials were essential. From Harriot's and White's time in Roanoke, to Ralegh's Guiana venture, and later at Jamestown, colonists sought to gain the confidence of investors at home by providing them with samples of ore and natural materials, such as sarsaparilla and tobacco, while those at home tried in earnest to separate fact from fiction. Material proof could be a particularly valuable accompaniment to letters and speaks to the larger phenomenon in early modern Europe of specimens from America functioning as "intellectual capital" in transnational networks of naturalists. Travel and colonization in America benefitted keen botanists like Charles de L'Écluse, who received "Drake's root" from a voyage to Virginia in 1580. Similarly, following one of his voyages to America, John White presented a Virginia grasshopper to Thomas Penny.[108] For most Virginia Company investors, however, specimens did not necessarily function as novelties or evidence of scientific discovery, but rather as material proof of future prosperity. In one of his letters to the Earl of Huntingdon, Macham enclosed "the relation of Lord De La Warr," published in 1611, and further reported that "within two days after the publishing hereof comes Captain Adams with a fair ship from Virginia, bringing word that Sir Thomas Dale with all his company safely arrived there." Presumably from the same "fair ship," Macham had news that the "plantation prospers now more and more; they want for no corn, for they have all in abundance." As if to confirm this, he enclosed "a little of every sort." Macham had probably acquired the samples from Captain Adams, who "hath brought great store of black walnut tree, sassafras; soap ashes and excellent sturgeon." The samples of corn, it seems, served to bolster the reliability of reports from the colony. If the

Earl of Huntingdon required further knowledge of Virginia plants and commodities, Macham promised that the unnamed bearer of the letter would be better placed to inform him, having "been long in London."[109]

Samples from America were not just evidence of the potential riches of the Continent, they functioned as gifts within networks of clients, patrons, and investors in England. The Earl of Huntingdon received specimens directly from the colony, not only from Macham, but from his agent in Virginia, Captain Nicholas Martiau, too. When a letter arrived in April 1624 it contained within it "a Prick of Tobacco and a great quantities of Sassafras." They were accompanied by "an Epitome of the present state of Virginia." These enclosed items were reassuring enough to solicit the response from the earl that "as all new plantations are troublesome and dangerous . . . after some few years I doubt not but this plantation will come to perfection."[110] Martiau again delivered commodities to his employee, sending a "proportion of sassafras" with a letter in 1625, as well as "a small token of tobacco," which his wife "is bold to present unto your noble lady," Elizabeth Hastings, Countess of Huntingdon.[111] It was not just investors, then, but their wives too who were charmed with delights from America. This may have been an especially astute gesture by Martiau and his wife, as elite women were valued patrons of the colonial project.[112]

One year after Jamestown was settled, colonists still believed they might find "golden mountains," or at least make people at home believe that this was possible. Writing to Sir John Egerton in 1608, Virginia settler Captain Peter Wynne reportedly sent samples of pitch, tar, soap, ashes, and dyes. "As for things more precious," he wrote, "I omit till time (which I hope will be shortly) shall make manifest proof of it."[113] Such gift-giving, between England and America was reciprocated, and it served to foster good relations between investors and those that managed their plantations. In exchange, the Earl of Huntingdon sent his agent, Captain Martiau, "a suit of apparel and a cloak of cloth six shirts two pair of black and two pair of russet boots and four pairs of shoes."[114] Their letters speak to the expectations that observers in England attached to Virginia, as well as the lived reality. Colonists hoped to find rich and valuable commodities that they could sell in England and Europe, as well as engage in profitable trade with the Virginia Algonquians. However, what actually materialized was an almost complete focus on tobacco cultivation. Despite pressure and attempts to develop other industries, as the earl's gift to Martiau indicates, the colony continued to rely upon trade with English and also Dutch merchants for essential goods and supplies.[115]

As well as receiving specimens from colonies, people in England could expect to receive the company of those who had experiences of America first-hand. It was common, as Macham suggested, for the bearers of letters to relate news directly to the recipients, including individuals of humble social status.[116] When writing to Martiau in Virginia, the Earl of Huntingdon noted that the "bearer your Servant Richard Jones did deliver your letters and tokens very safely, who hath made a very good relation of the Country, and I think is an honest poor fellow."[117] Again, Martiau's news was accompanied by "tokens" from the colony. Apparently responding to an earlier letter sent by Huntingdon in July 1624, Martiau wrote "news have we not in Virginia that may merit any relation." He did, however, promise to "report myself unto this messenger," his servant William Hutchinson, who could also provide "a more particular relation" of the earl's land in Virginia.[118] Messengers from various backgrounds became important conduits in the exchange of colonial news and knowledge. Lower-status eyewitnesses and experts were used to relate news about Newfoundland to potential investors too. William Payne was a merchant investor in Newfoundland and along with James Meddus was corresponding with Lady Conway about occupying a share of land in St. John's. In one letter, Payne told Meddus that he could arrange for Edward Conway to be visited by individuals who had traveled to Newfoundland, "Philips a Scotch and Mineral man . . . or Mr William Alexander a Scotchman belonging to the court hath been there, found the silver mine, and can fully inform my lord thereof; but may perhaps hardly do it to any other, then unto his honor's own self."[119] We can imagine how servants and patrons received these visitors into English households and heard (or overheard) their stories from the "New World," changing their own ideas and perceptions. First-hand experience and expertise were richly valued, but it was also important that witnesses were reliable and could bolster their claims with material proofs.[120] In a climate in which letters and even print could be untrustworthy, individuals who had seen, touched, and lived in America were the most reliable sources of intelligence and played a key role in mobilizing elite Virginia Company investors, such as the Earls of Salisbury and Huntingdon, Lady Conway and her husband, and Sir Walter Cope. Receiving objects and travelers were both ways that people in England tried to narrow the gap between their own experience and colonization in Virginia.

Fellow colonists from the British Isles were not the only visitors that investors received. Several leading investors in the Virginia Company and colonists, including its treasurer Sir Thomas Smythe as well as Sir Walter

Ralegh, Sir Walter Cope, Sir Thomas Dale, George Thorpe, Sir Ferdinando Gorges, Sir John Popham, and John Slaney, hosted Indigenous guests and captives in their homes. Indigenous peoples visited and were observed by spectators across London, in St. James Park, on the River Thames, and in the palaces of Westminster.[121] In the households of elite investors, their wives and servants also lived alongside Indigenous peoples, although there is little way of knowing what women like Sarah Smythe, Sir Thomas Smythe's wife, made of their guests. The Virginia Company's women investors, more broadly, likely shared similar experiences with Indigenous peoples. Isabella Rich, Sir Walter Cope's daughter, may have met the two Virginia Algonquians that he supervised and who rowed on the Thames in 1603. Elizabeth Dale, who was Thomas Dale's wife, Throckmorton's sister, and Thorpe's kinswoman, may also have encountered their Indigenous guests and captives. Surely, she met her betrothed when he returned to England in 1616 with Pocahontas and her Algonquian kinfolk. Cecily West, Baroness De La Warr, who oversaw plantation management in Virginia following her husband's death, also met Pocahontas when she visited England in 1616.[122] Women's experiences of the Indigenous peoples of America went beyond straightforward encounter: in 1596, Lady Ralegh demonstrated her cognizance of English and Indigenous relations, informing Cecil that "Topiawari the king that was her majesty's subject is dead and his son returned."[123] Even if we cannot say for certain what they thought about the Indigenous peoples they met, it is still important for our understanding of women's interest in, and investment in, colonization that we remember that these were experiences they shared alongside their husbands, fathers, and brothers. The presence of Indigenous peoples in England fostered opportunities for everyday encounters with Indigenous peoples, but it also led to Indigenous co-production in gentry households, as discussed above. The knowledge that they imparted on their hosts and captors infused promotional writing, changing understandings of colonization in America, including its geography and people. Their presence also corporealized, for people in England, the connections between the colonial discourses they read in print or heard in sermons and ballads, the money that they gathered in churches, the tobacco they smoked, and the colony itself.

Through print and manuscript sources, the tales of sailors, expertise of Indigenous peoples, rumor, and material samples, a picture of Virginia was forming in the minds of potential colonists and investors, as well as a broader public audience. Two particular discourses shaped news about English colonial efforts in America. The first centered around the unreliability of news, and the need to tackle this dilemma by drawing upon different kinds of eyewitness and expertise. Contrary to the claim that the "uncertainty" of news "could not be overcome by credible reporters," it seems that with the help of expert eyewitnesses and material proofs, like samples of colonial goods, people *could*, in fact, and at least in the context of colonization, *did* settle matters.[124] Commonwealth discourse was an additional dimension to the reception of news coming out of Virginia. Particularly in the first years of colonization, when the survival of Jamestown and Sagadahoc was precarious and very much contingent upon the continued injection of investor capital, reports that settlers were idle, disordered, and interested only in personal advance rather than the public good were damaging and potentially fatal. The realities of colonization in Virginia were often in sharp relief to the images portrayed in promotional literature, and the apparent failures of the colonial project led to investors defaulting on their promises. Investors' wavering confidence, because of news of faction in Sagadahoc, undoubtedly contributed to financial support falling short of what was needed.

How ideas about colonization in America diffused was both multifaceted and complex.[125] Whether you were an observer in England, or a diplomat posted on the Continent, you would have confronted and evaluated oral, written, and printed information not distinctly, but alongside, even in competition with, one another. This placed demands upon observers to be critical and cautious. For merchants, colonists, patrons, and diplomats, the continued supply of trustworthy news and proximity to news outlets was essential to conduct all kinds of business. They achieved this through the maintenance of epistolary networks, which allowed them to circulate texts and material proofs to inform, encourage, and persuade. The availability of print in provincial markets also enabled a wider and more dispersed audience to consume ideas about America. While Anthony Hilton was excited for his mother to get hold of the Virginia Company's latest pamphlet, ahead of his own Atlantic voyage, the owner of a copy of Robert Johnson's *New Life of Virginia* wondered if it was all nonsense. Different genres of texts about Virginia encouraged very different responses. While literary forms like promotional literature and, arguably, letters too prompted readers to be careful, colonists and company investors deemed the "day-book" or journal a more reliable form of written testimony. For that reason, colonial promoters like Nicholas Ferrar and the directors of colonization in Newfoundland and Sagadahoc urged colonists to keep thorough records, based on actual sensory experience: what they saw, heard, touched. Investors' own encounters with colonial goods, Indigenous peoples, and eyewitnesses, often within their own homes, added a further layer of texture, intimacy, and intricacy to their understandings of America. This varied experience, from speeches to samples and stories heard around ports, fed a growing appetite for colonization in America, not only ensuring that investors were willing to pour capital into the venture, but that a broader public were willing to adventure their purse and person in Virginia too.

CHAPTER 2

Adventuring Purses

Virginia Company Investors

Sometime in the 1630s, Lady Cecily West (née Shirley) sat for her portrait, clothed in lace and satin that shone with the same iridescence as the pearls that adorned her body. Between the thumb and index finger of her right hand, she gently held her long pearl necklace, a subtle reminder of the wealth and beauty that European empires extracted from the Americas. Her grasp appears to convey her own supposedly soft and feminine possession of "New World" wealth.[1] However, this portrait was completed in a decade when Cecily West, widow of Thomas West, the 3rd Baron De La Warr, was attempting to reassert, much more firmly, her hold on her family's wealth derived from colonization in Virginia. Around 1635, almost thirty years since the colonization of Jamestown, West petitioned Charles I for her pension on the grounds that her marriage jointure had been invested, at great cost to herself, in the Virginia venture. Cecily and Thomas married in 1596, exactly ten years before he joined the Virginia Company council and invested £500, the largest sum it received from any shareholder. But it is from Cecily's petition, rather than any extant Virginia Company records, that we learn of her substantial part in financing colonization in America.[2] Through petitions and depositions, representing the drama that unfolded in courtrooms, we can learn more about the everyday, prosaic nature of investing. The nature of investment in Virginia, as West's petition hints at, was also intensely gendered. Queen Elizabeth I granted the first patent for colonization in America, and Sir Walter Ralegh named the region after her, the "Virgin Queen." Throughout the late sixteenth and early seventeenth centuries, "possession" of Virginia continued to be framed in feminine, sexualized terms. Moreover, as Shannon Miller has suggested, through the motif of marriage to a virgin bride whose wealth, if intact, could be financially profitable, "the representation of Virginia" also effectively internalized "the financial organization of the project."[3] Cecily West's own wealth that she brought to her marriage embodied this motif, furthering our understanding of how women, in various ways, supported colonization. Gender shaped the practices associated with investment in trading companies, the management of plantations, and inheritance of wealth resulting from overseas trade and colonization. Women, as historians have established, carved out autonomous roles for themselves in early modern English society and its economy.[4] Yet, women's participation in the Virginia Company, as merchants and investors, was also a means of establishing autonomy; and, importantly, it enabled women to demonstrate their own independent interest in empire.[5] Focusing on how women's, as well as men's, networks and capital supported the company illuminates how gender shaped English enterprise in the domestic sphere as well as in Virginia.[6]

Exploring the sorts of behaviors that prompted and were promoted by men's and women's investment in the Virginia Company also reveals the extremely interpersonal, even intimate, practices that drove investment, and sheds light on how the company mobilized support across different spheres in early modern England, including the court, parliament, and livery companies. The mobilization of capital investment in the company worked alongside the mobilization of broader public approval and interest. This ensured that the Virginia Company would meet with the cooperation and collaboration of people and institutions across England, allowing it to develop the practices that sustained colonization in Virginia, not least lotteries and collections, forced transportation, and the tobacco trade, as discussed in the following chapters. The networks that were established through investment in the Virginia Company helped to lubricate domestic colonial enterprise, as well as empire formation overseas.

Entreaties to Invest

In the late sixteenth century, capital investment in English colonization was forthcoming from merchants and the monarch. However, in 1606, a new and unprecedented opportunity to invest in colonial enterprise emerged, with the advent of the Virginia Company.[7] For the first time, colonization in America attracted support and mobilized investment from a much broader swathe of English society. Joint-stock companies like the Virginia Company and East India Company did not, by their very nature, require all members to be experienced. Unlike regulated companies, it was the officers of joint-stock companies who directed trade, leaving investment open, for the first time, to non-merchant wealth.[8] This meant that the Virginia Company could entice investors with no previous experience of overseas trade and colonization, including men and women from various backgrounds. Between 1606 and 1624, the Virginia Company attracted more than 1,684 investors, made up of men and women, from aristocratic, gentry, and merchant backgrounds, as well as men who were trained professionals and members of livery companies. The cost of investing in the Virginia Company was, at £12 10s., relatively affordable, making it a potentially less daunting and risky venture.[9] Still, as Edmond Smith's work on the East India Company has shown, the price of investing in trading companies could be alleviated by investing in partnership with trusted associates and kin. Investing in groups was also a way to distribute and minimize risk, and also benefit from the experience of others, a practice that men and women in the Virginia Company also employed.[10]

Encounters in various places, from intimate domestic settings to opulent royal palaces, persuaded men and women to invest their fortunes. It is impossible, however, to speculate too much about how Virginia Company investors were initially drawn into parting with their money, although relationships forged with others through marriage and kinship, the livery companies, the Inns of Court, and even stranger churches certainly played their part.[11] For many, it was during their sojourn in London that their interest was sparked. During the first decade or so of the company's existence, investors would likely have ventured east in the City of London, to Philpot Lane, the residence of the merchant and company treasurer Sir Thomas Smythe.[12] There, they may have been welcomed by Smythe's wife, Sarah, before signing a share certificate. There are few records of how investors were actually enticed to part with their money, but the appeals, accusations, and contestations that were presented in Chancery Court, following investors defaulting on their subscriptions, describe some instances of how it occurred. They reveal that personal appeals, as we might expect, were sometimes necessary. In 1613, Phineas Pett, first Master of the Shipwrights' Company, who counted Prince Henry among his patrons, reported that it was through the "entreaty of some of his much esteemed friends as out of his own disposition" that he invested £37 10s. in the company.[13] Sir Thomas Mildmay, a gentleman investor, similarly described how, around 1609, "Sir Robert Mansfield knight came unto this defendant and entreated him to adventure into the said plantation."[14] Mathewe de Quester initially subscribed £50 in the first adventure, but "afterwards by earnest privation of some of the said company pretending good success and gain thereby" he agreed to subscribe a further £12 10s. for three years.[15] They were all dragged before the court because they had defaulted on their payments at a time when the company was trying to recover its reputation, in the years following the "starving time," and hastily trying to attract new investors with its Third Charter of 1612.

The Virginia Company struck up relationships with individuals and institutions through opportunities to invest, including town corporations and livery companies.[16] On 1 March 1609, the Grocers' Company discussed "extraordinary business," consisting of a letter from the Virginia Company council and a precept from the Lord Mayor of London, "to raise some voluntary contribution and of the best disposed and most able of the company towards the said plantation."[17] A year later, on 14 March 1610, Virginia Company agent William Leveson was present at a Grocers' Company meeting to collect "certain moneys by him supposed to have been promised by this company to be paid towards the plantation."[18] Leveson was specifically hired by the company to "solicit and procure [from] divers noble men bishops ladies knights gentlemen corporations merchants and others . . . such sums of money as they had agreed to pay in."[19] Shortly after Leveson's visit, on 25 April, the Grocers' Company finally agreed that £100 would be invested and paid to the Virginia Company treasurer, Sir Thomas Smythe.[20] Numerous investors had proved intractable when it came to paying up, so the company had clearly decided that additional pressure was required.

Livery companies were persuaded that their investment would immediately benefit the communities that they inhabited and were responsible for, chiefly by clearing the streets of the most destitute. But they were also persuaded by material gains, both personal and to society more broadly, not least by relieving ratepayers of the growing burden of poor relief. The Vintners' Company decided to adventure £100 in December 1610, but in the new year faltered on its initial commitment upon learning that the £6,000 that the company alleged it needed had already been collected. The Vintners' Company was prepared to invest what was necessary and no more. The claims that initially motivated the Vintners' Company were that plantation in Virginia would bring "honour" to England through "godly planting of religion amongst infidels" and "by amplifying the dominions [of England] thereof." To the "adventurers" would come "profit . . . by the commodities which that country may hereafter yield in short time." Of chief importance, however, was the potential to "disburs[e]" the realm of "many unnecessary members living . . . wherewith this land is always surcharged."[21] In March 1609, the Merchant Taylors' read a letter from the Virginia Company that moved them to help "ease the city and subjects of a swarm of unnecessary inmate[s]," who the Virginia Company alleged were "a continual cause of death and famine and the very original cause of all plagues," by making "some voluntary contribution for their remove into this plantation of Virginia." The Virginia Company imagined a close relationship between investment in the colony and local civic concerns, including the responsibility of corporations to alleviate the suffering of the poor in their parishes and wards.[22]

The livery companies were instructed how to respond to those impoverished and homeless individuals who claimed they had no option but to "lie in the streets." In Virginia, they could have "meat drink and clothing with an house orchard and garden for the meanest family and a possession of land to them and their posterity fifty acres for every man's person that hath a trade, or a body able to endure day labour, as much for his wife, as much for his child, that are of yours to do service to the colony, with the further particular and reward according to their particular merit and industry."[23] Tying investment in the company to civic duty and local obligations in such a way created bonds that were appealed to later on, when the Virginia Company sought support to host lotteries, transport vagrant children, or gather church collections.

The spread of investment in Virginia across England maps out how a broader public gained awareness of colonization and also how the Virginia Company forged connections outside the capital. Cities and towns across England, including London, Exeter, Bristol, Dover, and Plymouth, poured significant capital into the early Virginia Company. The town of Dover, for example, which later subscribed £5 toward the company lotteries, first invested £25 in the Virginia Company in 1610.[24] The city of Bristol received an entreaty from Sir John Popham to invest in the Sagadahoc colony shortly before the Virginia Company received its first charter in April 1606. In March 1606, the letter that Popham addressed to the mayor of Bristol, Thomas James, "touching the plantation in Virginia," was read aloud to the "common then present." However, the council decided that the city was "not to adventure any thing in that action unless it shall please the king majesty to undertake [the] same."[25] There must have been some pressure for the city to consent, as the following month the council recorded that "An yearly contribution for five years for the plantation and inhabiting of Virginia" would be made.

Bristol city merchants, Thomas Hopkins and Thomas Aldworth, would "confer and deal with the inhabitants of Bristol . . . what every man will adventure towards this action," which strikes up an image of Hopkins and Aldworth going house to house seeking contributions.[26] Over time, investment became more diffuse and less concentrated in the hands of wealthy merchants. As discussed in the following chapter, those who wanted to provide financial support to colonial ventures could also play at lotteries and contribute to collections in their parish churches, establishing a broader base of public financial support for Virginia.

Distance and the absence of proof made investors wary, and since at least 1612 many Virginia Company investors had defaulted on their payments, complaining that despite the company's promises "there came no profit."[27] As colonial ventures unfolded, investors and the public more broadly remained understandably wary about English endeavors in America, carefully picking through the information they gathered from their associates, sailors in ports, pamphlets, and letters, for evidence of success. In January 1613, Sir Thomas Mildmay reported that he had "heard by many credible persons that . . . divers returns have been made from Virginia into this realm of England and yet no profit yielded or given up by the said Treasurer or Company unto any the adventurers." Evidently there was mistrust between some investors and the company, with individuals like Mildmay believing that the dividends due to them were being withheld. The reality was equally disheartening, as he later learned that he "must expect no profit of his adventure by the space of twenty years contrary to the information given by the said Sir Robert Mansfield."[28] That investors expected a quick return underlines the commercial expectations associated with overseas colonization; while other claims were made, for many their investment was driven by a need for capital. Some, including Mathewe de Quester, quit their subscriptions and exchanged them with another, as they believed was "usual and lawful amongst merchants in like cases."[29] The testimony given in the court also underscores that investors gathered their information not just from the pamphlets they read or news they received, but were privy to discussions taking place within the Virginia Company itself. Sir John Sammes, for instance, had intimate knowledge of the company's decision making, including the fact that colonization in Virginia was proving to be "a matter of greater difficulty and charge then they before imagined and thought it would have been." A report from Sir Thomas Gates confirmed that "a greater supply of men and money was requisite," otherwise the venture "would fail and not take that effect as was desired." In 1610, Sammes learned that a further injection of capital, the sum of £18,000, was needed in order to guarantee success. But Sammes refused to hand over any more money to the company because he did not believe that it was, in fact, investing in Virginia.[30] He admitted to jumping ship before the whole venture sunk.

This window into investing underlines the very interpersonal character of investing, as well as the role of individual agency in shaping the development of trading companies.[31] Investment in the Virginia Company was influenced by the bonds that were established among young gentlemen at the Inns of Court, among courtiers in the royal palaces, and among statesmen in parliament.[32] Yet, we can extend our understanding of how such personal practices played out even further by focusing upon events in the halls of livery companies, in domestic settings, and in places outside of London. This brings into the fold a wider social spectrum of men who were investors, but it also points toward the social mechanics involved in enticing women investors, which were often in more informal settings. Women's intimate connections, namely the relationships they fostered with family, friends, neighbors, and fellow parishioners, can help us to understand how they were enticed to adventure their purses.

Women Investors' Intimate Connections

Early modern economic and legal practices shaped women's opportunities to invest in English colonial enterprise and determined how they managed their wealth and interests. Married women were constrained by the doctrine of coverture, which entailed a wife's legal personhood being absorbed by her husband's upon marriage. In theory, but not always in practice, she could not own her own property, make contracts, or represent herself in court.[33] Coverture also led to the development of legal mechanisms that were intended to protect a woman's wealth. Affluent women might have paid to have a premarriage settlement drawn up to establish a jointure that would provide her with an income during her marriage, or property might have been held in trust, so that a profligate husband could not whittle away her inheritance.[34] Coverture did not inhibit single women or widows, and married women in the City of London could formally adopt *femme sole* status.[35] Few actually went through the process officially, which meant appearing before the Lord Mayor and aldermen, but there is evidence that many more adopted *femme sole* status in practice, by hiring their own apprentices and receiving and extending credit.[36] Women's management of assets that stretched their financial interests overseas sat within a broader context of economic practice in the domestic sphere. As Alexandra Shepard has argued, women were at the center, rather than the margins, of economic exchange in early modern England. Women were responsible for household asset management, and they were also important creditors, extending credit to individuals engaged in business and civic corporations, in ways that cultivated trade as well as colonization.[37] In return, English colonial enterprise shaped women's lives as they gained access to new markets and opportunities to grow their wealth, extend their influence through investment and patronage, and form new personal and business ties that extended across the globe.[38]

Throughout the early history of English colonization in America, women's investment and patronage was privileged. Elite women's social capital was valued perhaps as much as, or even more than, the actual funds they provided.[39] Women of wealth and status who invested lent respectability and civility to colonial ventures, and they add an important gendered dimension to our understanding of investment practices too.[40] Focusing on the investment of women allows us to view the networks that elite investors operated within through a different lens, as women's relationships and patronage determined where nodes of influence existed, and how such influence was put into effect.[41] Elite women's investment in the Virginia Company followed a different pattern from that of men, prompting a different set of behaviors and outcomes. Unlike men, women were sometimes forced to invest through more informal, hidden channels because of contemporary legal and social constraints.[42] This means that there is sometimes ambiguity about whether women willingly gave their consent before their wealth was exhausted through colonization. Cecily West's jointure, discussed at the beginning of this chapter, is one example, but there are other indications that women's inheritance and capital was leveraged, with or without their say-so, to fund their husbands' colonial endeavors. Elizabeth Throckmorton, a Gloucestershire gentlewoman, and Sir Thomas Dale, a relatively obscure soldier, were married in 1611—the same year he ventured to Virginia and a year before he invested in the company.[43] Might her jointure also have furnished him with the funds he needed? The fact that both of these women later managed plantations in Virginia implies that there was greater partnership between wives and husbands than the Virginia Company's list of shareholders would suggest. Lady Ralegh was also said to have sold property inherited from her father in Mitcham, Surrey, to Thomas Plummer for £2,500, in order to fund Sir Walter Ralegh's last voyage to Guiana in 1617.[44] Again, Elizabeth Ralegh's continued interest in her husband's colonial exploits is suggested by her correspondence with the Earl of Salisbury. During the Financial Revolution, women frequently provided the financial resources for their husbands to invest, and there is certainly evidence that Virginia shareholders were also comfortable investing in this way.[45]

The proximity of women to company affairs prompted Nathaniel Rich to complain in 1623 that women were present at the Virginia Company court too often. Rich meant it as an attack on the corporation's governance under the leadership of Sir Edwin Sandys and Henry Wriothesley, the Earl of Southampton, at a time when faction was tearing the company apart. He claimed that for the previous four years there had been the "inviting of strangers yea of women to be present in a latticed gallery w[hi]ch looks into the place where the Courts . . . have been kept." There, they had been permitted to observe company business: "spectators of their [the company's] courses and hearers of their calumnies and to the end the rumour thereof might be more generally spread."[46] In 1619, meetings were relocated from the household of Thomas Smythe to the great hall of the home of Nicholas Ferrar, deputy of the Virginia Company. Located on St. Sythe's Lane in the City of London, Ferrar's home had emerged as the center of company operations.[47] The women who were supposedly so interested in overseeing and overhearing the company's business probably included those who were not investors, but who petitioned the company to collect the wages of their husbands, brothers, or sons. They included widows like Joice Lodge, lately returned from Virginia, who attended a company meeting, on 13 June 1621, to petition for "the Adventure of her person and her thirds out of the Land due for her personal Adventure ~~due for~~ of her said deceased Husband."[48] They could also have been women with independent commercial interests in Virginia, who were hoping to hear about the progress of silk production in the colony or whether new fines would be levied on the tobacco trade. Or they might have come because they had learned through sermons in their parish church about colonists' godly work to convert Virginia Algonquians to Christianity. While their identity remains obscured, much more can be said about the women who were not "strangers" to the company, but rather its investors.

In 1609, for the first time, the Virginia Company made its shares available to a broader membership, which expanded its number of investors into the hundreds and included women.[49] That year, only two women, both with merchant backgrounds, invested. The first was Katherine West (later Lady Conway), who bought two shares for £25, and she was joined by Milicent Ramsden (née Pickerd), who bought three shares for £37 10s.[50] At the time, as Katherine West was married to a City of London Freeman of the Grocers' Company, John West, she may have invested *femme sole*.[51] The widowed Milicent Ramsden had a similar mercantile background. She married first John Worsley in 1593, then Samuel Ramsden in 1603, who were both Freemen of the Brewers' Company.[52] Through her sisters, Katherine Lappidge and Ellen Parker, she had further familial connections to the Silkweavers' and Brewers' Companies, while her kinswoman, Milicent Young, was married to Richard Young, a "wine cooper."[53] Later she married Oliver St. John, and, in 1619, sold him three shares in the Virginia Company.[54] In 1612, with an expanded charter that included territory in Bermuda and authority to hold a lottery, the Virginia Company attracted a greater number of women investors. The social character of women investors was significantly altered too, perhaps signaling a change in attitude to investing in the Virginia Company. The new women investors were mostly aristocratic, including several who were in Queen Anna's circle.[55] Just one, Mistress Elizabeth Scott, a widow, had a more obscure background. The others were well known figures at court, including Mary Herbert, Countess of Pembroke; Margaret Clifford, Countess of Cumberland; Lady Elianor Cave (sometimes Carr); Lucy Russell, Countess of Bedford; Elizabeth de Vere, Countess of Derby; Lady Elizabeth Carey; Lady Elizabeth Grey; and Mary Talbot, Countess of Shrewsbury. Countess Bedford was the only woman to also buy shares in the subsidiary Somers Island (or Bermuda) Company in 1615.[56] But examining the company charters alone offers a limited view of women shareholders. Between 1615 and 1623, for instance, we know that at least a further fourteen women, including some, like Joice Lodge, from much more humble backgrounds, acquired shares in the Virginia Company. During this time, greater numbers of women became involved in the Virginia Company as shareholders, through the buying and selling of shares and also through the inheritance of shares from loved ones.[57]

The elite women who invested had a particularly influential position in the Virginia Company, wielding social as well as economic capital.[58] The Cavendish-Talbot women were three of nine elite women investors who bought shares in 1612, and they show how women's "intimate networks" facilitated investment in Virginia.[59] Lady Elizabeth Grey (neé Talbot), the wife of Henry Grey, later the Earl of Kent, invested £25 in 1612. She was also associated, through her sister Mary Herbert (neé Talbot), Countess of Pembroke, with several colonial investors. The Countess of Pembroke invested in 1612 alongside her sister Lady Grey, following her husband William Herbert, Earl of Pembroke, and brother-in-law Philip Herbert, Earl of Montgomery, who both invested in 1609. The countess's mother-in-law was Mary Herbert (née Sidney), the sister of Sir Philip Sidney, an early promoter of colonization in Virginia.[60] The Dowager Countess of Pembroke followed her sons' interest in Virginia, becoming involved in colonial affairs sometime before 1619. That year the governor of the Virginia colony, Sir George Yeardly, in a letter to Sir Edwin Sandys, wrote of the "service recommended unto me by you from the Countess Dowager of Pembroke," saying "I will not fail to perform [it] by the *Bona Nova*." What exactly that "service" was is unclear. Another matriarch, Mary Talbot (neé Cavendish), Countess of Shrewsbury, who was the mother of Lady Elizabeth Grey and Mary, Countess of Pembroke, invested £50 in 1612. She also had important familial connections to the Virginia Company: as well as her daughters, the Countess of Shrewsbury's brother William Cavendish, later the first Earl of Devonshire, and nephew William, who inherited his father's title, invested in 1612 and were active in the Virginia Company.[61] These elite women were connected to the most prominent noble influence in the company. The Earl of Pembroke, for example, invested £400, making him the second largest investor in the Virginia Company.[62] But, while marriage connected these families to one another, women's interest in the Virginia Company was not always determined by matrimony. Knowledge of investment practices was sometimes transmitted from woman to woman, such as mother to daughter, and Lady Grey's investment in the company was certainly independent of her husband, though not of the women in her kinship network.[63] In her experience, the familial connections held by her sister and mother to other company investors were key to engaging her interest. Women were not just connected to influence in the Virginia Company, then; they also exerted it themselves through familial networks of noble investors.

The legal impediment of coverture meant that it was requisite for married women to have access to their own capital if they were to invest in shares independently of their husbands. However, the Virginia Company records also suggest how husbands, or husbands and wives together, used women's capital to profit from colonization. In 1621, for example, Lady Pell and her husband Sir Anthony Pell sold two shares to William Savill. The fact that she was mentioned at all suggests that the shares belonged to her, or her

Table 1. Family tree of Cavendish-Talbot women in 1612, Virginia Company investors

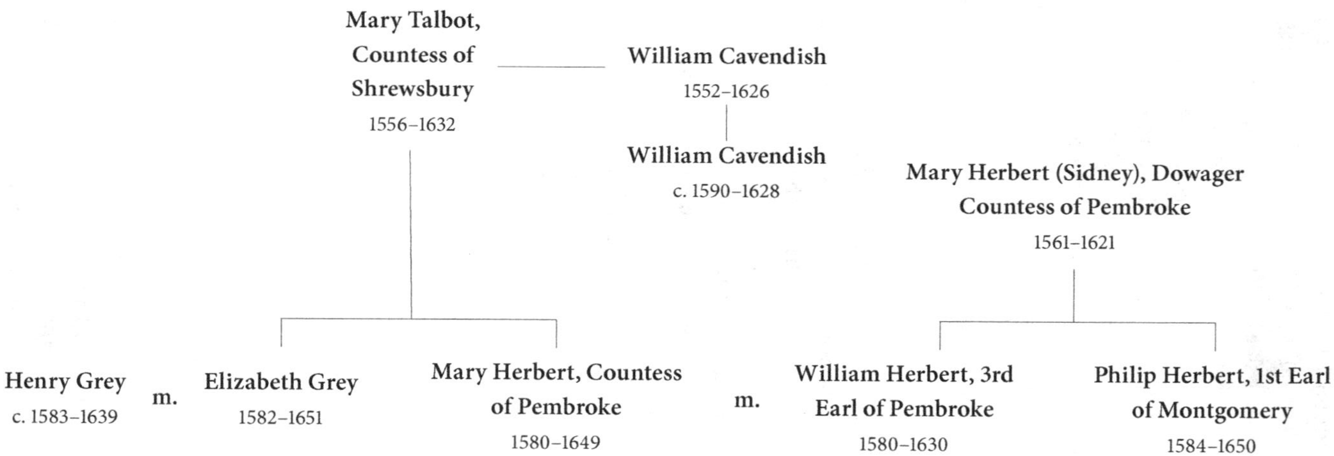

and her husband together, although it is unclear how they had acquired them.[64] The legal erasure of coverture creates silences in the company records that are difficult to recover. In 1622 Lady Isabella Rich and her husband Sir Henry Rich sold four shares to Mr. Henry Piercy, shares that had "descended" to Isabella Rich "as the sole Daughter and heir of Sir Walter Cope deceased."[65] In this instance, with such detail, it is possible to reconstruct more clearly women's associations with the company, revealing how the intimate networks of investors prompted shareholding in a direct and measurable way. When Cecily West petitioned Charles I, she asked him to continue her pension of £500 per annum, which had been bestowed upon her by his father James for a period of thirty-one years. She explained that she had seven children to provide for, including six daughters who required marriage portions, and she detailed how her own marriage portion had been spent by her husband on the Virginia venture. She wrote, "he disbursed great sums of money most of which were raised out of your petitioner's jointure."[66] A jointure was usually a cash portion that a woman brought to her marriage, which was used to purchase land and raise rents during her marriage, in joint tenure, with her husband. The terms were normally settled in a premarriage contract, meaning they were usually the preserve of the landed classes, who had property interests to protect and access to income in order to pay for the drawing up of such contracts.[67] West's petition suggests the possibility that there were other, unrecorded instances of women's capital being invested in colonization.

Women's investment in the Virginia Company was, overall, specifically gendered, as the number of women who inherited shares from a father or husband likely exceeded the number who directly purchased them themselves. Joan Reade received one hundred acres of land in Virginia and one share in the company following her father's death in 1622.[68] The daughter of the colonist Sir Ferdinando Weyman, who died in Virginia in 1610, was given eight shares "for adventure of his person" in 1620.[69] While he still lived, Katherine Fleete's father, William Fleete, decided to transfer her three shares in 1622.[70] Widowed women who received shares included Katherine Clarke, who sold one to Edward Harber in 1619.[71] Cecily West also inherited shares following her husband's death in 1618, worth £500. From 1620 onward, West began selling the shares, but while the company identified her as the owner of the shares, she was acting in part on her son's behalf, who was still too young to inherit his father's property.[72] As well as selling these shares, Cecily West took an active interest in their plantation in Virginia. In June 1620, Berkeley

Hundred planter William Tracy wrote to John Smyth, "I have made means to the Lady De La Warr to buy or borrow such things as she may fancy . . . her honour's land lieth next to ours."[73] Women did not inherit shares passively, then; they made decisions about what to do with their investment. For Cecily West, her concern was to manage her assets in the Virginia Company in order to make the best financial provision for her child.

Women's experience of investing in the Virginia Company was mixed, involving independent undertaking and identifiably interdependent partnership. In the instances when women bought shares in association with others, including individuals outside of their immediate kinship group, such as friends or neighbors, it was not necessarily because they did not possess the commercial acumen to conduct business alone. Rather, investing alongside trusted associates potentially signaled a shrewd decision to minimize the risk associated with overseas trade.[74] Lady Elizabeth Berkeley's decision to buy one Virginia Company share in 1621 and a further five and a half in 1622 was most likely influenced by her relationship with the Gloucestershire Berkeley Hundred planters, John Smyth in particular. Lady Berkeley was first married to Sir Thomas Berkeley, and Smyth served as steward on their Gloucestershire estate. She communicated with Smyth frequently, and it is telling that she turned to him in several household and financial matters.[75] Yet, Lady Berkeley also had kinship connections with other investors in this cohort, including Sir William Throckmorton, William Tracy, Richard Berkeley, and Sir Maurice Berkeley.[76] Mabel Collymore's investment was similar in this respect, as she also invested alongside associates who were connected through kinship and locality. She received a "bill of adventure" worth £50 and land in Virginia in 1616 as one of Captain Argall's "associates," transporting twenty-four individuals to Virginia.[77] The investors all resided in Kent, including Argall of East Peckham, who was an early colonist in Virginia and its governor from 1617 to 1619.[78] But they also appear to have been a tight-knit kinship group, as they included Collymore's father Sir William Lovelace, her kinsman Sir Anthony Aucher, John Argall, no doubt a relative of Captain Argall, and John Tradescant, who also had ties to Kent.[79] Women who were inexperienced investors in overseas ventures might have turned to trusted associates as a safer means to "adventure," but this was not always the case. Collymore was married to John Collymore, a Freeman of the Mercers' Company, so she was not detached from the world of commerce—rather, as we will see, she was able to independently navigate trade.

As well as the connections of family and locality that helped to generate investment in the Virginia Company, elite women were entangled in patronage networks, possibly even brokering interest in Virginia themselves.[80] Lady Elizabeth Grey acted as a patron to the lawyer and scholar John Selden, who lived in Inner Temple, which adjoined Grey's home in Whitefriars, from 1603 to 1620. Grey and Selden established a close relationship, and biographers suggest that she even took Selden as her lover. Their relationship may have preceded her investment to the Virginia Company, but it was certainly prior to his. Beginning in 1620, Selden was employed by the company for two years to work on the legal framework of colony and was arrested alongside his Virginia Company colleagues in parliament, Sir Edwin Sandys and the Earl of Southampton, at the end of 1621.[81] Selden may have benefitted from Grey's ties to substantial figures in the Virginia Company, including her Cavendish uncle and cousin.[82] Lucy Russell, Countess of Bedford, a literary patron, poet, and kinswoman of the Sidneys, was also embedded in a network of important Virginia Company patrons and investors. She benefitted from the patronage of Robert Cecil, Earl of Salisbury, and her brother was a close associate of Henry, Prince of Wales. She was also John Donne's patron from 1607, whose interest in Virginia intensified after this date. In 1609, John Chamberlain wrote to Sir Dudley Carleton that Donne "seeks to be preferred to be secretary of Virginia." Although Donne never subscribed to the Virginia Company he was elected as an honorary member in 1622, delivering a sermon for the company in the same year.[83] Elite women may have helped to bring men of humbler social standing, like Selden and Donne, closer to the center of the Virginia Company. Evidently, women were not altogether excluded from the networks associated with investment in overseas trade. Rather, they promoted interest and investment themselves through their familial and patronage connections.

Women, Commerce, and Transatlantic Connections

Women such as Mabel Collymore also relied on their own means to profit from investment in trading companies and plantations. Those with merchant backgrounds and expertise, such as Rebecca Romney, Lady Conway, and Milicent Pickerd (later Ramsden), brokered independent interests in overseas ventures using their own commercial expertise and networks.[84] In the Chancery Court on 26 January 1624, the merchants William Browne and Robert

Wright explained how they had conducted business with Samuel Argall and his associates, which included Virginia Company investor Collymore.[85] As discussed above, she invested £50 in the Virginia venture in 1616 as one of Argall's "associates" alongside her kin and neighbors in Kent. This group of associates did not include her husband, John Collymore, although she was married at the time. It was not unusual for husbands and wives to keep their investments distinct, although it is not clear whether that was the arrangement between Collymore and her husband.[86] The court heard that in 1624 Argall had lodged a complaint against Browne and Wright concerning a missing account book. Apparently, Argall suspected the merchants of mishandling trade. Browne and Wright answered that they had never seen the said account book, that Argall had supposedly delivered to John Collymore, and neither had Collymore delivered the same to them. If John Collymore was directly involved in this transatlantic trade network, then it is possible that Mabel Collymore's investment in 1616 was on the behalf of them both. That husband and wife were working in partnership is borne out by the evidence that Browne and Wright gave in court. In September 1618, Browne and Wright had exported around 265 pounds of Virginian tobacco to England, which they sold to Thomas Smith, a Freeman of the Skinners' Company in London, at the rate of 5s. per pound. They received a total of £66 7s. for the tobacco, and that day they put £25 straight into Mabel Collymore's hand. The next day she received the residue of the profits, totaling £38 17s., in the presence, they said, of her husband John Collymore.[87] But they were clear that it was her they gave the money to, and not her husband. For Mabel Collymore, at least, her interest in Virginia had turned to profit.

Similarly, Elizabeth Dale was not lacking in her own connections with Virginia Company investors, independently of her husband. Dale had an extended kinship network in the Severn Valley region, which included members of the Berkeley, Throckmorton, and Tracy families, and among them were some of the region's key backers of colonization in Virginia. Dale was closely connected to the Berkeley Hundred planters, which included her brother Sir William Throckmorton, her first cousin William Tracy, another first cousin Richard Berkley, and his son Sir Maurice Berkeley. Lady Elizabeth Berkeley, also associated with this network, was distant kin, related to Throckmorton on her paternal side through the Barons of Berkeley. Another associate, George Thorpe, was also distant kin, on Elizabeth Dale's paternal side, through the Denys family. The Berkeley Hundred investors, in turn, had mutual ties of blood and marriage.[88] Sir Edward Conway was also Elizabeth Dale's kinsman, through his first marriage to her cousin Dorothy Tracy.[89] Dale's familial network furnished her with the commercial connections that she needed in order to successfully and independently manage her property in the Virginia colony following the death of her husband in 1619.

Elizabeth Dale oversaw plantations in Virginia and attempted to recover her inheritance, through petitioning and litigation, in an effort to secure her future prosperity.[90] In 1621, she petitioned the Virginia Company to grant her a "patent for a particular plantation." The following year, she requested that the company send a letter to Sir George Yeardly, the governor of the colony, requiring him to assist her servant in the recovery of money owed to her by her tenants in Virginia.[91] Dale was also forced to defend her estate against the allegation that her husband was indebted in Virginia. Again, she turned to her servants for assistance, to conduct enquiries on her behalf in Virginia. Elizabeth Smalley (or Smallay), the widow of Robert Smalley, alleged that Thomas Dale had purchased sixty-three pounds of tobacco from her husband, valued at £10 10s., but had only paid 10s. while he lived. Smalley claimed to have tried to recover the debt from Elizabeth Dale twice already, in the Court of Common Pleas, but Dale retorted that she had not been able to produce any witnesses in her defense, because they were in Virginia. Elizabeth Dale did not believe that her husband would have bought any tobacco from Smalley, who she described as her husband's "servant." However, Elizabeth Smalley's claims were supported both by her husband's will and several witnesses. Under the weight of evidence against her, Elizabeth Dale promised that she would contact her servants in Virginia, and if they confirmed that the debt was owed, she would pay it.[92] Although she was remote from the colony, Dale also offered assistance to other planters, including those in her kinship network. In June 1620, William Tracy, her first cousin, wrote to his associate John Smyth that "I have silkworm . . . given me by my Lady Dale and she promiseth me to lend me kine."[93] Smyth told fellow planter, Richard Berkeley, that Tracy also had "goats from the Lady Dale."[94] Her Gloucestershire familial networks extended to, and were invoked on, both sides of the Atlantic. Without the ties provided by family and the assistance of her employees, it would have been impossible for her to manage her business at a distance in England.

Women actively managed their investment in the Virginia Company and plantations in the colony, but they were also more widely involved in shaping the company's affairs and even the material reality of the colony. Merchants like Rebecca Romney, who was married to a company investor, never invested in the Virginia Company herself, but she did lend it money on interest, money that was used to fortify the colony and provision ships that would carry colonists as well as supplies.[95] The Virginia Company's own records rarely capture the full spectrum of women's involvement in colonial enterprise as investors. But archival fragments, which tell us about women's involvement in the tobacco trade, supplying silkworms to their fellow planters, or attending company meetings, demonstrate that in the first years of English colonization in Virginia women were investors and entrepreneurs that were willing to take risks, adapt, and innovate. Women like Rebecca Romney and Elizabeth Dale also draw attention to the fact that they, like many of the men who invested in the Virginia Company, had much broader interests in English overseas trade and colonization, including the Northwest Passage Company and East India Company.[96] The ways that women invested in the Virginia Company are, therefore, just a small, but still significant, window into how women furthered English colonial enterprise in seventeenth-century England.

Between 1607 and 1612, William Leveson attempted to gather up the sums of money owed to the Virginia Company, some "forty thousand pounds at the least." Furnished with "divers books and notes . . . as also the names of the persons that should be solicited," he traveled around London, reminding ladies as well as merchants, of their obligations to the company.[97] Investing in trading companies was a public practice, insofar as investors relied upon knowledge and information that circulated in places of work, worship, and recreation across England, when deciding whether and how much to invest.[98] Investing was also a way to cultivate a "public economic presence," not least signal your virtue as a pious Christian.[99] Different kinds of pressure were exerted on potential investors, but some of it involved highlighting broader societal concerns about poverty and vagrancy, a tactic that seems to have been especially persuasive within the livery companies. Investing should be understood in relation to the communal practices of corporations and livery companies, but it also has to be viewed in relation to the more intimate practices associated with marriage and kinship. The character of the company archive guides us toward a more public understanding of investing, but as analysis of social networks, including women's, demonstrates, investing was very much a personal affair. The entreaties of friends and associates persuaded investors to adventure their purses, and individuals were also influenced by the interest of their kin and neighbors. For the Virginia Company, pursuing investors was advantageous not only because of the sums of money they endowed upon the colonial project, but also because of the connections that were fostered between the company, individual investors, and institutions across England. These were relationships that enabled the company to leverage the influence it needed to pursue the practices associated with domestic colonial enterprise, from lotteries to forced transportation.

Investing in the Virginia Company prompted different behaviors and responses from men and women. The methods that women chose, or were sometimes forced, to adopt reflected the constraints of coverture, but many women also invested freely with their own wealth and enthusiastically and independently managed trade and plantations in the colony, participated in new markets, and adopted innovative investment practices. Elite women lent respectability and civility to the colonial project, as well as generous sums of money. Promoters of colonial ventures in Virginia went so far as to invoke unnamed "gentlewomen" as investors, in order to entice others, but were insistent that their identity should remain a secret.[100] Women, therefore, were not a marginal influence in the company, especially if we consider that there might have been many women, like Cecily West, whose marriage portions provided the capital that allowed their husbands to adventure. Clearly, however, husbands and wives also established productive partnerships, as the commercial enterprise of Mabel and John Collymore suggests. Advancing colonization in Virginia required the input of many different social groups and communities in England, but the capital that investors, women as well as men, committed was essential for the company's success. Investing in the Virginia Company was an enticing opportunity for men and women to participate in colonization without ever leaving England. Certainly, for some investors, colonization felt like a remote, even obscure, enterprise, but the effects of their contributions had very real implications for colonists and the colonized across the Atlantic Ocean.

CHAPTER 3

Creating Capital

Lotteries and Charitable Collections

When the Virginia Company lottery visited High Wycombe, Buckinghamshire, on 27 May 1615, the clerk who was charged with recording the names of those who bought tickets wrote the phrase "Hope depends on chance" at the bottom of the list.[1] His phrase captures the mood that surrounded lotteries: the prospect of winning was not without hope, but players were equally resigned to the reality that winning was a matter of luck. A similar sentiment was embroidered with white beads on a contemporary drawstring purse, "HIT OR MISS / THERE IT IS."[2] The words that embellished similar purses, such as "REMEMBER THE POOR," reminded wearers of their charitable duty.[3] But this purse cautioned its owner, while reaching down to take a coin, on the fickleness of fortune. That such similar purses were embroidered with statements of this kind suggests the ways that donating money for charitable purposes and playing at lotteries had shared associations. The proliferation of lotteries in early modern England was often to pay for public works, and playing at the Virginia Company lotteries, in the period between 1612 and 1621, was equally framed as an enterprise for the public good or "common weal." The drawstring purse is itself an example, then, of how the material connections between public duty and private gain were established, which were not incompatible concepts in early modern England. The Virginia Company exploited this association in order to generate informal financial investment in the colony through lotteries and collections. Opportunities to finance colonization in this way traveled across England and were experienced by many close to home.

Lotteries and donations were informal mechanisms for financing colonization that percolated down into early modern society and seeped into

Figure 1. Purse, 1628, England. Object # T.250-1960. By permission of the Victoria and Albert Museum, London.

unexpected spheres of interest and influence, as both the rich and poor could "adventure" their purses. Through these means the colony penetrated the worldview of individuals who were far removed, in multiple senses, from Virginia, enabling those who had never voyaged to America to encounter colonization in a local setting. Through such means, the Virginia Company forged connections with civic culture and charitable giving in England, mapping investment in the colony onto wider concerns for the poor, while establishing its own reputation as philanthropic and socially responsible.[4]

Exploring the Virginia Company lotteries and collections indicates the social depth of informal financial investment in the colony. The responses of elite men and women who invested in the Virginia Company through shareholding have received much scholarly attention, as discussed above. Much less understood is how a much larger public financed the colonization of Virginia and how they were persuaded to do so. Donations were received from individuals of the smallest economic means, and the lotteries were similarly accessible. With a "blank" costing as little as 12d. to 1s., participation was affordable for the "common sort."[5] Individuals who spent sums of money on lottery tickets or made charitable donations drove the colonial project, and their participation illuminates the ways that economic mobilization for colonization became much more commonplace in early modern England.

London's Lotteries

Encounters with the Virginia Company lotteries were initiated in what proved to be a fateful year for the company. In 1612, two of the company's greatest patrons, the Earl of Salisbury and Henry, the Prince of Wales, died. In response to the prince's untimely death, John Holles wrote to Robert Mansfield in 1613 that "our uncertain fate hangs rather by a geometrical, then a natural thread, and in this lottery we have a million of blanks, to one lot of comfort: Virginia, the Northwest Passage, all brave undertakings by sea, or land for the honour, and benefit of this nation."[6] Holles and Mansfield were among the Virginia Company investors, discussed above, who had already "adventured" their purses in the colony. Yet, the uncertainty that followed the demise of Salisbury and Henry in the same year eclipsed their hopes. As Holles's analogy also suggests, there was general skepticism toward the new lotteries, and until the Virginia Company lotteries were terminated in 1621, these reservations persisted.[7] Lotteries were precarious things, based solely on chance, and yet, despite these misgivings, they proved a triumph. In London and England's provincial towns, £29,000 was raised—enough money to fund around thirty voyages or the passage of 3,625 "maids" to the colony.[8] So while the Virginia Company failed to make sufficient profit to pay dividends to its shareholders, it did profitably tap into public funding. In this respect, at least, the Virginia Company was a success. The lotteries were also an important means through which individuals across England were brought into contact with the colonization project, and a way for the company, by stating its own civic responsibilities, to forge connections between the colony and communities at home.

There were precedents for using lotteries when the Virginia Company adopted them in 1612. Supposedly influenced by their success in the Low Countries, one was first tried in England in the 1560s, in order to pay for the repair of England's harbors.[9] Their success stemmed from the immediacy with which they captured public interest; according to one account, people flew "like Wild-geese" to play at a lottery in London in 1608.[10] The Virginia Company was granted royal authority to hold a lottery with its Third Charter on 12 March 1612, yet plans to hold one began even earlier.[11] On 24 February 1612, "A book or thing called, *The publication of the lottery for Virginia*" was entered in the Stationers' Register for the price of 6d. Lots for the first "Great Standing" lottery were sold for 2s. 6d., and each person who ventured £3 was given a silver spoon worth 10s.[12] Supporters of the company, far and wide, attempted to court interest in the lottery. From Antwerp, John Wither wrote to the diplomat Sir William Trumbull, on 28 May 1612, "The lottery for Virginia is put off for a month. I have under-written for £5 hoping that I shall find some partners in Antwerp which I have offered." It is not clear whether his partners would have been other Englishmen, but the popularity of lotteries in the Low Countries suggests that Wither could have enticed participants from among his European associates. As well as the £5 he hoped to recuperate in Antwerp, Wither had also ventured £4, which he "presumed to write for my partner Brownlowe and myself in half, who I think will not refuse me."[13] This lottery was first drawn on 29 June, but took until 20 July to complete. In the end, because there was insufficient interest, 60,000 lots were "taken out and thrown away."[14] Not only did the tickets, at over 2s., still outprice many Londoners, but, as Robert Johnson has suggested, the colonization project, in the eyes of many, still "lacked promise."[15] Only two years earlier, colonists had been on the brink of abandoning the colony altogether.[16] Individuals who could have afforded to purchase tickets were unwilling to risk their money while the colony's future remained precarious. Undeterred, the company established running lotteries in August 1612, located in Smithfield, Southwark, and the Strand; with tickets that cost 12d., these lotteries were intended to attract the "common sort." Virginia Company investor Lady Conway, then Katherine Fust, was the stepmother of one of the administrators tasked with overseeing the running of these lotteries. The entire affair ended in controversy, however, when she was implicated in an apparent scam to defraud players.[17] Another lottery, "a little standing Lottery, consisting but of 12d. for every Lot," was originally planned for Candlemas term of 1613, but was postponed until 10 May 1613 and then again to 26 June 1613.[18] While the lotteries would achieve success in time, at first the Virginia Company struggled to generate enough interest.

The Virginia Company wrongly anticipated that the new affordability of the tickets would entice more players in London. In 1612, it wrote of its hope "that the inhabitants of this honourable City adventuring even but small sums of money, would have soon supplied so little a sum appointed to so good a work." Yet the company reported on the "slow bringing in of . . . money."[19] With similar disdain, Samuel Calvert complained, on 14 December 1612, that "the great lottery lies as if there were no life in the foundation." He interpreted the stagnation of the lottery as a symptom of the colony's lack of success more generally: just like the lottery, Calvert reported "Our Virginia plantations' motion is so slow that at this instant I can perceive no pulses to beat to purpose."[20] The second "Great Standing" lottery received some support from players outside London. In High Wycombe on 27 May 1615, the mayor and thirty citizens, including women and children, contributed £12 13s. 4d. toward the lottery.[21] A much more generous contribution of £97 was made by the citizens of Exeter.[22] At Great Yarmouth, its MP George Hardware bought lots worth £25 and included the poesy "Great Yarmouth Haven now in great distress, / Expects by Lottery some good success."[23] However, this lottery was not a roaring success either, and faced similar delays until November 1615.[24] Despite repeated attempts, then, to promote the lotteries across London and elsewhere, the company's efforts were largely fruitless in the beginning.

Across the City of London, the Virginia Company tried to garner the support of the livery companies, as well as individual players. The companies were central to urban life in early modern England, as bodies that regulated trade and helped to foster communal bonds through conviviality. They also shared a strong sense of charitable duty and administered poor relief not just among their own members, but also in the community more widely.[25] Freemen in the City of London "lay under a heavy responsibility of tradition and status to make large and useful charitable dispositions."[26] The Virginia Company treasurer, Thomas Smythe, and the Privy Council recalled this tradition, to good effect, by entreating the companies to remember their civic responsibility, both toward the city and Virginia. Indeed, on 18 May 1612, the Vintners' Company agreed, in order to uphold "the reputation and credit of the company," to adventure £40 in the first "Great Standing" lottery. Thomas Smythe had persuaded the Vintners' that the plantation would enrich the realm with new commodities, win souls to heaven and also disburden the nation of idle people.[27] The Clothworkers' Company also "adventured" £50, and its contribution was similarly secured "at the request and mediation of Sir Thomas Hewett," a Virginia Company investor.[28] While, "upon the earnest request of Sir Thomas Smythe," the Drapers' Company were persuaded to pay in £30, when called upon by the Privy Council to support the company lotteries again in May 1614, they gave a further £30.[29] Smythe also visited the Mercers' Company in the summer of 1612, when the company "fully agreed" to "adventure £50 in this present lottery for Virginia," and another £50 was "adventured" in 1614.[30] Finally, the Haberdashers' Company gave £20 that same year.[31] The Privy Council's letters to the livery companies in 1614, entreating them to contribute, were enclosed with copies of a company publication, titled a "true declaration."[32] The authority of the Privy Council, and oratory of the Virginia Company, certainly seems to have been persuasive. The Grocers' Company recorded, "Mr warden Dale with many forcible reasons for the general advancement of Christianity and good of our common wealth moved and persuaded the whole assembly then present to write particularly with their own hands how much every of them would willingly set down severally to adventure in the said lottery intended to so good a purpose." Among those who signed their names was the Lord Mayor of London, Sir Thomas Myddelton.[33] The Fishmongers' Company, which had adventured £25 in 1612, was similarly convinced, and gave £80 in 1614 to the second "Great Standing" lottery. The freemen did bitterly complain though that "very few of the adventurers did receive any profit thereby."[34]

The Virginia Company's supposed commitment to the "common weal" was emphasized across multiple genres of literature, which were used to persuade a broad swathe of English society to "adventure" in the lotteries. When, in 1619, the company drafted a letter to the City of London aldermen on the behalf of William Crashaw, it reiterated that colonization in Virginia was "a work not only of so public and general an use but of so high excellent and honourable a nature." Yet while there were wider issues at stake, the apparent profit to be gained by the lottery was often related to issues much closer to home. *Londons Lottery* promoted the potential for private, material gain as well as public good, claiming those who were lucky at the lottery would win "credit and good name" and, like London, would "live . . . famous long," at least in reputation.[35] The idea of "credit" was two-fold: as well as "good name," those who adventured in the lottery could find "fortune" and "great Riches." In humanist discourse, private gain and public good were not entirely at odds. For instance, a lottery held in Milan in the fifteenth century made an "appeal to private profit and wider civic loyalty."[36] While playing at the lottery offered amusement and the potential for huge winnings, *Londons Lottery* suggested participation also entailed a larger contribution to the prosperity of England.[37]

In the ballad, notions of public good were also entangled with Christian concern, with colonization in Virginia configured as a godly project. In the first instance, it was said that "God will favour Christians still, / and like the purpose well," but the ballad also provoked sympathy through the comparison and contrast of Algonquian and English society. It depicted England as presently well governed and enjoying "long-loved peace and plenty," yet it reminded audiences that the condition of Virginia was now as "England was once," "like a Wilderness." Virginia and its Indigenous inhabitants supposedly lacked a civil polity, with the ballad proclaiming that colonists would "plant that Land in government, / which never was before" and "build up fast Virginia's state." It was in both text and image that contemporaries were reminded that before Roman occupation their forbears had once inhabited a "savage place." Images of Algonquians were circulated alongside depictions of ancient Britons, who appeared with blue-painted, naked bodies, holding weapons and the severed heads of their foes.[38] The broadside published for the drawing of the second "Great Standing" lottery showed two Virginia Algonquians, Eiakintomino and Matahan, positioned on either side of an English man drawing rolled lottery papers, himself surrounded by rich prizes of gold coins and plate. Underwritten were the supposed words of the Virginia Indians, begging English audiences to bring the gospel to America:

> As *We*, were *Ye*; 'til *Others* Pity
> Sought, and brought You to *That City*.
> Dear *Britons* now, *be You* as kind;
> Bring *Light*, and *Sight*, to *Us*, yet blind:

Lead *Us*, by *Doctrine* and *Behaviour*,
Into one *Sion*, to one SAVIOUR.

Alluding to the Roman invasion and the civility they brought to Ancient Britons when they "planted" London ("*That City*"), the message was clear: "Virginia may in time, / be made like England now."[39]

In a letter to the City of London aldermen, the Virginia Company similarly entangled colonial discourse with evangelizing impulse, reminding them that the profits from the lotteries would help to fund a "Christian Plantation." Yet the company implied that colonization was a shared responsibility and admonished the aldermen that, until then, the venture had been borne upon "the shoulders of a few . . . many years to the care and burthen of the whole Land." This emphasis on the public, rather than private, nature of colonization was reiterated: "the benefit arising by the Lotteries belongs not to any in private but is consecrated to the public advancement of the work, and in particular to the building and endowing [of] Schools and Colleges wherein the Children of the Heathen are to be educated in Civility and Christianity and the knowledge of our language."[40] The Virginia Company presented the lottery as a Christian undertaking that also reaffirmed the responsibilities of the aldermen toward the poor and commonwealth more broadly.

Locating the Lottery House

From around 1616, the Virginia Company attempted to court new interest in the lotteries in provincial towns, which it did with some success. When the Virginia Company undertook these running lotteries in England's provincial towns, it had to do more than merely grab the attention of potential participants: it also had to gain the cooperation of town officials. To do this, it wrote letters to the mayors, recorders, and aldermen, some of which have survived in county archives, at Chester (1616), Norwich (1617), and Leicester (1618).[41] The letters introduced the appointed managers of the running lotteries, Gabriel Barbour and Lott Peere, and instructed how the lotteries should be organized. Writing to Chester on 15 June 1616, the company guaranteed the "fidelity, care and sufficiency" of Barbour and Peere and requested, "for so good a work as the upholding of that Plantation," that "a running Lottery . . . be kept in that your city." If the City of Chester officials had any doubts, they were assured that the Virginia Company "have now great hope and greater then heretofore" that the plantation would "stand and flourish to the honor and benefit of this Realm."[42] The company attempted to satisfy towns not only that the lotteries would be conducted with integrity, but also that the colony was worth their investment. The first samples of Virginian tobacco had recently reached England, grown by the colonist John Rolfe, the husband of Pocahontas. Their marriage in 1614 secured amity between the English and Powhatans.[43] In 1616, at least, the future prosperity and security of the colony seemed more assured.

Continued concern about the integrity of the lotteries stemmed, in part, from the reputation that the Virginia Company's lotteries had earned in London. In 1613, the company had accused William Leveson, the manager of the lottery at St. Paul's, of fraud, alleging that he had withheld £700.[44] In 1615, the Court of Star Chamber heard allegations of further corruption in the Virginia Company's lottery. Walter Fitzwilliam, who was Carver-in-Ordinary to the king, complained that John West, the manager of the running lottery in London, and an attorney named John Webb, had stolen winning lots and had coaxed two of West's servants to falsely claim the prizes.[45] To alleviate concerns, the company gave the City of Chester a series of clear instructions to avoid fraudulent practice: "receive this key herein sealed . . . [and] the prizes, and so see the mingling of them with the blanks . . . appoint one or two of your city (men of care) to lock up and open the same every morning and evening, and to permit a child (who shall be allowed for his pains) to draw out the Lots for all that adventure."[46] The custom of using a child to draw lots was common on the Continent too and was supposed to guarantee fairness; as the company explained, "so shall those whom we employ not be suspected of partiality."[47] The Virginia Company was tasked with reconciling several difficulties concerning the lotteries, but as well as insufficient interest and corruption, it found that conducting lotteries in provincial towns presented a new set of issues to resolve.

In provincial towns, the new affordability of tickets attracted players of small means, which was cause for further criticism. A 1608 pamphlet described how, playing at lotteries, "thus do a number of poor men labour with a kind of greediness to beggar themselves."[48] The laboring poor faced moral censure for gambling at lotteries. Writing to town councils, the Virginia Company proscribed "forbidding the poorer sort to make any adventures . . . as it is plainly set down in the printed Publications."[49] Heeding this advice, on 12 June 1618, the Leicester mayor and aldermen announced that the lottery was "free for all comers to adventure their money (poor people only excepted)."[50]

The prohibition of poor players was not completely effective, though. One way that players from all backgrounds were able to participate in the lottery was through the pooling of resources to buy tickets, much like Virginia Company investors who "adventured" together. In Wells, Somerset, Walter Cole reported that "he came to Wells to the lottery, and there joining his money with fifteen other persons . . . got a prize of six pounds, which some they divided between themselves."[51] For this reason, the charitable gifts that the Virginia Company gave to provincial towns have been viewed as a direct response to this issue, as "designed to create good will" and "material inducement."[52] Arguably, their purpose was more complex: they were intended to reaffirm the lotteries' association with public good and also to abate the concern of officials, that the lotteries were morally circumspect. Yet, when compared to the company's recruitment of artificers for Virginia, whose families were paid compensatory sums and children apprenticed, the company's actions fit within a broader pattern of behavior that was supposed to demonstrate charitable concern for the poor. The gifts served to emphasize the company's civic and social responsibility, as they helped the towns that provided support.[53]

The gifts that the company gave suggest that the colonization project was not wholly outward looking, across the Atlantic, but also concerned with issues at home. Moreover, the archival footprint left by the company's gift giving makes it possible to pinpoint the exact locations of the running lotteries. Gabriel Barbour gave the public library at Norwich, Norfolk, several volumes of theological works by Wolfgang Musculus, Clement of Alexandria, and Fulgentius of Ruspe in 1614. The library, which provided reading material to traveling preachers, was relatively new in 1614, and the works that the Virginia Company donated would have furnished the content of sermons in the city.[54] Similarly, when the lottery visited Maidstone, Kent, in July and August 1618, Barbour gifted a gilt cup, which the town clerk recorded would be used for communion.[55] In the years to come, material reminders of the Virginia colony would survive, exemplifying colonialism in lay spirituality. Several towns also received donations for the poor, including Leicester (£20), Maidstone (£20), Dorchester (£50), Devizes (£40), Reading (£40), Manchester (£30), Tiverton (£40), Cirencester (£40), and Warwick. These sums were used for various charitable purposes, including school supplies, hospitals, assisting poor artificers, and apprenticing poor children.[56] In Bristol, under disbursements for the parish poor in 1616, the churchwardens of St. Ewen's recorded "money given by the lottery £3 8s. 3d.," while in Gloucester, the "money given by the masters of the lottery" was "to be employed in provision of wood and coals for the poor of this city."[57] Profits from the Virginia lotteries would very literally sustain poor families, heating their hearths and stoking fires for their cooking.

The Virginia Company donations that were disbursed to poor tradesmen were carefully administered. In Bridgwater, Somerset, the mayor and aldermen recorded, on 1 April 1621, a "receipt for sixty pounds from the council of Virginia by . . . their deputy Gabriel Barbour . . . ten pounds thereof to be forthwith distributed to the poor; and the fifty pounds to be lent to some poor tradesmen inhabitants of your town, five pounds a piece for three years free without use; (Alehouse-keepers to be exempted from any part thereof) the said parties giving good security for repayment at the end of the three years, and other ten persons to have the said monies."[58]

The caveat that alehouse keepers were not to benefit added a further moral dimension to these civic loans, and proscriptions of this kind were not unusual.[59] If the purpose of the loans were to dispel negativity toward the lotteries, caused by the perception that poor people gambled away their earnings, then the company could not conceivably support individuals whose business was in drink. In Wells, the company also distributed civic loans. On 15 November 1619, Gabriel Barbour "tendered a book for lending the use of £30 by him given to be lent from five years to five years to six poor Burgesses for ever."[60] In December, a clerk noted that one of the chosen recipients was Henry Moorton, "notwithstanding that he is no burgess." The reason given was that Henry's wife "is a kinswoman of the said Mr Barbers."[61] In Devizes, Wiltshire, the loans were intended for "such honest tradesmen and artificers of the borough as will set the poor people on work and willingly take poor men's children of the same borough to be their apprentice." Here, the lottery would benefit a wider class of local people, including poor children, so that "they may be the better enabled to live."[62] Just as the company used the increasingly familiar model of charity briefs to collect money for the colony, an ostensibly unfamiliar cause, discussed below, it used lotteries, a relatively new financial scheme, to generate funds for familiar causes: the relief of the parish and laboring poor. Through gifts and loans the lotteries supported the colony in Virginia as well as the poor in England, and in doing so, the company demonstrated commitment to the public good—both at home and in Virginia.

The broad appeal that promoters of the Virginia colony wanted to generate is evident not only in promotional material and the cost of lottery tickets, but also in the actual locations chosen for the lotteries. During this period, the Virginia Company's lottery houses were afforded important spatial status in London, as they were woven onto existing sites associated with entertainment and spectacle in the hope of attracting participants. William Leveson was hired to oversee the "building erecting and setting up of a Convenient house for the said Lottery and furnishing of it with all hanging furniture and other stuff." The place the company acquired for this first lottery house was at the west end of St. Paul's, and it remained (as far as it is known) the location for the "Great Standing" and the "Little Standing" lotteries. St. Paul's Cathedral, both the building itself and the churchyard, was a significant site in seventeenth-century London, as a space for receiving news and gossip, a platform for sermons and a market for print. Even before the lotteries began, the preparations would have attracted attention: Leveson described how he bought timber and found workmen and paid for their "hire diet and wages" as they constructed a timber lottery "house." Administrators from the Virginia Company even regularly visited to check that the work was to their "liking."[63] The Virginia Company obtained a space for its lottery that was intended to attract the greatest amount of attention possible, enticing a broad body of spectators and participants from the multitudes that gathered on a daily basis in the aisles and yard of St. Paul's.

Running lotteries, as opposed to standing lotteries, were adopted in Smithfield, Southwark, and the Strand in 1613, in keeping with the entertainment and consumption associated with these parts of London and its environs.[64] The locations picked were prominent sites of spectacle, home to the conspicuous display of aristocratic townhouses, bloody sports, and performances on the stage.[65] They were places where the activity and entertainment of aristocrats, citizens, and the commons intermixed, meaning the Virginia Company could expect to attract an audience as diverse as those described in *Londons Lottery*. Through the ballad genre, the company attempted to convey a sense of universality among informal financial investors, as individuals from across the social spectrum were identified as lottery players. The ballad suggested the "highly democratic nature" of lotteries, as "Maids," "Country men," and "worthy Gentlemen" were all entreated to "venture now for Gold."[66] The higher social status of some players was suggested by the woodcuts for *Londons Lottery*, which depicted scenes from Archbishop Matthew Parker's 1572 translation of the *Books of Kings*. One woodcut, in particular, recalled an image of Powhatan (or Wahunsenacawh), an Algonquian leader and Pocahontas's father, who appeared crowned with feathers, sitting atop a throne in John Smith's 1612 *Map of Virginia*. As Margaret Aston suggests, audiences could not have missed the pictorial allusion to "regal presences."[67] This imagery was mirrored in the lyrics of the ballad itself, which claimed that "our most royal King and Queen . . . Hath granted grace and favours both" and "Prince Henry he, / in love is not behind."[68]

The greatest advantage of the running lotteries was the immediacy of the spectacle. Unlike participants in the standing lotteries held in St. Paul's, there was no need for participants to wait until the grand drawing to find out whether they had won, which could take months. Instead, lots were drawn immediately, meaning that players could potentially walk away, there and then, with their prizes. *The Great Frost* described a typical lottery player, who received "the papers of life and death . . . rolled up like Wafers," only to be confronted by "a pale piece of paper," hence, not a winning lot.[69] The theatrical staging of the lottery, which may have included the display of extravagant prizes, such as standing dishes or gold coins, but which certainly included the performance of children drawing lots, would have mapped colonization in Virginia onto these sites of everyday consumption.

The opportunity to invest individual fortunes in America through the lottery circulated even more widely than London, around England and onto the Continent. In English provincial towns and cities, civic spaces were designated as the lottery house; copies of advertisements were sent ahead by the Virginia Company to town officials in order to generate publicity; and the events themselves, which sometimes coincided with civic festivities, provided opportunities for performance, spectatorship, and participation in local settings. The Virginia Company connected with communities through opportunities to participate in colonization, raising awareness and interest, as well as capital. The provincial running lotteries began in 1616 and can be followed throughout England up to 1621, with research pointing to lotteries that were held across England. Lotteries in Warwick, Bristol, and Gloucester suggests there was an even wider dispersal of engagement with the Virginia Company than previously thought.[70]

Outside London, the Virginia Company lottery was a particularly appealing pastime. Writing from Exeter on 2 October 1619, Gabriel Barbour reported to Sir Edwin Sandys that the lotteries "prosper exceedingly in these western parts, where (I think) twill hold till Christ[mas]tide; I perceive small Towns & great markets, doth exceed the best Cities."[71] The provincial lotteries were very lucrative for the company too. In Leicester, the lottery consisted of 40,000 lots priced at 12d., generating £2,000 from ticket sales, and players had the opportunity to win 1,500 prizes, which were valued at £1,038 4s. 9d.[72] The running lotteries were successful because they mapped onto local civic culture too, by coinciding with important festivities, and appropriating meaningful spaces for the lottery houses. In Ipswich, the common hall was used as a lottery house, while in Norwich the council reported that, as Gabriel Barbour had requested, "[N]ewhall Chapel shall be appointed for that purpose."[73] In Chester, the lottery is likely to have taken place in either the common hall in the chapel of St. Nicholas or the Pentice, at St. Peter's church. The lower floor of the common hall was used for the storage of wholesale goods, but the upper hall served many purposes: it was a playhouse, the room where the corporation met, and the room where the quarter sessions were held. It was a significant, multifunctional civic space, importantly located in the marketplace of the city. The Pentice, on the other hand, was where the mayor conducted his business and where many civic banquets and games took place.[74] In Wells too, the lottery house was likely to have been located in the common hall, which was in the middle of the marketplace next to the cathedral.[75] The running lotteries did not take place in isolation then, but were made relevant and legitimated by their transfer onto symbolic spaces, representative of "civic honour," like the marketplace, and by their timing with cultural festivities.[76]

The timing of the Virginia Company's request to hold a lottery in the City of Chester was prescient.[77] Gabriel Barbour and Lott Peere, along with the company's letter, may have arrived as early as 17 June, right before an important period in Chester's civic calendar: Midsummer's Day.[78] The festival traditionally fell between 21 and 25 June, coinciding with the feast of St. Werburgh on 21 and 22 June, which from the thirteenth century was extended by the city so that the celebrations lasted for two weeks on either side of midsummer. During this period, the city reveled in festivities, holding a market and enjoying further entertainment from the Midsummer's Day show.[79] It is hard to believe that the timing of the company's letter was accidental, coinciding as it did with these celebrations. The Virginia Company tried to ensure that the lotteries were prominent and visible in English towns. It clearly anticipated that the lottery in Chester would be absorbed among the midsummer celebrations, as crowds descended on the city in search of exchange, consumption, and spectacle.

Richard Cokley was himself attracted to Chester at this time for the very same reasons. He ventured to Chester in June 1616 from his grandmother's home in Nantwich, located around twenty-two miles away. He told the city's

JPs that he traveled "intending to get some money of certain gent during the fair . . . by singing dancing and other . . . sleight which he useth." Cokley described how, on entering the city on a Friday, he had found lodging with two pipers, Francis and Thomas Willson, who had no doubt also traveled to Chester with the intention of entertaining the crowds at the market. As well as music, singing, dancing, tricks, and games to entertain visitors to the fair, there was the added spectacle of a lottery. Cokley himself, along with the Willsons, "went to the lottery." Approaching the "lottery house," Cokley may have been confronted by the image of a small child, surrounded by glimmering prizes, withdrawing rolled white papers from the tumbling baskets, and a hush may have fallen over the audience, as the papers were unfurled. We have Cokley's testimony about a lottery in Chester because the following day, another visitor to the fair, Peter Archer, accosted Cokley and accused the pipers of stealing his purse.[80] Richard Cokley was examined on 29 June (just fourteen days after the Virginia Company addressed a letter to the City of Chester) and deposed that he had been at a lottery in the city about 21 June, while the letter (Barbour and Peere with it) may have arrived around 17 June.[81] Through such incidental stories, we can begin to imagine how lotteries were experienced in these provincial settings, the timings and mechanisms that guaranteed their success, and the opportunities they presented for amusement as well as wrongdoing.

When locations were chosen for the lottery houses, the lottery agents, Barbour and Peere, were thinking about more than captivating audiences. The locations suggested that the lotteries were afforded legitimacy by civic authorities, and thus the claims that the Virginia Company made in promotional literature, that colonization would benefit the "common weal," appeared reinforced. Nevertheless, the connection between the Virginia Company lottery and local festivities was also problematic. In Chester and Wells the accounts of the lotteries only survive because they were associated with petty crime. The deposition made about a lottery in Wells can also be identified as the Virginia Company's. Officials in Bridgwater received a letter from the Virginia Company, and a lottery was held in the town before 1 April 1620; however, a gift from Gabriel Barbour shows that a lottery was also held in Wells, twenty-one miles from Bridgwater, some months before.[82] In October 1619, two depositions, given by Walter Cole and Ruthe Pittman, also point toward this. They described going to the lottery, together with four others, and celebrating their shared winnings of £6 afterward in a tavern, by drinking ale and eating cake. However, Pittman stated that after they were "late at the lottery held in Wells," Cole stole from her "with violence . . . the sum of six shillings." Cole denied the charge, instead insisting that he last saw Pittman at the tavern with a group of male youths before he returned home.[83] The lotteries had a prosaic impact upon life locally, then, creating opportunities both for pleasure and subversion.

Through their statements, we learn how inhabitants of provincial towns, the "common sort," might have encountered the colonization of Virginia as players in the company lottery. It was said that "a very great and almost infinite number of several persons" had taken part in the lotteries.[84] But what did it mean to part with your money and gamble in the Virginia lottery? Did the circulation of print, including ballads, mean that playing in the lottery was understood as saving the souls of Native Americans? Was walking away with a prize like winning your own share of American wealth? As she celebrated with her ale and cake, was Ruthe Pittman thinking about her fellow countrywomen in Virginia? We have no answers, but the popularity of participation in lotteries suggests that a large number of English subjects, whether at home or overseas, deemed it worthwhile to venture in the lotteries—either to win "credit" or support the colony. Unfortunately, the incidents of petty crime that allegedly flourished around the lotteries, as described by Ruthe Pittman and Richard Cokley's accuser Peter Archer, kindled by the larger festivities in which they were situated, no doubt helped to cement their negative reputation and eventual dissolution.

The termination of the lotteries in March 1621, therefore, was determined by factors that were not altogether in the company's control. Even while members of the House of Commons, including Sir Dudley Digges and William Beecher, defended the lotteries on the grounds that they were to "so general a good," wholly "voluntary," and ultimately "to a public end," there was no denying the accusations that they were maligned by corruption or that the poor gambled away the little earnings they had at the lottery house.[85] A proclamation issued on 8 March 1621 suspended the Virginia Company's lotteries, and all others, stating that while "Our eye fixed upon a religious and Princely end and design, yet the said Lotteries, having now for a long time been put in use, do daily decline to more and more inconvenience, to the hinderance of multitudes of Our Subjects."[86] So it was that the lotteries, which had, according to the Virginia Company, been the "real and substantial food" that "nourished" colonization, came to an abrupt end.[87] While it is possible to imagine that the proprietors of the Antelope and the Swan in Wells, where Ruthe Pittman, Walter Cole, and their associates spent their winnings, may have been pleased with the increased patronage that the lotteries supported, it is also easy to understand why onlookers may have resented the new-found wealth that enabled the poorer sort to become inebriated.[88]

Although the Virginia Company's lotteries were prematurely terminated, observers of the colony, colonial projectors, and colonists themselves understood that they had supported and even helped the colony to flourish. In his 1622 diatribe against Thomas Smythe and the former government in Virginia, colonist Captain John Bargrave noted that the foundation of the colony was upon "public servants, planted by the lotteries."[89] John Guy, a Newfoundland colonist, similarly complained "the plantation of Newfoundland never had [a] penny help, but from the adventurers purses, nor ever had any lotteries."[90] Then, when Somers Island Company investors revolted against the Virginia Company's proposed tobacco contract in 1623, they appealed to the Crown that special care had to be taken toward Bermuda: it had not, unlike Virginia, had the assistance of lotteries and donations.[91] That the lotteries had helped to sustain the colony was recognized at the time, and this supposedly successful model of drawing on public finances was even considered for future colonial ventures. Sometime between 1629 and 1630, one anonymous colonial projector (possibly for Carolina) reminded the Crown that "Virginia hath been furthered by many lotteries, and public requests in all the parish churches." They came up with their own model to similarly draw upon "public" money.[92] This association between the lotteries and parish collections, noted at the time, is an important one. As with the drawstring purse, there was a material connection between playing at the lotteries and public collections. Both had charitable, even pious, undertones. While the Virginia Company lotteries were never revived after 1621, the company did, until its dissolution in 1624, continue to receive public financial support in the form of public donations.

Charity and Public Piety

In churches across England, parishioners were entreated to part with their earnings for Virginia. This was not the only time that parochial charity complemented state policy in early modern England. Supporting Virginia fitted within a much larger nexus of local giving to more distant causes, not least England's Protestant allies, including French Huguenots, refugees, and mariners captured by Turks.[93] Money was frequently gathered to help release captured Christian mariners, replace someone's property lost in a fire, or even fund the passage of destitute Irish travelers to return home.[94] So as well as supporting the poor and vulnerable in their own communities, parishioners helped to relieve the suffering of people further afield. It is not surprising, then, that in the years following the colonization of Jamestown, the public was urged to support the colony too. Colonization evoked public piety and, in the words of William Crashaw, stimulated "the stirring up of so many Honourable and worthy persons of all conditions, to disburse so freely and so willingly, such far sums of money, and some of them even a good part of their estate, and that without any certain or apparent hope of speedy profit."[95] Printed literature was circulated widely to entreat the public to aid the colonial project through collections. A brief issued in 1616, for example, instructed ministers, "in your sermons or otherwise, by exhortation, to stir up the devotion of godly people, to the advancing of a work so much tending to the glory of Almighty God."[96] The donations that the company received from churches and elsewhere shows that the capital that flowed into the company was, as with the lotteries, similarly geographically wide, and provided by individuals from a range of social backgrounds.

This phenomenon can be explained, in part, by understanding the collection of money in church as an inherently *public* practice, with parishioners facing pressure to contribute. The fabric of the church itself, furnished with the poor box, book of remembrance, and alms dish, "recorded" collections and also reinforced the relationship between charity and worship. The congregants of St. Alphage, in the City of London, where the treasurer of the Virginia Company Thomas Smythe was a vestryman, may have been particularly compelled by the material realities of their church. In 1616, an "Indian dish" was purchased for 12d. Whatever its original intended use was, the congregants had refashioned it as a collection plate, "to gather money in." So, when the church made a collection for Virginia in 1618, it is possible that its parishioners placed their coins in this Indigenous ware.[97] We can only imagine how encountering a Virginia Indian object during the collection might have reinforced the Protestant evangelizing mission that was so familiar from company sermons and even persuaded some to dig deeper into their purses.

In order to foster such practices, which included the issuing of a charity brief in 1616 and a precept from the Lord Mayor of London in 1618 to collect money for the colony, the Virginia Company had to secure the Crown's support. This, it appears, was generously forthcoming. A royal letter patent, drafted in 1620 with the intended purpose of raising funds for the colony, stated that Virginia was of "high import, tending much to our honour, the perpetual safety of our kingdoms, and the good of all our subjects."[98] The granting of such privileges underlines that the Virginia Company and its members were a powerful lobby at the Jacobean court. Mechanisms for levying funds, such as the charity or church brief, "show how personal appeals, patronage, and impersonal agencies fitted together in a distinctively early modern way."[99]

As well as national efforts, throughout this period there was sporadic charitable giving for the colonization project too, from individuals as well as parish churches. Most commonly, churchwardens supported, on a case-by-case basis, strangers returning from Virginia, or their own parishioners who were about to embark on journeys to the colony. Additionally, one estimate puts bequests from individual donors in London to the North American colonies, including Virginia, Bermuda, Massachusetts, New England, and New Hampshire, in the period up to 1660 at £1,942.[100] Arguably, however, when it came to public contributions, the Virginia colony was preferred above other American ventures in the first decades of English colonization. This apparent success, did, however, have an adverse effect, by stunting the efforts of later colonial projectors. The Privy Council noted in 1623, that in order to assist Virginia the kingdom had been "drained by former gathering in churches."[101] This was the unfortunate consequence of the great outpouring of public piety toward Virginia. True or not, this perception had implications for prospective ventures not only in the Chesapeake, but in New England and the Caribbean too.

Promoters of the colony carefully mediated appeals to public duty and to private as well as spiritual gain to persuade people to make donations. The Virginia Company promoter and preacher Patrick Copland argued, in a publication that described his recent collection of money for the colony, that "public actions of virtue, besides that they are presently comfortable to the doers, are also exemplary to others . . . while our souls live in glory in heaven, our good actions may live upon earth."[102] His notion of the public good, delineated as virtuous actions, shaped the rhetoric that surrounded the donation of money to the colony. William Crashaw similarly proclaimed that by donating to Virginia "we may show our selves good common-wealths-men." While other actions might "enrich our purses," this, he said, would enrich "our consciences."[103] But as well as for their public good, donations were exemplified for the opportunity they provided for spiritual edification.

When sailors aboard an East India Company ship, on which Copland traveled, donated to the Virginia colony, the apparent conversion of the whole ship toward this godly cause was presented as a profoundly Christian act: "*they that turn many to righteousness, shall shine as the Stars for ever and ever*, Dan. 12. 3."[104] Yet, the framing of donating to the Virginia colony as an act of "common weal" collided, at times, with private interest. A draft royal letter of authorization warned parishioners that if they failed to donate to the colony then their ability to receive any material benefit from Virginia would cease.[105] Thus, promoters of colonization in Virginia adopted a strategy for persuasion that wedded public duty and private gain and relied on an everyday understanding of commonwealth: that it entailed the preservation of resources for the whole of society.[106]

The sermon was a key device for inspiring public piety. In this respect, that sermons were printed to be both read and heard was significant, as from the pulpit ideas about colonization, the godly commonwealth and the spiritually "regenerative effect" of Virginia were diffused to audiences across England.[107] Sermons made claim to the godly justifications for colonization, but they also mused on the act of donating itself. Daniel Price praised London, "this Honourable City," for its "liberal contribution," while William Crashaw credited "assistance by the *purse*," arguing that each person "is bound to assist . . . according to that ability of his."[108] The necessity of monetary contributions was not ignored in sermons, and we know, of course, that praying in church for the success of the Virginia colony was not "in lieu of 'purses'" either, despite Crashaw's verse "Some engage their persons, and more their purses; but our petitions shall do more good then our persons, and our prayers then our purses."[109] Clearly the sermons delivered by Crashaw and others effected collections in parish churches across England. There were, however, apparent barriers to donating. According to Crashaw, a man was "bound first to maintain himself and his family, and to bear his part . . . where he lives." Yet, as we will see, the Virginia Company attempted to overcome such anxieties, of local versus ostensibly global charity, by suggesting that money proffered in the parish could bring longer-lasting material benefits to families at home. Moreover, audiences were pleaded with to consider what they spent on "*vanities*" and "superfluities" and think how such sums could have "done much good to this godly business."[110]

As well as the application of rhetorical tools, the company needed to employ actual mechanisms to collect donations. The Virginia Company used the parish church, and specifically the charity or church brief, to gather contributions from ordinary people. A brief was a writ from the monarch that authorized the bearer to travel far and wide to seek donations. Often then, when individuals confronted parish churches with their paper licenses, the causes that they entreated for, could be far removed—geographically and emotionally—from the immediate concerns of the parishes they had recently entered. This was no barrier, however, to parochial generosity.[111] In 1616 a brief was issued to raise funds to build a school and church in the colony, in order to educate the "Children of the Infidels."[112] In 1617, the company gave £100 to Rebecca Rolfe (or Pocahontas) and her husband John Rolfe, "out of the moneys collected for works to be performed for the planting and propagating of Christian religion in those heathen parts." It was hoped that the "good example of her conversion" would "encourage other of her kindred and Nation to do the like."[113] By May 1619, the Virginia Company reported that the total amount received so far for the college was £1,500, which had risen to £2,043 2s. 11½d. by the following year.[114] The 1616 writ itself, penned in the voice of the king, instructed the Archbishop of Canterbury to "write your Letters to the several Bishops of the Dioceses in your Province, that they do give order to the Ministers and other zealous men of your Dioceses, both by their own example in contribution, and by exhortation to others, to move Our well-beloved Subjects . . . to contribute to so good a work, in as liberal a manner as they may."

George Newman, the Commissary General for the Archbishop of Canterbury, added to this text, inserting a printed instruction for individual parishes below. The surviving example was sent to the minister and churchwardens of Bethersden, Kent, who were instructed to seek collections four times a year for the next two years, from "well disposed people of your Parish from house to house."[115] So, as well as exhortation in church, where parishioners were literally "captive audiences," local people were confronted at the private, domestic threshold to make donations to the colony.[116] The letter that the Archbishop of Canterbury attached to the 1616 brief suggested that ministers keep an "Accompt of each man's benevolence, set down in writing." Ian Archer has illustrated the ways that parish churches served as public "theatres of memory," spaces where charitable acts were commemorated to encourage charity in others.[117] With charity briefs, a similar aim was fulfilled, although the impulse was to persuade others to donate by shaming those who had not. The means of gathering the collection was ostensibly public, even while it physically took place at the threshold of the private realm, and public memory itself would be inscribed and preserved in the "accompt."

In 1620 the Virginia Company once again considered raising funds through parishes and drafted a royal letter of authorization. This document was written in the voice of the monarch, referring to "these our letters," and described how for several years the Crown had been petitioned "to take into, our consideration two worthy projects of great consequence": Virginia and Bermuda. While the two colonies may have been imaginatively cast together on this occasion, colonists in Bermuda certainly felt that they had not benefitted from public collections as much as their fellows in Virginia.[118] The Crown was now determined "to put to our princely and assistant hand, with purse, care, charge and comfort." The collection of money from parishes was not framed as a tax in the same way that compulsory poor rates were. Rather, it was described as a "friendly assistance" and likened to a Christian, charitable act: "it is no meaning nor intent of ours to demand this small sum of any man as any tax at all upon any our loving Subjects; but to entertain it as a friendly assistance for the term and time expressed for the furtherance of so honourable godly, and good work . . . Moreover our pleasure is that a Register for remembrance may be kept in every parish, that who so refusing the said laudable and honourable assistance of so small a matter may be utterly disabled themselves, and their children to receive any benefit or comfort by the said Plantation hereafter."[119] So, this apparently free plea for assistance was not wholly without censure, as those who failed to support the company's godly venture would have their names recorded in the parish register. As well as facing public pressure, the added caveat that whoever failed to donate would find themselves and their children prevented from benefitting in any way from the colony most likely alluded to migration to the colony. There are numerous examples of the poor receiving charity to be transported to the colony, which was often mediated through parishes.[120]

The Virginia Company was casting a wide social and economic net for such donations. The circulation of the brief was intended to not just persuade wealthy parishioners to give money to the colony, but poorer people too, whose primary point of contact for the Virginia colony was their church and immediate local community. As charity briefs circulated nationally, the one issued in 1616 further intimates that the Virginia Company intended for the geographical range of donations to be similarly wide. The parish church, as the Virginia Company no doubt expected, proved to be fertile ground for monetary contributions. In its own records, the Virginia Company detailed the amounts that were collected from the diocese of London and more widely across England. By 2 March 1617 the company had received £300 "for the education of the children of those Savages to the true knowledge of God and Christianity."[121] Parish churches in London continued to give even after this apparently widespread and generous donation, with collections for Virginia made to transport vagrant children from the City of London to the colony between 1618 and 1621, discussed further in the following chapter.[122] In 1618, the Lord Mayor of London, Sir Humphrey Weld, issued a precept that stated that £500 was needed to transport one hundred children, and that overseers of the poor, churchwardens, and constables were ordered to collect the sums from those who usually paid poor rates throughout every parish in the City of London and its surrounding liberties.[123] In theory, then, the Virginia Company was relying on the generosity of better-off citizens, who could afford regular contributions. Furthermore, the means chosen to determine who should pay, and how the sums should be collected, even more closely tied together the issues of colonization and parish poor relief. There is some evidence in churchwardens' accounts of this collection. The ratepayers of All Hallows, Staining, contributed 18s. to the Lord Mayor "for Virginia boys" and a further 11s. 3.d "towards the setting forth of children to Virginia" between 1618 and 1619. Between 1622 and 1623 the parish again collected 6s. 4d. for the transportation of vagrant children.[124] St. Alphage raised 12s. 3d. in 1618, also "to answer the collection for Virginia and the Lord Mayor's appointment."[125]

Other parishes were more giving. In St. Christopher-le-Stocks, the parishioners paid 19s. 3d. to the Lord Mayor in 1619, followed by a collection of £3 10s. and £4 5s. 6d. paid to the chamberlain in 1621, and a further £3 9s. 3¼d. in 1623. Compare this to the £27 16s. that the same parishioners contributed toward the relief of the poor in 1621, and the amount they gave for "sending the children to Virginia" appears paltry. It was much more though than the £1 9s. they raised in the same year for the relief of maimed soldiers.[126] In St. James Garlickhythe, too, a more generous amount of £5 11s. was gathered in 1618. Such sums were raised in spite of, or perhaps because of, the pressures that parishes themselves faced to care for vagrant children.[127] The churchwardens of St. Bartholomew-by-the-Exchange recorded two collections in 1619 and 1620 for the Virginia colony. The first, amounting to 14s. 3d., was "Paid to My Lord Mayor for so much as was gathered short for the Children sent to Virginia"; they collected a further 16s. 3d., which was "Paid unto Sir William Cockayne, Lord Mayor of London for the hundred Children to be sent to Virginia," with a note "more then could be received which Mr

Cottisford should a paid in."[128] Finally, St. Helen Bishopsgate gathered £7 3s. 4.d "for Virginia business" from 1618 to 1619 and paid £5 7s. 7d. "unto the chamber of London for children sent to Virginia."[129] As many as twenty-one London parishes, and perhaps more, contributed toward this particular project.[130] The collective effort of parishioners probably surpassed the £500 the Lord Mayor had hoped for, as according to the Virginia Company's account, up to 17 May 1620, £400 was already gathered.[131]

The donations that London parishes made were conceived of in wider terms than the transportation of vagrant children from the streets of the city. St. Helen Bishopsgate, for example, gave 2s. "for two books for the Virginian poor."[132] Similarly, St. Michael Cornhill paid 10s. toward the relief of the poor in Virginia, which they levied "in discharge of part of the ratement [*sic*] assessed upon the parish."[133] Other parishes discharged their charity for the transportation of their own parishioners to the colony. St. Botolph Bishopsgate, for instance, gave 5s. so that Goodwife Norman could send her daughter to Virginia, and a further 9s. to William Smith for his apparel and "setting him forth to Virginia."[134] Donations to the Virginia colony were not limited to the capital either. The Virginia Company received money from collections across England. The parish of Cheriton, Hampshire, raised £25 between 1622 and 1623, while in 1617 the brief that was issued in 1616 raised £7 19s. 1d. from the Diocese of St. Albans, Hertfordshire, and 5s. from the parish of Warfield, Berkshire.[135] Parishes in Cornwall also responded to the 1616 brief. The churchwardens of Cambourne spent 1s. in 1616 on the "conveyance of the money to Virginia" (although there is no record of how much), and Liskeard parish made three payments in 1617, totaling 30s., "for the building of churches in Virginia," and another 10s. was collected in 1618.[136]

The personal donations that the Virginia Company received, including from the very wealthy, cut across society. Some of the smaller donations that the company received, made up of shillings and pence, suggest that it benefitted from the benevolence of a broad social base of donors, including people in society who were far removed from the elite. Sometime before 1622 Nicholas Ferrar, who was a successful City of London merchant, investor in the Virginia Company, and also the father of company administrators John and Nicholas Ferrar, bequeathed £300 toward the establishment of a "College" in the colony. The money was given on the condition that "ten of the Infidels children [are] placed in it." Ferrar also promised an annual stipend of £24 for the keeping of "three discreet and Godly men in the Colony, which shall honestly bring up three of the Infidels children in Christian religion." A further £550, "together with a godly letter" "for the bringing up of children of the *Infidels*: first in the Knowledge of God true Religion; and next, in fit trades," was donated anonymously to the company; and at the Virginia Company's quarter court, an anonymous benefactor donated a further £25 for the school.[137] Plans were also underway to build a church in Virginia, aided by a donation of £200 in 1619 from the recently deceased Mary Robinson.[138] As well as monetary donations, the colony received expensive "gifts" from wealthy donors. A company pamphlet described numerous items "given to the Colony this year by devout Persons" that were intended for the school and church. Included were gifts of "Plate, and other rich Ornaments for two Communion Tables . . . one for the College, and the other for the Church." For use in the colony "a small Bible with a Cover richly wrought, a great Church-Bible, [and] the Book of Common Prayer" were also donated.[139] The donations reveal the concern that children in the colony should receive a Christian education; indeed, the drive behind the project to build a school was Patrick Copland's belief that education was fundamental to the process of civilization. On 15 November 1620, "a stranger" to the company donated to the school key Christian works including "*S[t.] Augustine De ciuitate Dei*, [and] Master *Perkins* his works," as well as "an exact Map of *America*," suggesting that worldly edification was important too.[140] These larger donations made by wealthy individuals enabled them to cement their social standing, and were duly celebrated and praised by the Virginia Company at its court meetings and in print.[141] Yet, the contributions they made do not belie the fact that many more of the donations that the company received were much smaller.

The donations that were made by sailors aboard an East India Company ship started at 1s., a sum that a skilled tradesman could have earned for a day's work.[142] Patrick Copland traveled on voyages with the East India Company before he set his sights on the Virginia colony, and it was aboard an East India Company ship named the *Royal James* in 1621 that he collected £100 8s. 6d. for the "Free School" in Virginia. Considering that the sum total of all benefactions from London donors toward education in the American colonies was £960 in the period 1480–1660, the ship's donation of just over £100 was not insignificant. A total of 143 individuals including Copland donated, and all of the individuals were named, although it was only in a handful of cases that their position aboard the ship was recorded. There were, for example, two surgeons named William Wilie and John Long who gave £1 10s. respectively, and groups of merchants and master's mates donated larger sums (£20 and £6 13s. 4d.). Individuals up and down the hierarchy of the ship donated, including its captain, Martin Prince, who gave £6 13s. 4d.[143]

Donations on the ship cut across rank and included small amounts from more than one hundred sailors, ranging from just 1s. to the £1 5s. given by Henry Smith, a purser. Donations of and above £1 were rare aboard the East India Company vessel; most of the sailors (one hundred of them) gave donations amounting to no more than 5s. The number of individuals who made these smaller donations indicates that they comprised the ship's lower-ranking officers and sailors, who might have been pressured to donate by those higher up the ship's hierarchy.[144] No doubt too, Copland, who had earlier heard stories about the fledging colony and its Algonquian converts from the Virginia colonist, Sir Thomas Dale, personally entreated the sailors, not least during his sermons.[145] In another pamphlet, Edward Waterhouse's *A Declaration of the State of the Colony*, there is further evidence of East India Company sailors donating to the colony. Again at the Cape of Good Hope, "Gentlemen and Mariners" who were homeward-bound on the *Hart* and *Roe-Buck* gave £66 13s. 4d. toward the free school, and in light of these donations the masters of the ships, Mr. Swan (*Hart*) and Mr. Browne (*Roe-Buck*), were made freemen of the Virginia Company.[146] At a court meeting the Virginia Company also determined that "in honour" of the generosity of the sailors, the school would be named "The East India School" and East India Company employees would "have precedence before any other, to prefer their children thither, to be brought up in the rudiments of learning."[147] Their donations highlight that the social make-up of donors was wide-ranging, including the learned and those who were likely to have been illiterate, as well as members of the political elite, for whom philanthropy was an integral aspect of their public self, and those who may have, at one time or another, been the beneficiaries of charity themselves.[148] For most, their ordinary experience of charity would have been the parish church, even while the concept of donating to distant causes was not alien to them. The East India Company sailors, then, were geographically far removed from the colony; yet plans to provide a Christian education for children in Virginia clearly struck a chord with their spiritual concerns and charitable impulse. As Alison Games has suggested, East India Company sailors may even have imagined that their own children would be the beneficiaries of this new, godly enterprise.[149] Whatever their thoughts, colonial philanthropy shows how a range of English global interests intersected.

After 1621 there is no further evidence of state-sponsored, large-scale collections being made for Virginia.[150] Arguably, the colony seemed to be on firmer footing as the Virginia Company had generated enough informal investment to nourish the colony in its infant state. But also, with the establishment of new colonies in North America and the Caribbean, the English public found that their philanthropy needed to stretch even further. Increasingly, Virginia had to compete for the goodwill of parishioners. In 1623, for example, St. Christopher-le-Stocks raised, "by order of parliament," £17 2s. 5d. "for the agents of New England."[151] In 1621 Richard Whitbourne, the author of *A Discourse and Discovery of New-Found-Land*, secured support from the Privy Council for a collection.[152] The Privy Council sent letters to the archbishops of Canterbury and York, asking them to raise "voluntary contributions as shall be willingly given and collected for him within the several parish churches of the said province." Whitbourne had first sailed to Newfoundland in 1579, and in 1615 was commissioned to hold the first vice-admiralty courts in Newfoundland. He returned again in 1618 when he was hired by William Vaughan to reorganize his patented colony, which he removed to Renews. But his efforts had left him broke, having "spent much of his time and means (having formerly been a merchant of good estate)."[153]

Under Crown control from 1625, colonization in Virginia did continue to receive financial support, though it was more sporadic and increasingly individualistic. For example, the churchwardens of St. Thomas the Martyr in Bristol spent £10 1s. in 1634 to send four pauper boys to Virginia.[154] This appears to have been a one-off and was not precipitated by an official order, more an extension of parish poor relief. Similarly, when Sir Richard Grosvenor gave 2s. in 1637 "to one Mr. Calvert a poor minister born in Malpas and coming from Virginia," it was one of many small acts of charity that he administered that year.[155] There is evidence, too, that in the same way that bequeathing money to certain institutions in wills was rather formulaic—including the parish, the house of correction, or the hospital—giving money to help settle the poor in Virginia may have become commonplace too. This is neatly illustrated by the will of the London merchant Nicholas Abdy, who, when he died in 1642, left £120 to send vagrant children to English colonies: in Virginia, New England, or the Caribbean. Both his brother and father made identical bequests.[156]

The more expansive outlook displayed by Nicholas Abdy's bequest is reflected in subsequent schemes that were put forward to generate funding for colonial ventures. They reflect the expansion of English colonial ambition into other parts of North America and the Caribbean, yet they also show that the Virginia Company influenced the schemes of future colonial projectors. The company had made an example of how best to engage the English public, and their purses, in such ventures. In 1634, projectors proposed a plan to settle a "populous and well governed plantation in the West Indies." Apparently learning from the failures of Virginia's early settlers, the Caribbean planters would not "seek for a mines of gold or silver to make a country desert and to bury millions of men." There was something that they did intend to emulate, however: "use the poor men's hands and the rich men's purses." In order to raise investment, the projectors proposed issuing "a brief as such as in use commonly upon occasion of fire." Of course, a charity brief had been successfully trialed by the Virginia Company in 1616. Similarly, it was suggested that a collection should be gathered for three years, with "leave to every parish to employ their own liberality . . . to the end they may be sure to be disburdened of such number of their poor as their charity shall be able to send over in the said plantations."[157] Like the Virginia Company had done before, the projectors suggested that through "voluntary collection" there would be an opportunity to disburden parishes of their poor.

A projector for colonization in the Carolinas also believed "we must begin to lay the foundation of this our design by a commune charity to our poor." The projector suggested that their proposal, penned between 1626 and 1628, along with a petition, should be printed and "pass[ed] openly among the people before the gathering of this alms to prepare and dispose the people to be liberal in a work of sovereign importance." The collection of "alms" suggests that they imagined that the parish church would be the focal point of gathering donations. Rather than seeking investment through the setting up of a joint-stock company, this projector clearly thought that Crown patronage and the charity of England's parishioners would be enough to establish and sustain a colony. They anticipated, however, that parishioners might feel overburdened by charitable expectations and resist this call for alms, and so they posed the question of whether "we who have often freely opened our purses for strangers should now harden our hands against those of our nation."[158] The parish church was also the proposed loci of collections for another plantation (its location was not specified) between 1629 and 1630. The author of the proposal suggested "that all communicants within the realm of England, when they receive their tokens, before they repair to the Lord's table, do each of them give one penny more, then they are accustomed to do." The collection was to be publicly recorded too, as with earlier proposals for

Virginia, this time in the bishop's register.[159] Donating to colonization would thus become an embodied experience, associated with taking Holy Communion and receiving the body of Christ.

There was a clear consonance between the models for public collections mapped out during the lifetime of the Virginia Company and those tried by later colonial projectors. Nowhere are these forms of persistence and adaption more apparent than in Captain Baily's schemes. Baily's proposal for a new plantation in Virginia, dated around 1623, suggests that he was influenced by, or indeed was the author behind, an earlier project penned by the Virginia Company: its 1620 draft royal letter of authorization. That document had described the Virginia Company's collection not as a "tax," but a "friendly assistance" and also suggested keeping a "register for remembrance," so that the children of those who refused to contribute would be barred from receiving the benefits of colonization.[160] Baily adopted not only the same ideas, but the exact phrasing, suggesting that his collection was "not in the way of any tax at all, but to be left to their charitable gift." He confronted the apprehensions that the laboring poor might have but suggested that if "one penny a piece" should be given by each family they would be "as free of the plantation made in Virginia, as he that shall give any far greater sum." Like the Virginia Company had earlier suggested, Baily proposed that there should be a public element to this giving so that parishioners could be shamed into contributing. As he suggested, "he could not be a good subject that would shut his purse strings against it." Therefore, he proposed that two register books should be kept in every parish to record the names of those who did, and those who did not, donate. The latter register would be used to ensure that those who failed to contribute "may be disabled himself and his children to receive any benefit of that plantation ever hereafter."[161] Yet, Baily's scheme was, perhaps not for the first time, rejected. This time it was on the basis that earlier collections had, in fact, been so effective. Thomas Smythe, John Wolstenholme, Humphrey Handford, and Robert Johnson, who all had ties to the Virginia Company, told Secretary Sir Edward Conway, himself an investor, as was his wife Katherine, that they did not "approve of any such course as is propounded to that end." The reason they gave was that during their earlier involvement in the Virginia Company they had witnessed "the kingdom drained by former gathering in churches and lotteries for the support of the former plantations."[162]

Collections worked alongside the company lotteries, raising public consciousness and engendering responses from a broad swathe of English society. The result was not only increased awareness about colonization in Virginia but also further capital for the project. Both were necessary for practical as well as ideological purposes. Through parishioner generosity the evangelizing mission was supported, but so was the transportation of England's poor who would serve in the colony as bound laborers. The association between Virginia, public works, and Christian piety also served to lay the foundations for an expanded vision of an English Christian commonwealth. While colonists in Virginia were dispersed from their native English parishes, their Christian kin in the domestic realm were encouraged to think of their counterparts in the colonies as spiritually and emotionally close to home. Personal adventure, either your person or your purse, was the only means to gain membership of this expanded, global community. The East India Company sailors, who made their living within this connected web of English colonial expansion, exemplified this more global understanding of what it now meant to be English.[163] Those who refused were readily excluded, an isolation that, if colonial projectors were believed, could last a lifetime: "ever hereafter."[164] Of course, the wealth that collections generated could not have materialized without the application of specific mechanisms, like charity briefs and mayoral precepts. The Virginia Company was successful at securing wider state support in order to employ these tools, and the tools were themselves an effective means for gathering public donations. To galvanize the flow of capital from parishioners to the company required a whole nexus of individuals working in sync across the nation, from churchwardens and bishops to agents and accountants. The Virginia Company achieved this with such apparent ease that later projectors who attempted to lay foundations in new colonial arenas modeled themselves on similar practices.

Informal investment in Virginia through the lotteries was similarly conferred with formal approval, not least through the bestowing of Crown and civic authority. However, throughout this period, there was persistent tension between the private and public tenets of informal investment. While in public discourse private gain and public good were harmoniously wedded (*Londons Lottery* proclaimed "they that thus for Country doth, / can never live in lack"), this did not entirely reflect reality. The lotteries roused moral censure, as the poor were expressly forbidden from playing, thus denying them their own personal opportunity for economic advancement out of America. Such prescriptions and the articulation of "public good" did, of course, also serve to uphold the socially responsible reputation of the Virginia

Company. This status was further strengthened by the company's own efforts to better the lives of the English poor, through dispensing charitable gifts and civic loans in the places that its lotteries visited. Such acts also enabled the company to forge civic connections in provincial settings through the appropriation of symbolic spaces for the lottery houses and, in reciprocation, charitable gift giving. Yet, while the practices that the Virginia Company adopted to garner financial support for the colony were ostensibly "official," they affected responses that were both socially and geographically diverse. Playing at the lottery, a broad spectrum of individuals in early modern England made informal investments in Virginia. Through these transactions they were not only drawn into a web of colonial activity and made actors in it, as their money was mobilized to fund colonization, but they themselves may have gained new awareness, and were also the beneficiaries, of overseas expansion. A broad swathe of English society was drawn toward the colony despite its distance, and, perhaps without fully realizing it, they became enmeshed in domestic enterprises that supported colonization.

CHAPTER 4

Mobilizing Labor and Welfare Reform

On Fleet Street, in the City of London on 24 August 1618, a small child named William Larratt was arrested for the crime of vagrancy. On this summer evening, William was in the city apparently unaccompanied, although he later said that his mother was alive and "dwelleth in the country at Westminster," perhaps some two or three miles from where he was found. It was a watchman, whose job was to walk the streets of London at night scouring the city for vagrants and nightwalkers, who stumbled upon the boy. At the behest of the Virginia Company, the Lord Mayor of London had recently issued a precept to all aldermen in the City of London, ordering them to instruct constables to "forthwith walk the streets within their several precincts, and . . . apprehend all such vagrant children both girls and boys as they shall find in their streets and in the markets or wondering in the night to be apprehended by the watch, and them to commit to Bridewell." A constable named Cleyton took William to the Bridewell house of correction, which was no more than a few minutes' walk from where he was found. That night, William was admitted to Bridewell and no doubt whipped and punished for his vagrancy, but not before the governors ordered him, "a little boy," to be transported to the Virginia colony and bound there as a servant.[1] Vagrants who were admitted to Bridewell were usually punished and put to work, perhaps thrashing hemp or cleaning the streets, before they were—often quickly—released. This time, William's fate was to be bound for one of the newly established English colonies in the Atlantic world, like thousands of poor children in England over the course of the seventeenth century.[2]

The mobilization of labor for Virginia required the cooperation of individuals across society, including, but not limited to, Virginia Company merchants, judges, constables, and churchwardens. This did not, however, guarantee that the mobilization of forced labor for the colony would be without issue, as it was, sometimes, impeded, resisted even. The forced migration of subjects from the domestic to the colonial realm was viewed as a paternalistic measure to palliate social and economic ills at home while ensuring that newly founded colonies like Virginia could flourish. Individuals would be saved and the health of the domestic body politic simultaneously restored through a raft of measures that fell under the rubric of social reform and improvement, of which transportation "beyond the Seas" was just one.[3] It was not only England's poor that were affected, of course, but criminals, too. However, as vagrancy was considered to be a crime, the line between pauper and rogue was often blurred. This practice of transporting prisoners and the poor overseas received wider public support, from collections, as seen in the previous chapter, as well as in sermons and print. In promotional literature, writers substantiated the view that colonization would prove to be transformative for the lives of the poor in England: in Virginia, a new world of opportunity and redemption awaited them.[4] The experiences of those who migrated voluntarily and involuntarily has often been examined in the context of the societies for which they were bound, especially the high demand for labor to produce crops like tobacco.[5] Yet, such an interpretation should not come at the expense of exploring the pressures in England that drove, and sometimes hindered, the forced transportation of criminals and the poor.

Mobilizing labor for Virginia shaped practices in seventeenth-century England, particularly in relation to the development of welfare reform policies.[6] Previous scholarship on migration in the English Atlantic world has tended to focus on how the flow of English people overseas shaped colonial societies, or how English laws on labor and servitude, including indenture, shaped the development of unfreedom and slavery in slave-holding societies like Virginia and Barbados.[7] However, the emergence of forced transportation to Atlantic world colonies, especially the forced apprenticeship of vagrant children, helps to explain the development of welfare reform policies in early modern England and the subsequent change in attitudes toward the poor. Whether considering the forced transportation of criminals or the children of poor families, it is clear that the practices of transportation developed in close relation to domestic contexts and attitudes and cannot be explained by colonial interests alone. Instead, the decisions of ordinary people across England, whether they were Justices of the Peace or magistrates, poor parents or poor children, determined how policies around coerced and forced migration developed in the English Atlantic world, and had a lasting impact on English attitudes toward the most vulnerable in society.

Condemned Persons

In 1606, two laborers from Kent, Richard Ley and John Shepton, confessed to and were found guilty of trespass at the Assize Court. In its widest sense, this meant that they were guilty of a non-treasonable or felonious crime, but it could also mean the trespass of another's person, goods, or land. In usual times, a person found guilty of trespass would be expected to pay damages, but now the colonial project shaped judicial outcomes. The assize judges decided that instead of receiving punishment in England, they would be transported to Virginia.[8] There is no evidence that they ever made it to Virginia, but the company had set a precedent for the forced transportation of criminals to English colonies. This practice has been interpreted as a desperate measure, concocted by those with colonial interests.[9] In the first few years of settlement, colonists were anxious to get a foothold in Virginia, which proved impossible due to famine, disease, and conflict with the local Algonquians.[10] The company needed young, able, and skilled men, both to work and to populate and protect the settlement. Yet, the practice of transporting criminals was not so straightforward, as legal procedure and the status of an individual could determine how vulnerable they were to transportation. Not all were petty criminals that no one would miss, and some criminals found ways to mediate against transportation too. Importantly, the forced transportation of criminals was also given legitimacy because of domestic concerns and interests. It was not presented as a wholly punitive practice that would benefit the colonies alone. Rather, it was framed in terms of paternalism, as a practice that would benefit the individual as well as English society more broadly.

Early practices developed on an ad hoc basis, without the support of any official policy. In 1611, Thomas Dale, the interim governor of Virginia, wrote to the Earl of Salisbury, recommending that prisoners who were condemned to die should be forced to labor in the colony for three years instead.[11] It seems that Dale's request did not fall on deaf ears. In March 1611, Tristram Conyam reported to Thomas West, Baron De La Warr, that instead of losing out on the benefit of the spring weather, the Virginia Company would send "such [men] as we could get of a sudden choosing rather to take worse men into this supply" than none at all.[12] Until 25 March 1617, when an act of the Privy Council officially sanctioned the practice of transporting criminals overseas, the process was negotiated unofficially between the Virginia Company and local magistrates. The 1617 act provided legal instruction, sanctioning judges "to Reprieve and stay from execution such persons as now stand Convicted of any robbery or felony (wilful murder, Rape, witchcraft or Burglary only excepted)," stipulating that if the accused should refuse to go to Virginia or return from abroad "before the time limited by us his Majesty's Commissioners be fully expired," they would be "subject to the execution of the Law." The warrant, they claimed, was not applicable to all felons, just those "who for strength of body or other abilities shall be thought fit to be employed in foreign discoveries or other Services beyond the Seas."[13] Even the 1617 act failed to provide uniformity, as those found guilty of burglary were, in fact, ordered for transportation to the fledging colony.

The individuals whose lives were affected by this decision making were caught up in a web of overlapping interests between the Virginia Company, the courts, and houses of correction. The instructions authored by magistrates and governors reveal that individuals from different social backgrounds, who had committed crimes of various sorts, came up against the authority of the Virginia Company. A number of individuals were guilty of serious offences and not the "petty" crimes that Paul Griffiths's research on Bridewell suggests.[14] A case in point is Harry Reade, who was ordered for transportation to Virginia in February 1619 after being found guilty of highway robbery. Where similar evidence of robbery survives, many items that were stolen were of very high value, such as horses.[15] Also in 1619, a group of prisoners from Newgate were deemed "fit for service in foreign parts," including George Gascoigne and William Sharpe. Gascoigne was guilty of housebreaking in London, while Sharpe was found guilty of breaking into the property of William Paget, 4th Baron Paget, and "stealing of diverse parcels of linen from thence."[16] Baron Paget was an investor in both the Virginia and Bermuda Companies, so he may have had some involvement in recommending Sharpe for transportation.[17] William Clapham was also a burglar, who with four other men was found guilty of burgling Lord Digby's property in St Martin's-in-the-Field. They were described as "parish yeomen" and were accused of stealing several items of silver, including spoons, basins, ewers, flagons, tankards, pots, bowls, a trencher plate, and a chaffing dish. They were sentenced to hang on 2 April, with only Clapham apparently escaping when he was subsequently ordered for transportation.[18] Even the most violent criminals, including John Fyerbrasse, who was charged with a stabbing, were ordered for transportation.[19]

Transportation orders intersected with concerns for the domestic sphere, or commonwealth, more broadly. Transportation was presented as an opportunity to rid the commonwealth of "the most notorious ill livers, and misbehaved persons," thus restoring the body politic to better health.[20] The criminals who were ordered for transportation were not just guilty of crimes against property and individuals, but those considered more politically subversive too. John Haydon, for example, was imprisoned in Bridewell in 1635 after being found guilty of preaching abroad in contempt of court, and of several attempted escapes from prison. On 18 June, the governors recorded that he would go to Virginia voluntarily, on the condition that he was, for the time being, set free. This was risky, considering his previous record, but apparently, he gave "sufficient sureties" that when his time came, he would return.[21] Thomas Brice, a Westminster yeoman, was "sentenced to be drawn to the gallows and hung" in June 1634 after he was found guilty of having "feloniously filed clipped and diminished six pieces of lawful current money called King Charles shillings, and seven pieces of lawful current money called King Charles sixpences." At the end of the following month, however, Brice also received the "King's mercy" and was instead sentenced to transportation to Virginia.[22] They were both ordered for transportation because of the threat, symbolic or otherwise, that they posed at home. While Haydon had disrupted the peace of the commonwealth through his sermons, Brice had attacked the king's authority by defacing his minted image. A more acute example of the political threats that the commonwealth faced was witnessed in Northumberland, Cumberland, and Westmoreland in 1617. There were reports of outbreaks of violent disorder, and a proclamation ordered the worst offenders to be sent "into Virginia, or to some other remote parts," where they could "no more infect the places where they abide within this our realm."[23] While the Virginia colony was on unsteady foundations itself, it was still perceived as a suitable outlet for subversive individuals who posed a threat to the domestic sphere.

Individuals across the social spectrum were transported, not just "the rags of scum of the people," as George Donne observed in 1638.[24] Some were landholders, including the group of yeomen who robbed Lord Digby of goods valued at more than £155.[25] The position of yeomen conferred some status and a degree of prosperity, because, as landholders, they were entitled to hold office in their parish, such as the position of churchwarden.[26] More importantly for the Virginia Company, their skill as agriculturalists made them ideal candidates for transportation. On 22 September 1634, George Sandys, a gentleman, was accused of stealing a "gray gelding worth five pounds" from Sir Peter Temple and was ordered for transportation to Virginia.[27] He was the son of Sir George Sandys, who was himself a well-known felon and cousin of Sir Edwin Sandys.[28] On this first occasion, George Sandys was acquitted, but he was evidently unperturbed by the threat of transportation and went on to murder Jane Wright by strangling. He was acquitted again, but then boasted of his guilt to Honor Rudston, while he and two accomplices raped her: her evidence put him firmly on the scaffold.[29] Sandys's repeated violent offences distinguish him from poor women like Hester Clements and Mary Williams, who were sentenced to transportation to Virginia in 1637 by the Bridewell governors after they were caught "seizing upon a man in an unseemly manner as he was making water."[30]

While magistrates might not have discriminated on the basis of status, not all instructions for transportation were treated with equal urgency. As the case of George Sandys demonstrates, commands were not necessarily followed through and orders for transportation were just that: "orders not outcomes."[31] A warrant dated 8 July 1635, which instructed fourteen prisoners to be "delivered" to Captains Thomas Hill and Richard Carleton, "to be transported by them into Virginia," illuminates this issue. Although fourteen prisoners in the Newgate gaol were ordered for transportation to Virginia, as few as four appear to have actually set sail for the colony.[32] This document is also a rare example of women, who were convicted of felonies, being sentenced to transportation. Elizabeth Williams, for instance, appeared before the court at Newgate on 25 June 1635, on suspicion of "receiving stolen goods" from another woman called Tomson Hall.[33] On 2 September 1635, she was further charged with being an "accessary to a felony committed by Isabel Landay," who was described as being "at large."[34] Yet, there is no further evidence that Elizabeth was transported to the colony in 1635.[35] One explanation for the failure of the magistrates to follow through is that "receiving stolen goods" was not a statute crime until 1691, meaning that it was rarely recorded and prosecuted before then.[36] Williams's transportation may have been obstructed because of the difficulty of determining whether or not she had actually committed a felony, but there was clearly also slowness and even ineptitude in the management of criminal transportation.

Transportation to Virginia was sometimes a positive choice for prisoners, and one that they independently pursued. This is suggested by the petition of Elizabeth Cotterell, who pleaded with Charles I to release her from Marshalsea, where she "hath lain here these 18 months." Although it had been eight months since she was "reprieved," she had "not yet obtained her liberty." Cotterell was "desirous to be transported to Virginia." Enclosed with her petition was a warrant that would authorize Sir Edmond Verney, the Keeper of Marshalsea, to in turn authorize William Fleming, a City of London Freeman of the Saddlers' Company, to transport Cotterell to the colony.[37] John Carter also petitioned the Privy Council in 1622, begging that, having received a reprieve after being found guilty of stealing a horse, he would be transported to Virginia.[38] Henry Robinson, a pirate, was also reprieved after helping magistrates prosecute his accomplices and return stolen goods to merchants, but rather than stay in England, he asked for a fresh start in Virginia. He asked to be allowed to voyage to Thomas Place, a planter, and as his servant "take honest pains for his living."[39] Individuals like Elizabeth Cotterell, John Carter, and Henry Robinson played a role in both the enforcement and obstruction of their transportation, meaning that not only did colonial interests not have full sway over decision making in England, but that it could be a drawn-out, rather than swift, process.

Johanna Howell was one of the fourteen individuals named on the warrant, discussed above, who never voyaged to Virginia. In April 1624 she was found guilty of stealing goods but avoided transportation to Virginia by employing a method that was available only to women: she claimed to be pregnant. On inspection by a jury of matrons, they found that she was, "though not quick," meaning she was in the early stages of pregnancy.[40] She might have also been pregnant in the summer of 1635 and used this as a means to avoid transportation again.[41] If the magistrates were lenient, it was certainly not because of her otherwise good reputation. She had already been tried in 1633, and in 1637 she was again found guilty of stealing goods, including a petticoat and waistcoat.[42] There was nothing inevitable, then, about transportation orders, and it was even possible for prisoners to obstruct them. For women, one possible avenue was the use of their bodies as a site of negotiation.[43]

Of course, transportation orders were not always thwarted, and others who were named on the above 1635 warrant certainly did go to Virginia.[44] John Humfreys, aged twenty-three, traveled to Virginia soon after the above warrant was issued on 24 July, aboard the *Assurance*.[45] Elianor Sutton traveled next on 27 July, aged twenty, aboard the *Primrose*.[46] She, too, had tried pleading that she was pregnant, though unsuccessfully.[47] On 1 August, Marie Burback, aged seventeen, sailed on the *Elizabeth*.[48] Jane Prym, who was found guilty of theft, was also transported. On 10 April 1635, Prym had also tried pleading, unsuccessfully, that she was pregnant, after being found guilty of stealing a cloth cloak, brooches, a felt hat, a pair of worsted stockings, and an apron from William Cooper. Added at a later date was the allegation that she had also stolen a pair of sheets, a shirt, a smock, and a neck cloth.[49] She was aged eighteen when she was transported to Virginia, and traveled aboard the *Primrose* along with Elianor Sutton.[50] This selection of individuals, who were together ordered for transportation in 1635, suggests that outcomes were not straightforward, but instead often rested on a number of factors, including the outcome of legal debate and the status of the criminal in the English courts. Even as the practice of transporting sentenced criminals developed, a certain amount of flexibility and room for negotiation remained.

Transportation was not a linear process, and the practice was not entirely driven by the needs of colonists in Virginia. Instead, the concerns of people at home shaped orders. As the practice of colonial transportation developed, magistrates had to take into consideration established customs concerning labor and consent. Stephen Rogers, who was charged at Newgate with the manslaughter of George Watkins, is a case in point. A range of interests intersected and were negotiated in Rogers's case. At the request of the Virginia Company's treasurer, Sir Thomas Smythe, Rogers was reprieved from execution and instead ordered for transportation on 3 April 1617. Rogers was a young apprentice carpenter, so his youth, physical strength, and "art" made him a valuable addition to the colony. Yet, his voyage to Virginia was delayed because the magistrates decided that he was first to be "re-prisoned for one year" and then "flogged on two market-days at Brainford [Brentford] and to be put on one day in the stocks at Acton." Then, on his knees "in the open porch of the church," he was ordered "to ask forgiveness of his master."[51] The length and nature of his punishment exposed Rogers to the opprobrium of his entire community.[52] It also suggests that the magistrates did not consider servitude in Virginia punishment enough. In this instance, they were unwilling to let the company convey Rogers to an uncertain future without immediate reprisal, at least before he had atoned to his master and parish.[53]

These kinds of domestic and local concerns similarly affected the decision to send John Adis, who was also an apprentice, to the colony. On 29

July 1626, the Bridewell governors recorded the charge that he had "used the body" of Katherine Bukill several times, and while Adis denied it at first, when Bukill brought evidence in court, in the form of witness statements, he admitted his guilt. Because Adis was apprenticed to Thomas Ridiard, a haberdasher, Ridiard's consent was required before he could be transported.[54] The process of gaining a master's consent sprang from two issues: firstly, Bridewell was thought to be on shaky legal standing; it was "legal Bedlam without parliamentary consent," and so the governors needed their authority bolstered.[55] However, the Statute of Artificers (1563), in force to protect the interests of both parties by criminalizing the premature termination of apprenticeships, would also have been a consideration.[56] The Bridewell governors rightly anticipated that transportation should be legally deliberated, but it also forced practical, even economic considerations. Gaining Ridiard's consent was a matter of satisfaction to conciliate an injured party, as it was him that would be forced to apprentice and retrain another person.[57] In this way, the cases of Rogers and Adis suggest that the patriarchal and economic concerns associated with the apprenticeship system meant that they were less vulnerable to transportation orders. Their swift removal to Virginia was not tolerated in the same measure as that of vagrant children, for instance.

Individual interests were increasingly afforded particular significance, especially in relation to apprenticeship and consent. Over the course of the 1620s, the Bridewell governors more regularly recorded the consent of a master before ordering an apprentice for transportation.[58] As Sonia Tycko argues, the importance of recording consent also sprang from the concern that those bound as colonial servants might seek to break their contracts, by claiming that they were coerced.[59] That even during this early period such reassurances were deemed necessary speaks to the pressures that people were already under. Gill Richardson had run from her master, taking with her "money to carry her to Virginia," but although she was eager to go to Virginia, the governors ordered on 7 August 1619 that she should be "kept here until her master be ready to give at the charge of the prisoner."[60] Similarly, John Saken was arrested for vagrancy in Fleet Street on 22 August 1628, and expressed his willingness to go to Virginia, but he was returned to his master instead.[61] John Gardner, who had run away from his master nine times, was brought to Bridewell on 30 August 1628. When they sought out his master, he actually consented to Gardner's transportation, probably because he was so troublesome.[62] This shows that the young people who were transported were not, as Alison Games has suggested, "vagrants and waifs" that no one would miss, but often individuals whom others had invested in.[63]

Yet, this entanglement of different, patriarchal interests in the lives of poor youths engendered a confused and often inconsistent approach to transportation. On several occasions at least, young vagrants were transported apparently even without the consent of their parent or master, contrary to the above examples. Richard Lichfield was ordered to go to Virginia alongside James Wray on 23 June 1627, both allegedly being "set by for that purpose." This was despite the fact that Lichfield had run away from his father, who lived in the country, and Wray was a runaway apprentice.[64] William Coolape had also "run from his master . . . about a week since" when he was arrested on 18 October 1617 in the Old Bailey, reportedly for vagrancy. However, without any further interference he was "kept to go to Virginia."[65] In these instances it could be that the governors were facing unrecorded pressure from Virginia colonists and merchants to transport youths who could be indentured with immediacy.[66] Under these circumstances, the servants' recorded consent may have been enough to persuade masters that the contracts would be enforced.

The tensions surrounding the terms of apprenticeship and consent that were revealed when youths were transported to Virginia were not unique but are apparent in other colonial contexts too. In Somerset, on 28 April 1637, William Morice of Burton was examined about an apprentice, John Stile, who he had employed as his servant to go to St. Christopher's in the Caribbean. Stile was apprenticed to Robert Elliot, a tailor, but one day, in the presence of his master, attempted to negotiate wages (£30) for six years' service with Morice on the island. Morice replied, "you are too little," but as Elliot had not openly objected, Morice assumed "he consented to the boys going." Soon after, Stile visited Morice and they struck a bargain: Stile would receive £20 at the end of six years' service, only "if his master Elliot thereunto consented." His master's consent was apparently forthcoming, as Elliot replied "he [Stile] is a naughty boy let him go whither he will." Stile was presently sent to Bristol and, at the time of the examination, "yet is in the ship and stays."[67] That Morice had been required to recount this story in front of the JPs, and his emphasis on Elliot's consent, suggests that Elliot had challenged Morice's own version of events. New considerations were forced upon masters and apprentices alike, as they navigated a new, expanding world of English labor across the Atlantic. Even while colonists put pressure on domestic institutions to encourage forced or coerced transportation, local, social, and economic conditions in England could not be ignored. This climate dictated how the practice of forced transportation developed across the English Atlantic world.

Poverty and Paternalism

Early promoters of colonization in Virginia, including Humphrey Gilbert and Richard Hakluyt, galvanized upon concerns about overpopulation and underemployment in sixteenth-century England. Colonization in Virginia offered solutions that would put men, women, and children to work. Central to Hakluyt's recommendations was the rejuvenation of the English cloth trade by extending it into America and using forced labor in the colony to develop the shipping industry and employ hands in silk cultivation, mining, pearl diving, and farming.[68] The anxieties that stemmed from supposed overpopulation continued into the next century. In Robert Johnson's *Nova Britannia* (1609), the threat that the idle poor posed to the body politic was conveyed with enormous imaginary power, England being a "land abounding with swarms of idle persons." He suggested that, inevitably, they would be tempted to "swarm in lewd and naughty practices," "having no means of labour to relieve their misery." He concluded that "if we seek not some ways for their foreign employment, we must provide shortly more prisons and corrections for their bad conditions." By describing the "swarms" of people, Johnson conveyed the popular feeling that overpopulation was both "grotesque" and a dangerous threat to the body politic.[69] His remarks also seemed to echo the fears and anxieties about vagrancy, which affected mostly young, single men moving across the country in search of work. The number of individuals being apprehended for vagrancy rose by 65 percent between the 1570s and 1630s, suggesting it was growing at roughly the same rate as the population.[70] In his sermon, *A Good Speed to Virginia* (1609), Robert Gray similarly suggested that the commonwealth was under threat: "Our multitudes like too much blood in the body, infect our country with plague and poverty."[71] His audience would have understood Gray's allusion to Galenic theory, as the "humours" of the body politic, he suggested, were dangerously imbalanced. In *A Plain Path-Way to Plantations* (1624), Richard Eburne also complained that whereas "England . . . heretofore admirably flourished in plenty and prosperity," now there was "great misery and encumbrance . . . by reason of the excessive multitude of people."[72] Productivity was key to the health of the commonwealth, and while opportunities were scarce at home, in Virginia Robert Johnson argued that "such as are of no trades (if they bee industrious) . . . shall have there employment enough, for there is a world of means to set many thousands a work."[73] Colonization in America, as Gilbert and Hakluyt had claimed, presented a bounty of opportunities.

Writers' use of natural imagery conveyed the idea that the English commonwealth and body politic functioned as "an organic social order," a worldview that "implied the mutual interdependence of all subjects" within the commonwealth.[74] As they saw it, and as Johnson explained, this order was under threat. He wrote, "it fares with populous common weals, as with plants and trees that be too frolic, which not able to sustain and feed their multitude of branches . . . admit an engrafting of their buds and Siences into some other soil, accounting it a benefit for preservation of their kind, and a disburdening their stock of those superfluous twigs that suck away their nourishment."[75] Richard Eburne also described purging the "Land of evil weeds."[76] The imagery that writers used suggested that transportation was a natural process, but one that would require careful cultivation. In a 1624 petition to parliament, Eburne cautioned that English colonists had yet "taken but weak and slender roots in the soils they are planted upon."[77] Articulations of this kind extended to the analogy of the bee hive or "colony."[78] Eburne urged his readers to recognize that "like Stall that are overfull of Bees," the poor of England should be "transplanted into some other soil, and removed hence into new Hives."[79] Drawing upon the same analogy, Robert Gray argued, "so doth the master of the bee-garden, when he sows a hive pestered with multitudes of bees, he drives the hive, and so reapeth . . . greater gain by his ware and honey."[80] The beehive was, of course, also representative of productivity, and it was implied that England could once again be a land of milk and "honey" if the poor could be employed. This way they would cease to be a burden on the commonwealth.

The tone adopted by Johnson and Eburne was also sympathetic, with Eburne suggesting that the idle poor had only been driven to "commit such crimes, for very need and pure hunger." He argued that they could still make a contribution to the commonwealth, "being first chastised, and then well governed, and of better means provided, [they] may prove honest and good men and women afterward."[81] Here, Eburne imitated the same language of reform and improvement seen in a proclamation issued in 1617. The proclamation declared that criminals "in their punishments . . . might live, and yield a profitable Service to the Common wealth in parts abroad," there "they might be rather Corrected then destroyed."[82] Eburne argued that transportation was not a purely punitive measure, but rather a solution that could alleviate the desperation of England's poor, including those who had turned to vagrancy. Pamphlet writers suggested that transplanting subjects overseas was a way to exercise paternalism and simultaneously ensure that the commonwealth, at home, could flourish.

The Virginia Company intervened in parliamentary debates in order to persuade the government that transportation was a real solution to England's poverty and vagrancy problem. On 30 April 1621, a bill in parliament proposed "That no Poor man should resort to dwell in any Town Corporate that was not worth £5 in goods or 40s. per annum in Copy or Lease[hold]." Straight away, the bill was firmly rejected by Virginia Company treasurer, Sir Edwin Sandys, who argued that they had discussed and dismissed the same bill once before, adding that he deemed it unsound because it would restrain "works of nature and Charity." It was not right, he argued, "that a man should not be able to give relief either to his father or Brother."[83] Here Sandys played on the commonly held view that neighborly charity was in decline, contrary to tradition and custom.[84] Another point of contention was whether towns or the countryside were best placed to receive vagrants, and Sandys suggested that venting the poor into towns from the country would be "like the turning of a sick man from one side of the bed to the other, the malady still remains." Instead, Sandys pressed the case that "the poor that can not be set on work may be sent to Virginia": "Never was there a fairer gate opened to a nation," he argued, "to disburden it self nor better means by reason of the abundance of people to advance such a plantation."[85] Sandys built upon claims made by the Virginia Company a decade earlier in *A True and Sincere Declaration of the Purpose and Ends of the Plantation in Virginia* (1610), that for the poor "there is left no vent, but age." "By trans-planting the rankness and multitude of increase in our people" to Virginia, both England and the poor could be relieved.[86]

Before the first Virginia Company ships even set sail for the colony, company investors discussed the utility of transporting poor, but skilled, workers to Virginia. In a letter to the Earl of Salisbury, Sir Walter Cope said that Sir John Popham had noticed the plight of "poor artisans that would, and cannot work," for whom plantation in Virginia would provide employment. He promised to invest £500 for five years, "if the action prosper," in a "project" to transport them.[87] The colony needed skilled craftsmen just as much as craftsmen needed the opportunities that settlement in Virginia offered, and there is detailed evidence of company investors and colonists finding this skilled labor between 1619 to 1621. In the process of hiring poor craftsmen, the company also displayed paternal care toward their new employees and the families they left behind. In the first months of 1621, for example, company agent Roger King recorded his expenses from an expedition he went on to Sussex to hire men for the colony's ironworks. The craftsmen employed were smiths, colliers, finers, carpenters, and founders, who negotiated with King to ensure that their families would be compensated in their absence.[88] The recipients were almost entirely women, individuals who speak to colonists' affective connections to home and their anxieties about leaving loved ones behind. These were concerns that, at least in part, were subsequently palliated by the company's "relief" payments.

The receipts for money show that not all poor male migrants who ventured to Virginia were unattached and relieved by their release "from the social and familial constraints of parish life," as Alison Games has suggested.[89] In fact, many had to rely upon, and negotiate, the charity of the Virginia Company in order to ensure the welfare of the wives, mothers, and children they left behind. Roger King recorded that "I have promised to send down unto Lambard's mother my finer 10s." and "unto one of my carpenters wife 10s."[90] In August 1619, the company also recorded that 5s. was paid to "Broxe wife a smith that went to Virginia" and 6s. to "Payne Bayles wife who went to Virginia."[91] Between July and September that year, the Berkeley Hundred colonists were preparing for the departure of the *Margaret,* and in their receipts was 14s. given to William Clement "for the relief of his wife in his absence and for redemption of his tools that were pawned."[92] Clements was clearly in desperate financial straits before his departure if he had been forced to pawn the tools of his trade. Among the family members that such men left behind in England were children. Roger King's expenses in Sussex included a note of £2, given "to my founder to bind his daughter [ap]prentice seven years," a symbol of how affective ties to kin were severed by migration.[93] It is unlikely that this founder ever returned from Virginia, and perhaps in full knowledge of this he did as much as possible to ensure his daughter's safety and prosperity. In this sense, the receipts register the personal impact that the colonization of Virginia had on communities because of these departures. Men were persuaded to "adventure" with the reassurance that their families would not be left completely destitute.[94]

Colonial projectors outside of the Virginia Company focused their attention on poor families too. In 1623, Captain William Baily put forward a proposal to the Privy Council to establish a new plantation in southern Virginia. Baily suggested that the poorest class of men, the "day labourer" with "great charge of wife and children," might be persuaded to give 4d. toward the new plantation if he could have one of his children above the age of eight years "transported" to the colony. In Virginia the child would be "clothed, and furnished withal necessaries, never to trouble thee more, and when he comes to years of understanding he shall have a proportion of land, and all kinds of household stuff to begin the world." Would not the poor man, then, think his "money well bestowed"?[95] Richard Eburne, was also enthusiastic about the potential of colonization in Newfoundland to alleviate the crisis of poverty. Eburne, a vicar who lived in the parish of Henstridge, Somerset, drew on local examples when he petitioned both parliament and a local gentleman, Sir Robert Phelips, the MP for Somerset, in 1624 and 1625. In his petition to parliament, he wrote of the possibilities that colonies provided to strengthen England against other nations, including Spain, and also dispose of "the excessive and intolerable number of the poor people that burden our land." In his letter to Phelips he stressed the latter point, enclosing with his letter "an instance or example of it, and for it in the parish where I dwell." He clearly anticipated that this local evidence would stir the interest of Somerset's MP, who could petition the House of Commons for reform. In this note, Eburne argued that, although fifty or sixty years before the majority of the parishioners in Henstridge had lived comfortably on farms and in cottages, now families were dwelling in cramped, put-together coach-houses built on waste ground. Poverty was preventing the settling down of young men and women, and, as a consequence, the formation of new households. For the first time, too, there were "inmates," where previously there had been "not at all," as well as a charge of £40 per year on the parish for poor relief, which before was "not a penny." No doubt, in the course of serving his parishioners, delivering sermons at church as well as overseeing poor relief, Eburne had become intimate with the realities of life-cycle poverty. There was no denying that the material lives of the laboring poor in England had greatly worsened.[96] But, as Eburne argued, "a great and speedy plantation other where is most expedient and necessary for our land."[97]

Projects to settle poor families in English colonies in the Atlantic world extended beyond Virginia, into Newfoundland, New England, Carolina, and the West Indies too. At a meeting of the Council of New England in 1622, it was recorded that a "letter" would be sought from the lieutenants of English shires "for the setting forth of their poor sort of people to New England."[98]

The projectors for a Carolina plantation, south of Virginia, also suggested using official mechanisms to encourage the transportation of the poor to the colony. Alms would be collected in parishes and, "by a commune charity to our poor whom we behold daily by our eyes increasing in number," the destitute would be drawn from idleness and set to work in the colony.[99] In 1634, a project for plantation in the West Indies was also under consideration, and the transportation of poor families was once again on the table. A voluntary collection was proposed, but the petitioners also recognized that in order "to erect a plantation it is equally necessary that we use the poor men's hands and the rich men's purses." The proposed collection was considered just as essential as investors' capital. The petitioners also acknowledged that there was some skepticism about the advantages of transporting poor people to a newly established colony. Yet, they hoped that the poor would "of their own accord and wisdom . . . give themselves to such labour and to that good husbandry." That they imagined sending family groups is suggested by the proposition that while men would till the land, women could be employed processing flax and hemp.[100] As will be discussed in further detail below, changing attitudes toward the poor in England went hand in hand with the development of colonial policies toward coerced and forced migration. As the anonymous projector suggested, "poor men's hands" were needed for the establishment of colonies.

Binding Poor Children

In the sixteenth and seventeenth centuries, there was a raft of new welfare reform measures that ordered the relief and regulation of the poor. The introduction of the English Poor Laws in 1598 and 1601 was especially significant for providing a framework for provision in local parishes. They established guidelines for the punishment of vagrancy, provision of work for the able-bodied, and assistance for the "impotent," as well as foster homes and apprenticeships for children.[101] Their implementation promoted a change in attitude toward the poor, who were no longer seen as a threat, but "an opportunity."[102] Thousands of poor children in London were put to work making pins, while Bridewell inmates were tasked with thrashing hemp, spinning cloth, and cleaning the streets. These reforms were not always successful, but the binding of parish poor children as apprentices proved to be an exception, even if not always popular among the wider community.[103] This scheme was first introduced under the 1547 Vagrancy Act, which stipulated that girls up to the age of twenty and boys up to the age of twenty-four should be forced into apprenticeship. Under the 1563 Statute of Artificers, the practice of forcing youths into work was once again revitalized. This time, children aged ten to eighteen without occupation were entered into the service of a master until they were at least twenty-one.[104] Pauper apprenticeship was legislated again under the Poor Laws. Now, a child's consent was not a requirement, and apprenticeship was targeted at children who were deemed, by the parish authorities, to be a burden on their parents. Legally, they could be bound as apprentices from the age of seven, up to the age of twenty-four for boys, and twenty-one (or the age of marriage) for girls. They were bound out by their parish to a master, usually in menial trades, and usually received some training.[105] While their parents could not, legally, be compelled to consent to their apprenticeship, according to Lord Chief Justice John Popham, they could be coerced.[106] Toward the end of the 1610s, there was a concerted effort to enforce the practice, with instructions in articles to Justices of the Peace in Norfolk and Suffolk in 1617 and West Riding and Lancashire in 1618, showing that there was increased pressure.[107] Parish apprenticeship was firmly planted in the English welfare system, and, as Sandra Dahlberg argues, it was this particular aspect of the Poor Laws that forged a pattern for the forced migration of poor children to Virginia.[108]

The English were familiar with the concept of forcibly binding, or indenturing, poor children into service, and the Virginia Company directly drew upon the precedence of the Poor Laws as well as the authority of houses of correction, local constables, and churchwardens to smooth the way. In one respect, the Virginia Company and the English state were not acting in entirely innovative ways. In 1609, the Virginia Company had discussed sending vagrant children to the colony, influenced by the recruitment of 1,500 poor children in Lisbon to serve as indentured servants in the Portuguese East Indies.[109] In 1616, poor English youths were also sent to plantations in Ireland.[110] Recruiting servants from among England's poor would continue to be practiced across English North America, too. The Council for New England, a joint-stock company that was chartered in 1620 and granted authority to colonize the region, pressed the Crown for permission to do the same in 1622 and 1623, as discussed below. Under the Virginia Company, Dahlberg suggests that this was the first time that English children were indentured by their parishes for overseas apprenticeships. Dahlberg analyzed this practice in relation to the parish of St. Dunstan-in-the-East, and the surviving letters of one of its indentured children, Richard Frethorne. The Virginia Company discussed introducing a bill to parliament in 1621 that would authorize parishes, at their own charge, to send the "poor with whom they are pestered into Virginia." There is no evidence that this bill was ever submitted to parliament, even if MPs widely approved of the idea. Yet, parishes like St. Dunstan-in-the-East were clearly in support too, with evidence of both Richard Frethorne and William Galloway being "put an apprentice" and bound for Virginia.[111] More widely, as the contributions in Chapter 3 suggest, parish apprenticeship was pursued.[112] Examining in detail how this practice unfolded in the City of London, several years before the company's proposed bill, demonstrates that it could be a fraught and not necessarily straightforward process.

To implement parish apprenticeship, the Virginia Company appealed to the relevant authorities, whose support was forthcoming. It first petitioned the Common Council in July 1618 "for taking up of vagrant boys and girls that lie and beg in the streets of this city having no place of abode nor friends to relieve them and for the transporting of them to Virginia to be employed." One of those who approved of the scheme was Robert Batemen, the vestryman of Richard Frethorne's parish of St. Dunstan-in-the-East.[113] The petition prompted a flurry of activity across the City of London. What ensued was propelled by, and tightly integrated with, poor relief policies in England. In September, City of London aldermen instructed the constables in their wards to arrest any vagrant children they found and commit them to Bridewell.[114] Soon after, the Common Council agreed that one hundred children "such as have no means of living or maintenance shall be taken up and transported to Virginia there to be educated and brought up at the charge of the said company." The money for their transportation, which amounted to £500, would be collected by the "churchwardens, collectors for the poor and one of the constables in every several parish of this city," and "paid over to the alderman of that ward." Children, "such as have no means of living or maintenance," aged eight to sixteen, would be taken up and transported to the colony, at the charge of ratepaying citizens, and bound as servants until the ages of twenty-four for boys and twenty-one, or at marriage, for girls.[115] The logic, terms, and financial apparatus used to implement this scheme clearly took its instruction from the Poor Laws.

Although binding poor children as indentured servants was discussed in redemptive, even paternalistic, terms, such language did little to belie their cruel treatment, as many were forced to go to English colonies against their will. Yet, despite the apparent disregard for either the children's or their parents' consent, the decision to transport vagrant children from London to Virginia did entail some consideration for their welfare. Discussion between the Virginia Company and the Common Council of London over the terms of their indenture demonstrates there was scrutiny of the conditions that the children would live under in Virginia. The Virginia Company had to assure the council that the children would fare better in the colony than in the City of London, promising that they would "get their living and maintain themselves when they shall attain their several ages or be out of their apprenticeship." The company, on the other hand, agreed that, at the end of their indenture in Virginia, the children would be granted tenancy on fifty acres of land and provided with a house, a year's worth of corn to eat and more to plant, a cow, clothing, household items and tools, and weapons to defend themselves. After a further seven years, the company would provide them with their own "bound apprentices . . . to help and assist them in their labour." To ensure the terms, it was decided that "covenants shall be made by indentures" between the company and council. Following this agreement between the Virginia Company and the Common Council, the Privy Council proclaimed on 31 January 1620 that "the City deserveth [*sic*] thanks . . . for redeeming so many poor Souls from misery, and ruin." Although conditions in the colony would be trying, servitude in Virginia was presented as an opportunity for both moral and material betterment.[116]

In December 1619, it was agreed that one hundred more poor children, this time aged twelve and above, from the City of London, would be sent to Virginia with money supplied by local citizens. Whereas the governors of Bridewell ordered seventy-five boys and twenty-four girls for transportation to Virginia in the winter of 1618 and early spring of 1619, in the winter of 1619 to 1620, the children ordered for transportation numbered fifty-eight boys and two girls. Reports soon reached the company that these children had attempted to revolt, possibly with the assistance of their distressed friends and family.[117] Sir Edwin Sandys, the company treasurer, wrote to the secretary of the Privy Council, Sir Robert Naunton, on 28 January 1620, entreating that those who were unwilling to go to Virginia could be forced. Sandys complained that although one hundred children "out of their superfluous multitude" were ready to be "transported" to Virginia, "now it falleth [*sic*] out that among those children, sundry being ill disposed, and fitter for any remote place than for this city" refused to comply. He pleaded that they were individuals "of whom this city is especially desirous to be disburdened; and in Virginia under severe masters they may be brought to goodness."[118] His plea was not ignored, and the Privy Council granted the council and the company authority to transport the youths against their will, ordering on 31 January 1620 that if any continued to be "obstinate" they could be punished and shipped to Virginia "with as much expedition as may stand with conveniencie [*sic*]."[119] This event suggests that, from the very beginning, there was open hostility and defiance toward this scheme.

Across parishes, it was widely believed that binding pauper children to the Virginia Company would relieve taxpayers and overseers of their responsibilities toward the local poor. Although the city was faced with an initial cost of £5 to outfit each child on their voyages, taxpayers avoided what was potentially a lifetime of financial support. Echoing the language of the Poor Laws, the Lord Mayor of London ordered aldermen to instruct churchwardens to find out which families in their parishes were "overcharged and burdened with poor children," and whether they would consent to the transportation of these children to Virginia, "thereby to ease them of that charge where they shall be well used and provision made for their good education and future maintenance." Parents were threatened that, if they did not consent to the transportation of their children, their parish poor relief payments, which they relied upon for sustenance and survival, would be suspended: "Take such order that they receive no further relief from the parish wherein they inhabit." The coercion of poor parents and their children was masked as paternalism, or what Patricia Crawford described as "civic fatherhood." Despite community resistance, the number of children apprenticed in the seventeenth century suggests that this practice received sufficient support from local administrators, who may have understood this practice not so much in terms of bolstering the colonial project, but as benefitting their communities.[120] The individuals who usually carried out arrests, the local constables, beadles, and night watch, had personal, vested interests in the transportation of vagrants. Constables, for example, were elected by, and held accountable to, their community.[121] As they policed their own neighborhoods, there was a real sense that they had the power to dispel disorder from their own doorsteps.[122] In the crowded, disease-ridden environment of London especially, parish authorities may really have been persuaded that by sending poor children to Virginia, they were doing the most compassionate thing.[123]

The children that were sent as servants to Virginia were themselves aware of the care and conditions they could expect. Richard Frethorne, for example, attempted to have his indenture redeemed by writing about the insufficient clothing and food that he received.[124] However, it seems that despite the company's promises, many arrived in a terrible physical state and languished in desperate conditions. George Thorpe, a colonist at Berkeley Hundred, complained in 1621 that "of those few boys" that had been sent to him, two were in such bad health, "diseased with old ulcers," that they were unfit to work; another was "broken-bellied"; a fourth "maimed in one of his hands"; and a fifth child was "so diseased in his whole body that he hath not been able to help himself ever since I had him."[125] Yet, this scheme was clearly understood as a success and continued to receive the support of the Common Council, even after the Algonquian attack on the Jamestown colonists in March 1622. Despite its catastrophic consequences for the colony and colonists, the Virginia Company once again persuaded the council to raise £500 and send one hundred children to Jamestown. Instructions were drawn up for poor relief ratepayers to contribute an eighth of their usual assessment to the scheme, and any who refused would have their property distrained for three days and then sold to raise the levy. The deadline for the collection was the end of August, making this an incredibly swift response to the disaster.[126] Any of the eight boys who survived their first winter in Jamestown probably languished with George Thorpe at Berkeley Hundred, who was killed during the Powhatan attack on the colony in March 1622.

The relationship between the transportation of vagrant children to Virginia and provision for the poor became, over time, closely entwined. In October 1632, the City of London responded to a request from the Privy Council for 30,000 quarters of corn by complaining that in the last year they had already spent great sums of money on the relief of the poor and setting them to work. As well as apprenticing seventy vagrants to Bridewell and forty to trades, and housing 773 poor children in Christ's Hospital, they had also bound fifty vagrants to merchants in Virginia and Bermuda.[127] Transporting the poor to English colonies was now part of a well-developed system of welfare provision. That the transportation of the poor to Virginia was related to innovations in welfare reform was not lost on commentators. Writing in 1624, Eburne discussed how transportation to Virginia might be achieved with reference to "Statute": the Elizabethan Poor Laws. He argued for the transportation "of all such vagrant persons, as now contrary to the Statute wander about the Country loitering, begging . . . of which sort many are strong and able persons, such as could and would work and labour well." Those who were "strong and able" should be sent "at the common charge of the place, either where they are apprehended, or ought to be relieved," thus reiterating that parishes were responsible for the poor. Concerning poor children, he suggested that "boys and maids, but maids especially of nine or ten years old and upward, be taken up," and this was justified in relation to the Poor Laws: "the Statute of 43. *Eliz.* 2. and 1. *Jam.* 25."[128]

The Council of New England took note of the Virginia Company's practices concerning forced transportation, and between May 1622 and February 1623 developed its own policies to grow the population of its fledging colony. First, it recorded that youths "that have not been tainted with any villainy or misdemeanour" would be transported and "placed out and bound apprentices, to such as shall have occasions and means to employ them."[129] That they wanted youths who were "untainted" suggests that they did not envision, at least initially, transporting children who were vagrants. It could be that attracting suitable youths proved more difficult than the council anticipated, because soon they looked to "tak[e] away poor children," just as the Virginia Company had done. The council drafted a proposition to the City of London to transport one hundred poor children aged fourteen and above to New England.[130] As the Virginia Company had done before, the council decided to use the precedent set by the Elizabethan Poor Laws, specifically the "statute made the . . . year [1601] of Queen Elizabeth for the binding forth of poor children apprentices." This particular suggestion was made by council member Sir Henry Spelman, the uncle of Henry Spelman, who was a child himself when he traveled to Virginia.[131] He argued that such a method, if employed "in every county . . . will be very easeful to the country, and beneficial to the plantation."[132] Several years later, around 1629 or 1630, Captain Harvey also made a proposal to the Privy Council that "the City of London be invited to send over a hundred poor boys and girls, to Virginia, at the general charge of the city, which (by his majesty's gracious letters directed to the Lord Mayor and Court of Aldermen) may be effected, *seeing they have done as much at the request of the late company.*"[133] The Privy Council deemed this "very reasonable and requisite," and ordered that "letters be written accordingly."[134] English welfare reform policies were a toolset that colonial projectors continued to draw upon in order to further the peopling of plantations with a cheap, indentured, labor force. Whether or not further numbers of children in the City of London endured this same practice at this time is unclear, but it was certainly not the end of the coerced transportation of children to English, and later British, colonies.[135]

The process of transporting the London poor to Virginia was not so straightforward, and it involved the interests of parties outside the Virginia

Company and the Common Council. Transporting poor children did, more often than not, demand the mediation of multiple interested groups, even prompting broader conversations about who was responsible for the lives of the poor. Between 1617 and 1626, the Bridewell governors issued 381 orders for transportation to Virginia, and its court book shows that on many occasions transportation orders were avoided, obstructed, or rescinded.[136] Bridewell's president in this period, Sir Thomas Myddelton, was a founder of the East India Company and an early investor in the Virginia Company, and on at least one occasion he directly interfered in the transportation of a child himself.[137] In June 1619, for example, he returned to Bridewell one William Smyth, who had previously been arrested and ordered for transportation. However, the governors recorded that before embarking to Virginia, Smyth had "run away and took with him divers things belonging to others."[138] The records reveal that other unwilling youths had also, for a time at least, managed to evade transportation. Following the Lord Mayor's instructions, a beadle named Britten arrested Roger Setherne on the charge of vagrancy, and he was duly ordered for transportation to Virginia on 25 September 1618. But Britten returned Setherne to Bridewell again on 3 October, and, for a second time, Setherne was ordered for transportation.[139] Similarly, Gryffin Beale was brought by warrant from the Middlesex House of Correction to Bridewell on 24 August 1618 and kept to go to Virginia.[140] But he was arrested again on 29 January 1619, and once again detained for transportation to Virginia.[141] While Arthur Chaundlor also avoided transportation when a deputy named Harper arrested him on 10 October 1618, he faced the Bridewell governors again on 12 February 1620 and this time was not so fortunate: he was ordered for transportation and was living in Virginia "in the main" in 1624.[142] There are questions about the unseen social and legal mechanisms that caused transportation orders to be bypassed. In this period, A. L. Beier suggests that Bridewell was not always fulfilling its purpose of putting the poor to work; instead individuals were sent away soon after admittance and punishment.[143] It appears that the discretion of the governors was also in play concerning transportation orders.

Here the domestic context of the orders, including the Elizabethan Poor Laws, provides some explanation. At times, it seems that the orders for transportation prompted a reconfiguration of who bore responsibility for vagrant children, and whether they should be transported to the colony. In the first instance, it seemed that transportation would relieve parishes of their responsibility to poor children, but on some occasions, it seems that the governors of Bridewell attempted to reassert parish responsibility for their poor. William Larratt, for instance, the "little boy" who was first arrested in August 1618 and ordered for transportation, discussed at the beginning of this chapter, subsequently appeared before the Bridewell governors on 26 February 1619 and 3 July 1619. The entry in February recorded that he had been brought in from Fleet Street (again), but this time they ordered him to be sent to the "churchwardens and overseers for the poor, where he was born."[144] On the third occasion, the frustration of the Bridewell governors can be felt, as the entry is brief and only repeats that he should be sent to the churchwardens. The governors wanted his parish to provide for him, rather than to transport him to Virginia. If William was returned to his parish, he could have been fostered and even educated, and for such a young child, maybe the governors felt this was a kinder fate.[145] In the 1620s, the Poor Laws, which made the parish responsible for poor relief, were enforced more regularly, and it seems that on this occasion the Bridewell governors were determined to compel the parish authorities to see to it that William was provided for.[146] It is also likely that the governors knew of the macabre tales about the starving time in Virginia, even if more recently the colony seemed to be on firmer footing. Perhaps they, unlike their fellows on the Common Council of London, were not always willing to relent to the pressure of the Virginia Company.

The Bridewell court book paints a picture of how multiple interests in early modern London were entangled in the processes of transportation, and often it was not the will of the institution alone that determined the outcome. Sometimes transportation orders were made at the demand of private, rather than "public," interests. This is evident in several cases where youths were transported as servants in the employment of named individuals. A marshal named Davies, for instance, arrested Robert Rogers and brought him to Bridewell in July 1627, where the governors authorized that Rogers could be kept for Davies's "friend" and bound for Virginia.[147] Sometimes the arrests themselves were pursued for personal interest. "Deputy Steward," for example, arrested a runaway apprentice, Daniel Barnes, in September 1627. It was then revealed that Barnes was actually apprenticed to Steward's son and destined for Virginia, a prospect he clearly did not relish. Regardless, it was ordered that Barnes would be forced to "stay till Dep[uty] Steward's son be here next week."[148] Similarly, Rowland Truelove, a Virginia Company investor, arrested Christopher Robinson in July 1627, and the governors ordered Robinson to be apprenticed for ten years in Virginia to none other than Rowland

Truelove, who was a citizen of London and Freeman of the Clothworkers' Company.[149] As a process, transportation accommodated diverse interests, including those of individuals who wanted a personal stake in colonization. Yet, it seems that even at this later date, after the dissolution of the Virginia Company, authorities in London continued to arrest and forcibly bind vagrant youths. It is no longer clear that a levy was being raised among the citizens of London; rather it appears that individual merchants were using a system, previously put in place by the Virginia Company, to their own advantage.

Following the Elizabethan Poor Laws, Paul Slack argues that the next watershed in ideas toward the poor occurred in the mid-seventeenth century. With the publication of Samuel Hartlib's *Londons Charity Enlarged, Stilling the Orphans Cry* in 1650, alongside other contemporaneous works, there was greater "sensitivity to the sufferings of the poor, and particularly of children . . . difficult to find earlier." Slack gives Hartlib's woodcut for *Londons Charity* as a particular example of this, quoting the "pictures of pity" that were meant to stir "every pious heart." This renewed sympathy apparently engendered a whole new language of welfare reform: a house of correction was now a "Nursery" or "Magazine of Charity."[150] However, Hartlib's woodcut was actually influenced by Michael Sparke's 1636 pamphlet *The Poor Orphans Court, or Orphans Cry* (1636). Not only are the titles very similar, but the imagery and verse used in Hartlib's text borrows directly from Sparke's earlier work. Both employ the rhyme "The orphans cry, we perish, we die," and images of starving and sick vagrants similarly speak to their audiences: "As we you see/ So may yours be" (Figure 2 and Figure 3). Hartlib would have been familiar with Sparke's work as they had an established professional connection. Sparke printed one text written by Hartlib, *England's Thankfulness,* and another, John Drury's *A Motion Tending to the Public Good of this Age and Posterity,* that he published. They collaborated on the publication of *A Reformation of Schools* by John Amos Comenius, and Sparke also received books from Hartlib, who was described by Sparke as "a great Scholar."[151]

There is also an important connection between Hartlib's ideas for welfare reform and transportation to Virginia that has previously gone unnoticed, again concerning Michael Sparke. Sparke was actually a promoter of transporting the poor to Virginia, which can be explained, in part, by his personal web of connection to the colony. His brother Thomas Sparke and nephew Daniel Sparke were investors in the Virginia Company, and it was one of them, "now bound for Virginia," who transported four "pauper

Figure 2. Michael Sparke, *The Poore Orphans Court, or Orphans Cry* (London, 1636), Frontispiece. Call # STC 21509 Bd.w. STC 6981 Copy 2. By permission of the Folger Shakespeare Library under a Creative Commons Attribution-ShareAlike 4.0 International License.

Figure 3. Samuel Hartlib, *Londons Charitie Inlarged, Stilling the Orphan's Cry* (London, 1650). © British Library Board (General Reference Collection E.598[4.], sig. A1v). Image published with permission of ProQuest as part of Early English Books Online, www.proquest.com. Further reproduction is prohibited without permission.

boys" from Faversham, Kent, in July 1634.[152] An even earlier work of Sparke's, *Grievous Groans for the Poor* (1621), was dedicated to the Virginia and Somers Island Companies, whose Christian charity, he wrote, had "transported . . . mean and decayed persons." Sparke also praised the work that the Virginia Company had already done to employ the poor, who he described as a "Rotting sore [which] hath run far of late," in that "famous Plantation." Similarly to Gray, Johnson, and Eburne, Sparke framed his arguments in relation to the body politic, but perhaps more so than his contemporaries he argued for sympathy toward the poor: "the Impotent with the lame foot, is to be defended and sustained by every member of the body of this Commonwealth."[153]

In his later work *The Poor Orphans Court*, published a couple of years after his kinsman transported poor children, he demanded help for "these poor Orphans, whose Court is kept in a Cage, or under a Stall, or in St Paul's amongst the forms."[154] He disparaged the current welfare system, under which "these miserable wretches . . . are cast off by wicked parents, or being placed out to apprentices in the Parish, or put to Masters, are cast off from one to another."[155] His recommendations on how reformation might be achieved was closely tied to England's colonial expansion in the Atlantic world. He suggested employing children in shipping and also that every parish should raise a "stock" to employ poor children until they were strong enough to be transported to the "Plantations," there to be employed by "some careful Master . . . and they to give a true account of the children." He also advised that ships bound to Virginia, New England, and other colonies, should carry six boys and six girls each, their passage paid for by their parishes, and at their arrival, "he that takes them into custody or service, give bond to pay the charge of their fraught [*sic*] . . . to the Parish." If this condition was met, "they might have them but six years *apprentice*." Surely, Sparke questioned, wasn't this a much better use of the money that parishes currently spent on "banqueting" and "feast[s]"?[156] Like the Poor Laws more generally, Sparke advised that the parish should take responsibility for the transportation of the poor. But, clearly, he was also influenced by the earlier connection forged between the forced transportation of children to Virginia, under the Virginia Company, and the system of parish apprenticeship.

This web of connection between Virginia colonists, London printers, and social reformers, across the later sixteenth and early seventeenth centuries illuminates how the transportation of the poor was not just about providing labor for English colonies in the Atlantic world, but also formed part of a much larger and sustained debate about welfare reform in early modern England. Promoters including Richard Hakluyt, Humphrey Gilbert, and Sir John Popham had meditated on the advantages of settling the poor and unemployed in English colonies in America, but their plans were only brought to fruition through the planning and negotiation of the Virginia Company. The realization of their vision came at a time when the orders of the Poor Laws were being pursued with greater urgency, and with significant impact on contemporary attitudes as well as policymaking. In Sparke's writing on the transportation of the poor, we find evidence for more sympathetic attitudes toward the poor much earlier than Paul Slack's suggested turning point of 1649, and with the same material evidence—the sorrowful woodcut—in mind. But the participation of Michael, Thomas, and Daniel Sparke in the practice and promotion of apprenticing and transporting poor children also reveals the very interpersonal connections between the ideas that were communicated in print by promoters of transportation, with the views held by individuals who had interests in America, and those who were directly involved in the practice of forced transportation itself. Rather than seeing ideas in print as the observations of armchair colonists, there was perhaps a more direct resonance with practices on the ground. It also reminds us of the thick web of overlapping influence and interests that are mediated through print and archival sources, helping us to imagine how events were shaped by individuals at the time.

Forced transportation was not a wholly outward-looking colonial policy, but one that was deeply rooted within English social practice, including the Elizabeth Poor Laws and welfare reform during the early seventeenth century. The process of transporting individuals to the colony led to the entanglement of a range of issues in the domestic sphere and engendered debates in which multiple contemporary concerns intersected, including authority and consent, charity and relief, and population and poverty. Through discussions on transportation, contemporaries disentangled ideas about society and social reform, drawing upon metaphors of the body politic and images of the commonwealth to do so. The coerced and forced transportation of criminals and the poor to English colonies cannot be understood without reference to English law as well as social and economic practice, something that historians have long since acknowledged. However, much less appreciated is how practices that were developed in order to mobilize labor for the Virginia colony, especially in relation to the transportation of poor adults and children, were intimately tied to developments in English welfare reform more broadly.

English customs and policies did not just shape the development of free and unfree labor in the burgeoning Atlantic empire, but colonization itself determined attitudes and policymaking in England. Not only that, but the practices tested in the context of Virginia influenced the next generation of colonial projectors too. The nature of English migration, both free and unfree, in the Atlantic world is often framed in oppositional terms, of stable family formation in New England, versus young, unattached men in Virginia and Barbados.[157] Yet, the reality was much more complicated, and the New England colonists actually drew on the precedents set by the Virginia Company in ways that have gone largely unnoticed. The practices that developed around forced transportation engendered another sphere of colonial enterprise in early modern English society too: in parish churches where collections were made, in courts around the country, on the streets of the City of London, and in the Bridewell house of correction where decisions were made about the fate of individuals. Despite the powers they were up against, some individuals found ways to exert agency and mediate situations, including actually expediting their transportation to Virginia. As we have seen, such experiences also had wider repercussions. Colonization had meaning in peoples' lives, whether it was the poor man who had pawned his tools and struggled to provide for his family, or the wealthy parishioner who provided charity to the local poor. The processes associated with forced transportation provide glimpses into the very intimate, interpersonal, and emotional qualities of their experiences, as they faced up to the realities of colonization in Virginia. Forced transportation altered the reality of the world in which they lived and also, through their eyes, tempered the social fabric of the communities they inhabited.

CHAPTER 5

Domesticating Tobacco and Moral Economy

In *A Counterblast to Tobacco*, penned in 1604, James VI and I complained "a man cannot heartily welcome his friend now, but straight they must be in hand with *Tobacco*."[1] There was no denying the ubiquity of tobacco consumption in early modern England, especially following the successful cultivation of tobacco in Bermuda and Virginia. Yet, as the king's complaint suggests, English smokers were familiar with the sight, smell, and taste of tobacco long before the establishment of English colonies in America. It was through encounters with Indigenous peoples in the Americas over the preceding century that Europeans had gradually learned how to first consume, and then cultivate, variations of the plant *Nicotiana*. In the late sixteenth and early seventeenth centuries, it was sweet tasting tobacco from the Spanish Empire that fulfilled European demand.[2] Across the Continent, a corpus of medical literature on its various properties abounded, while the tobacco pipe itself emerged as a popular component in Dutch genre paintings. In John Gerard's *Herbal*, a botanical work first printed in 1597, *Nicotiana rustica* was described alongside other native plants growing in England.[3] But tobacco was not just encountered in paintings and printed work; English towns and villages, alehouses and theatres, were subsequently consumed by smoke.[4] By the turn of the seventeenth century, a complex economy and culture of tobacco consumption, which pervaded world cultures, had taken hold.[5]

Tobacco was the first English imperial commodity that was widely consumed, preceding tea, coffee, and sugar in this respect.[6] Lauren Working has demonstrated that this symbiotic relationship, between tobacco and the burgeoning English empire in America, was not lost on consumers. Smoking was a subversive means for English gentlemen to engage with Native American cultures and simultaneously project their own "imperial-minded masculinity."[7] Through the practices associated with tobacco consumption, the empire became commonplace, and this was, in part, the problem with tobacco: the susceptibility of subjects, including the rural poor, to its "evils" was "likened to the temptation of rebellion."[8] Tobacco also had a particular role in Stuart imperial policy and political culture, as the tobacco trade served as a crucial conduit for the English state's intervention in Virginia, through which successive Stuart governments sought to manage and profit from the colony.[9] Focusing on the mobilization of the English tobacco industry provides a unique opportunity, then, to study the impact of colonization in Virginia on domestic society and politics.[10] While there were certainly debates about the monopolization of other goods in the early Stuart period, like currants and finished cloth, tobacco presented a distinct set of problems.[11] The Atlantic world was still the only place that colonies were established, and tobacco was the most widely dispersed and profitable cash crop from these colonies. But, uniquely, there was also a well-established domestic market in tobacco, including its cultivation. Policies on tobacco brought into conflict and entangled, for the first time, the interests of subjects in England and those in its empire, including around the contested issues of political and moral economy. Exploring the controversies that developed in the English tobacco industry focuses attention on the role of non-elite men and women in forcing these debates. It highlights how, through the development of a domestic tobacco industry, the priorities of Virginia Company shareholders and colonists clashed with the concerns of the "common sort" in England. Yet, it also demonstrates the significant ways that Virginia colonial enterprise, both materially and immaterially, changed society in the metropole.

Culture and Cultivation

English colonists recognized the potential lucrativeness of tobacco cultivation, and when they colonized Jamestown in 1607 a taste for tobacco was exported with them. The tobacco pipe-maker Robert Cotton voyaged to Virginia in 1608, and archaeologists have discovered around 1,550 fragments of his pipes, stamped with a recognizable fleur-de-lis pattern.[12] Although *Nicotiana rustica* was cultivated by Virginia Indians in the Chesapeake, and the English certainly joined in smoking it, when colonists began their own experiments with tobacco cultivation, they used seeds of the sweeter *Nicotiana tabacum* they were accustomed to, found growing on the coasts of Venezuela, Hispaniola, and Trinidad.[13] In 1615, before any English colonial tobacco was exported, 100,926 pounds of Spanish tobacco were received in the Port of London and 1,351 pounds in the out-ports along the English coast.[14] John Rolfe began his trials shortly after arriving in Virginia in the summer of 1610, after having spent ten months stranded on Bermuda. According to Spanish sources, tobacco was growing on the island in 1603, and the colonists might have collected seeds and samples before their departure. Whatever the source of his seeds, Rolfe's efforts were successful, and the first sample of his Virginian tobacco was exported to England in 1612.[15] In 1616, just 2,500 pounds of tobacco from Virginia and Bermuda made its way into England, but in 1617 this grew to 18,839 pounds. From then on, exports rose sharply, to 49,668 pounds in 1618 and 119,021 pounds in 1620.[16] In 1619, John Pory, who was secretary of the colony and a company investor, claimed that a farmer in Virginia who could afford the assistance of six indentured servants could earn £1,000 per annum. "These be true, yet indeed rare examples," he wrote, "yet possible to be done by others."[17] In 1631, imports reached 1.3 million pounds and by 1633, if not before, tobacco was recognized as the "chief commodity" of Virginia.[18] During the 1630s, tobacco emerged as an intoxicant of mass consumption: prices fell dramatically in England as the transatlantic trade in colonial tobacco grew, and the consumption of a single tobacco pipe emerged as a cheap and transient "hit" for customers.[19]

Following John Rolfe's early experiments, tobacco cultivation flourished in Virginia, altering the entire material world of colonists. Plantations, which had previously been tightly packed around the fort of Jamestown, began to spread along the James River, enabling ambitious colonists to acquire the fertile land they needed for tobacco production to flourish. As tobacco was shipped in large, heavy hogsheads, settling beside navigable portions of the river was essential so that their crops could be easily transported to boats and then shipped overseas.[20] The lower James River basin was said to produce an inferior quality of tobacco leaf, whereas the tobacco grown between the James and Rappahannock Rivers was considered to be the best quality.[21] The cultivation of tobacco in Virginia also had a significant demographic impact on the colony. Tobacco production was labor intensive, and planters demanded a cheap workforce. This need was met first by the use of tenant farmers, later indentured servants and, from 1619 onward, the toil of enslaved Africans.[22] Unfree laborers also lent their expertise to English tobacco cultivation in the Atlantic world. In 1616, Bermudians sought Indigenous peoples and Hispanic Africans who were experienced in the techniques of tobacco cultivation in the Spanish Empire. Drawing on Indigenous knowledge and African

Table 2. Imports of tobacco in pounds (lbs.) from the English colonies of Virginia and Bermuda

Date	*London*	*Outports*	*Total*
1616	2,300	200	2,500
1617	18,839	0	18,839
1618	49,518	150	49,668
1619	45,764	0	45,764
1620	117,981	1,040	119,021
1621	73,777	0	73,777

SOURCE: "Lord Sackville's Papers Respecting Virginia, 1613–31, I," *American Historical Review* 27 (1922), 493–538, at 526.

Table 3. Tobacco prices per pound (lb.) in the Chesapeake and England

Chesapeake farm prices		*English wholesale prices*	
Date	Price	Date	Price
1615	27d	1618	8–9s
1625	11.6d	Late 1620s	2s
1630	5.3d	Late 1630s	<1s
1632	2.9d	1660s	6–8d
Late 1630s	5d	1680s (better quality)	4d

SOURCE: Russell Menard, "The Tobacco Industry in the Chesapeake Colonies, 1617–1730: An Interpretation," in Paul Uselding, ed., *Research in Economic History* (Greenwich, CT, 1980), 5:15; and Russell Menard, "Plantation Empire: How Sugar and Tobacco Planters Built Their Industries and Raised an Empire," *Agricultural History* 81 (2007), 309–32, at 321.

expertise gave Bermudians a distinct advantage, and colonists there grew more tobacco than their Virginian counterparts until 1625.[23]

Against this context of cultivation in English America it is easy to overlook the much longer history of tobacco cultivation in England. Before 1597, John Gerard had observed *Nicotiana rustica*, or yellow henbane as he called it, "sown in gardens, where it doth prosper exceedingly, in so much that it cannot be destroyed where it hath once sown it self, and it is dispersed into the most parts of England."[24] Tobacco was probably introduced into England around the middle of the sixteenth century, when English sailors and merchants returned from voyages to the Americas.[25] The introduction of tobacco smoking was a gradual process, with tobacco first penetrating maritime communities before its breakthrough into urban centers.[26] By the 1580s, however, tobacco smoking was certainly popularized outside of maritime communities, something that has long been attributed to Sir Walter Ralegh's influence, who was reported by his contemporaries to have made smoking fashionable at court.[27] By the turn of the century, sailors and courtiers were certainly no longer the sole consumers of tobacco. Individuals in Cornwall and Carlisle—far flung from the capital and the major ports of Bristol and Portsmouth—were enjoying pipes.[28] Sailors, too, are likely to have played a role in introducing tobacco cultivation to England and across the Continent.[29] Within this European-wide context, cultivation occurred in various settings, including the gardens of physicians, known as physic gardens, while sailors probably grew "hardier varieties" in their herb gardens.[30]

By the time, then, that Jamestown was founded in 1607, tobacco had probably been grown on English soil for several decades. The first recorded attempt to grow tobacco on a commercial scale was 1619 in Winchcombe, Gloucestershire. In this region, tobacco cultivation had even given rise to local place names such as "Tobacco Piece" in the parish of Hailes.[31] Following the establishment of plantations in the colony, tobacco planters sought to cultivate the experience of people from this region, transporting twenty men and women from Hailes to Virginia in 1620.[32] Gloucestershire investors in the Berkley Hundred plantation, including John Smyth, took advantage of their Virginia connections. A list of "remembrances" for Captain Woodleefe during his voyage to Virginia in 1619 included "Mr Smyth's particular request is, That you forget not to furnish him, with some good Tobacco seed."[33] Growers in England may have taken instruction from *An Advice How to Plant Tobacco in England,* published in 1615, a text that suggests sufficient appetite for cultivating and consuming English tobacco in order to supplant the trade in tobacco from the Spanish Empire.[34] Experiments were undertaken by Virginia Company administrators John and Nicholas Ferrar, who kept their own tobacco garden and recorded receipts for gardeners and manure.[35] In 1613, Henry Bluett sent tobacco seeds from America to his uncle Richard Weekes in Somerset, along with instructions for their cultivation. He had received the seeds from "a friend of mine that came lately from Guyana," and advised, "if you will make trial of it," to plant the seeds in ground that is "very fat and made very clean from weed and grass." Henry gave further instructions about how the seeds, *Nicotiana tabacum,* should be sown, raked, and replanted once established ("grown four inches high"). Yet, he wrote "I will write you more there after because I have not yet the perfect instructions for it."[36]

Prospective tobacco growers who were unfamiliar with botanical literature relied upon knowledge gathered from those with firsthand experience of its cultivation in America. As colonists learned firsthand, tobacco cultivation required a specialized "tool kit." In 1621, items including "20lb. of string packthread to dry tobacco" were sent to Virginia, as well as a "gross" (144) of "tobacco pipes from Lambeth Marsh which are very large." The disposability of pipes meant that enormous quantities were required to satiate demand, but the supplies also reflected colonists' experimentations with processing their crops. On 10 March 1618, Captain Argall had written to the Virginia Company that colonists found that tobacco cured better on lines than in heaps and requesting more string to be sent.[37] Enough experience, no doubt partly through trial-and-error efforts, was generated to allow tobacco cultivation in England to flourish. A proclamation dated 30 December 1619 to "restrain the planting of Tobacco in England and Wales" lamented that tobacco growth had "by the Inland plantation become promiscuous, and begun to be taken in every mean Village, even amongst the basest people."[38] In spite of the proclamation, tobacco cultivation continued throughout the realm with growth in at least twenty-six counties in England, Wales, and the Channel Islands between 1620 and 1680.[39] In 1621, Thomas Dawson made efforts to sell four hogsheads of his Gloucestershire-grown tobacco, receiving around £8 from John Stratford, which he thought was a poor price.[40] In Lincoln in 1626, Michael Batterby was growing tobacco, "not to bee intended for medicine but to bee taken in the pipe."[41] This may have been the alias of Michael Bland, of Ketsby, Lincolnshire, who was reported by Francis South to the Privy Council as growing "horse tobacco for medicine and pipe tobacco about the tenth part of the acre."[42] As far as John Gerard was concerned, tobacco grown on native soil was far better for the English constitution, and, it seems, others agreed.[43]

In this period, the consumption of tobacco birthed a new material culture and was also associated with a novel kind of sociability. In tobacco's development from the pastime of sailors to a widespread habit, there were processes of introduction to, and education about, tobacco smoking. Tobacco shops appeared as early as 1605, forming "a crucial link between the production and consumption of tobacco, connecting metropolitan consumers of American goods to an English, and then British, empire."[44] Retailers, including tobacco pipe-makers, probably instructed customers in how to prepare and smoke their pipes.[45] But there were many other potential points of contact with tobacco in English towns and villages. The introduction of retail licenses in October 1633, and the investigations that followed into whether people continued to retail tobacco illicitly, reveal that individuals took to exchanging tobacco discreetly in homes and even in a "calf house" in a field. Smokers could buy tobacco by the pipe or penny-worth, sometimes wrapped up in brown paper, from grocers, innkeepers, tipplers, and vintners.[46] In *The Works of John Taylor the Water Poet* (1630), vintners' customers were said to call for a "pipe, pint, and a candle too" throughout the night.[47]

Londoners in search of tobacco had to navigate an array of hanging shop signs. In 1623, a letter from Virginia colonist Richard Norwood was addressed to Mr. Marshall in London "at the sign of the Tobacco Roll in Tower street." Trade tokens such as these were numerous across the city.[48] The visual language associated with retailing tobacco suggests how Londoners would have come to associate the tobacco they smoked with the colony of Virginia, as well as with Africans and Native Americans. Catherine Molineux traces this relationship in late seventeenth- and early eighteenth-century London through trade cards and tobacco papers that included images of "New World" people and colonial plantations, arguing that producers "often employed Virginia as a metonym for tobacco."[49] Yet, that earlier consumers grasped the origins of the tobacco they smoked is suggested by several mid-seventeenth-century trade tokens. One was probably issued for a tobacco shop, "At the New Virginne [*sic*]" in Pancras Lane. It depicted a Native American figure wearing a feathered headdress, smoking a tobacco pipe, and holding a tobacco leaf. Two other tokens depict "hybrid" Native American–African figures, who "specifically reflect the association of Africans and Native Americans with the tobacco trade and smoking."[50] On both tokens, a male holds a tobacco pipe and tobacco leaf, and one of them is inscribed with "At the Black Boy Inn."[51] If we consider the artisans who crafted such images and their place in the material fabric of the city, where they were seen by thousands, an impression forms of the "complex interaction among ideologies of empire, the social experience of smoking, and the cultural meanings of tobacco."[52]

Smoking a pipe also came to characterize interactions and cement social relations in the "Old" and "New World," for gentlemen and the "poorer sort" alike, including women. William Barclay, a physician, claimed that tobacco "worketh never so well, as when it is given from man to man, as a pledge of friendship and amity."[53] The motto chosen by the Company of Tobacco Pipe Makers when it was reincorporated in 1663 was "Let brotherly love continue," a reflection of the fraternal bonds that incorporation granted, as well as the sociability associated with smoking.[54] In places including Carmarthen, Wales, and Leicester, England, young men described drinking jugs of beer and smoking tobacco by the pipe while playing at cards in local alehouses.[55] Across the Atlantic, when a ship landed at Jamestown in 1623, the new arrivals were duly welcomed with tobacco. Colonists went aboard to greet friends and hear the latest news from England, and were described as "being aboard merry," "drinking tobacco" in the cabins and gunroom. However, "through negligence of their fire," they "blew up the ship" resulting in the loss of fourteen lives, including sailors, servants, and one woman.[56] Tobacco was sometimes an accompaniment to more reckless behavior. In Somerset, local villagers were dragged before the Justices of the Peace after apparently getting a dog "drunk" on beer and a tobacco pipe.[57] Smoking could also be associated with personal intimacy, stimulating an affective response. One Mr. Anthony received tobacco from his friend, Captain Thomas Stockwell, on several occasions, and wrote to him "Tasting your tobacco makes me remember you, at meals your knife, between meals and at night again your tobacco."[58]

Women who craved the effects of tobacco, for pleasure and its medicinal properties, shaped the creation of local economies of exchange. In Southampton, James Mason accused his servant Christian Smith of stealing "about 7lb. weight of *Virginia* tobacco" from his cellar, something that she admitted to. She described giving away and selling the tobacco several times to local women, including another servant, Elizabeth Wheate, and Ann Drake, a spinster. Elizabeth promised Christian "half a yard of lace at the next fair" in exchange for about two and a half pounds of tobacco, or as much as Smith could "hold between both her hands." These illicit exchanges took place during periods when her master and his apprentice were absent, and when the other women hoped to avoid prying eyes. They came once on a Sunday, "a little after the beginning of evening prayer," and another time "on shrove Sunday . . . at evening prayer time."[59] That smoking tobacco had a potentially corrupting influence on women is illustrated in a 1628 woodcut. In it, a young woman stands behind a table littered with tobacco pipes, gripping a goblet of wine in her left hand; her young lover touches her breast with one hand and holds a pipe to her mouth with the other, all while her right hand points across the image to a scene that symbolizes her abandoned role and duties: her husband spinning yarn while her young children watch.[60] Such moral censure did not stem women's appetite for tobacco. In Sussex, Lady Earlsfield sent her young servant, Elinor Waller, to buy four ounces of tobacco, perhaps not for the first time. However, when Lady Earlsfield heard that Elinor would be examined by the officers looking into the retail of tobacco without license, she instructed her to say that the tobacco had been bought "at London."[61] Women's consumption of tobacco fed into the contemporary idea that women were preoccupied with exotic goods. As John Gerard himself noted, "according to the English Proverb, Far fetched and dear bought is best for Ladies."[62]

In medical literature, too, tobacco engendered an adverse debate. Smoking was not considered, as it is today, to be a purely palliative remedy; rather tobacco was understood, if taken "correctly," to be a cure for many ailments. William Vaughan, writing in 1600, argued that when "well dried, and taken in a silver pipe . . . [tobacco] cures the migraine, the toothache, obstructions proceeding of cold, and helps the fits of the choler."[63] Claims like this bolstered a body of literature, in circulation in Europe since the early sixteenth century, which attested to the healing properties of tobacco. Although

Figure 4. *English Customs. 12 Engravings of English Couples with Verses* (London, 1628), Image 4. Call # STC 10408.6. By permission of the Folger Shakespeare Library under a Creative Commons Attribution-ShareAlike 4.0 International License.

tobacco was relatively new to Europeans, the idea that smoke and fumes could be curative was not. Those living in the seventeenth century were aware that in ancient Greece and contemporary China substances were burned for medicinal purposes.[64] Within England also, tobacco smoking was thought to have built upon "a cultural wisdom about psychotropic plants . . . concentrated in the folklore of urban and rural populations." Goodman has argued that this type of knowledge was "a phenomenon of a particular social class," among those who were familiar with what has been described as "female medicine" or the "medicine of the poor."[65] During her interrogation, Christian Smith alleged that one woman, a Widow Smith, had bought "a piece of tobacco her child being then sick of an ague to make a medicine withal."[66]

As early as 1606, English women recorded recipes containing tobacco, which suggests just how quickly its use was subsumed into lay medical practice. Mrs. Corlyon's recipe book included an "Ointment of the herb Nicotiana, good for any Cut or Wound, and for any Ache in the Bones." For this remedy she wrote, "Take in the month of Auguste as many of the leaves of the herb *Nicotiana* as shall weigh six ounces," which suggests that it was English tobacco that she had in mind.[67] Johanna St. John's recipes, dated from 1680, were borrowed from her friends, doctors, grandmother, and "an old woman." One was Lady Roberd's recipe "to prevent miscarrying," and next to it a "Tobacco Salve." While it is not clear if this recipe was also a preventative for miscarriage, its location in the text might guess that it had a related use. This is further suggested by the recipe itself, which contained tobacco leaf, red wine, hog's grease, and, crucially, birthwort, a plant associated with preventing complications in childbirth because of its resemblance to the birth canal. However, the recipe is also almost identical in its ingredients and method to an ointment for wounds and ulcers included in the 1633 edition of Gerard's *Herbal*.[68] Uses for tobacco were passed down through multiple generations, and may have, as recipes were recopied, taken on new meanings and associations.

While some used tobacco's supposed medical benefits to justify continued consumption, others were concerned that tobacco could have an ill effect on the body politic itself. In his *A Counterblast to Tobacco,* James likened "the vile use (or rather abuse) of taking Tobacco" to the "naturally inclined corruptions . . . natural infirmities . . . idle delights, and soft delicacies" of "commonwealths," which were often "the first seeds of the subversion of all great Monarchies."[69] Tobacco was socially subversive because of the potential harm it posed to the English body politic, as well as the country's poor population. In the House of Commons, Sir Peter Frescheville argued that "Tobacco is the cause of drunkenness, drunkenness of idleness, idleness of beggary, so Tobacco of beggary." Yet he advised against prohibiting tobacco altogether, instead suggesting that parliament allow the continued importation of tobacco from Virginia and Bermuda. This would resolve several problems simultaneously: provide support for the colonies, increase England's coffers, and rid the nation through migration "of that *inutile pondus* of unprofitable members in the Commonwealth" who were most likely to be, in his eyes, the worst abusers of tobacco.[70] Peter Frescheville was an investor in the Virginia Company, so his stance is unlikely to have been entirely altruistic, but his argument does encapsulate the contradictory nature of political debate on the tobacco trade at this time.[71] Whether James liked it or not, by the end of his reign, tobacco inflected social relations, cultural responses to gender and the Indigenous peoples of America, lay medicine, and parliamentary politics. It was established as both a key colonial commodity and a domestic crop, which would be difficult to uproot from the English landscape.

It was against this cultural backdrop that conflict arose in the transatlantic tobacco industry. Encroachments on the domestic tobacco industry brought into conflict, for the first time, the economic interests of subjects at home and colonists in the burgeoning English empire. Policy makers were made to confront the domestic consequences of an imperial economy, under pressure, in many instances, from those lobbying for colonial interests. More or less as soon as colonial tobacco was established in England's economy, the domestic tobacco industry began to shift. Whereas English tobacco growers were previously unhindered, they now found their activity threatened; similarly, the manufacture of tobacco pipes, which had prospered under James, was similarly encroached upon as the trade became more tightly regulated. In towns, villages, workshops, and their homes, men and women responded, sometimes with violence, to innovations enforced from above. How the debates surrounding the tobacco trade played out between the crown, parliament, and projectors is much better documented and understood. But getting at the experiences of the "common sort," as they confronted the possibilities and difficulties of colonial expansion, not only enables us to glean how a broader English public was made to engage with the economies of English colonies; it also gives us a chance to understand how those with "limited access to a public voice" appealed to their constitutional rights to property and customary rights to subsistence in order to resist the impact of colonialism on their livelihoods.[72]

Pipes, Monopolies, and Free Trade

Walking through the street in early modern England, a person's first visual encounter with tobacco was probably not the leaf itself, but the object in which it was most commonly consumed: the tobacco pipe. The pipe was essential to smoke tobacco and as it was fragile, affordable, and thus disposable, enormous quantities of them were required to satiate demand. As early as 1570, pipes were produced in London, and by 1640 substantial manufacturers were also operating along England's main trade routes, in Bristol, Gateshead, and Newcastle.[73] However, in 1619 a "society" of London tobacco pipe makers, in business for seven years, expressed their concern that some craftsmen were producing inferior wares, and that many apprentices were failing to finish their training.[74] A proclamation stated that, as a result, the industry was without "policy or good government." The king's personal view on smoking is clear from the proclamation, which disputed the utility of pipe manufacture altogether, as it "concerneth not any Commodity of necessity for our Commonweal, but a superfluous pleasure." Nonetheless, the society received a Royal Charter and from 1620 onward a monopoly on pipe manufacture. Concealing or "harbour[ing]" illicit wares or their makers was now unlawful.[75] Although granting the pipe-makers a charter was seemingly contradictory, considering the king's view on the trade, the king expressed his hope that it might deter others from leaving more established trades in order to manufacture pipes.[76] This innovation in the pipe industry was entirely connected to the lucrativeness of tobacco-related products, which had greatly increased in the space of a few years. While the amount of Spanish tobacco annually imported into London had remained more or less the same between 1616 and 1618, tobacco from Virginia and Bermuda had more than doubled year on year.[77] And yet, the new monopoly on pipes was not an uncommon development. As Jeremy Boulton has shown, large manufacturing firms in London increased during this period, at the expense of "small independent masters across a range of enterprises and in most sectors."[78]

The monopolization of tobacco pipe manufacture was, then, the first encroachment on the freedom of men and women to operate in a domestic manufacturing trade as a direct result of English colonial expansion. Tobacco pipe making in England could be a family affair, with wives working alongside husbands in the workshop, so it is also likely that family members stood side by side in protestation.[79] In 1619, for example, a group of pipe-makers "fortified themselves in their houses with weapons" against Justices of the Peace in Surrey and Middlesex, who had come to enforce the charter and suppress their continued manufacture of tobacco pipes.[80] Another group who were excluded by the monopoly petitioned parliament in 1621, complaining that their houses had been "violently broken open" by the patentees, who "by force and against their wills . . . have broken down their furnaces, carried away their works of very good value, with their Moulds and Tools and have forbidden them to work in their Trade for fifteen weeks together, and have imprisoned divers." They claimed that since the halt to their work, and damage or removal of their tools and wares, they had been unable to support their families, and wanted an opportunity to "make proof of the great oppressions and grievances" that they had suffered at the hands of the patentees. They made an emotive plea, by claiming to be "very poor people," for whom the monopoly had been "the undoing of their wives and children, whereof divers have died."[81] In doing so, they appealed to the expectations of paternalism in two distinct ways, first through supplicating themselves to parliament as humble petitioners in need of relief, and second by highlighting their inability to support their own families, as both a husband and father should.[82]

Through their description of the suffering and injustice they had experienced, the tobacco pipe-makers also participated in a much more pervasive political discourse of corruption, related to monopolies and patents, that was prevalent in Jacobean England, and that reached a climax in 1624 with the Statute of Monopolies.[83] Their petition suggests that debates concerning monopolies were more widespread than previously thought, and even that the petitioners had some knowledge of the climate of political debate in parliament at the time. According to Ian Archer, we should not be surprised that they lobbied parliament, since the "voice" of artisans was often "heeded" at Westminster.[84] However, the example of the pipe-makers is unique, because, according to Christopher Dent, there is no other recorded example of artisans directly petitioning parliament about a monopoly in the Jacobean period.[85] The fact that they did so at all suggests that they could afford the costs associated with petitioning, and had at least some access to political patronage. Moreover, the revocation of the patent in 1621, along with others, suggests that they achieved sufficient leverage with MPs.[86] The pipe-makers provide an example, then, of the different tools, or "petitionary styles," which were often communal and direct, that early modern subjects had at their disposal to affect political change.[87] They showed an apparent awareness of constitutional rights, which under the common law meant that they were at liberty to work in the trade of their choice; and nor could their rights to property be infringed, without a "dangerous imbalance resulting."[88] But they also addressed this particular grievance in terms of paternalism, a concept that was as deeply ingrained in English society as custom and the "common weal."

The patent on tobacco pipe manufacture and clay suggests how widely the industry surrounding the smoking of a pipe expanded during the early seventeenth century. Both James VI and I and Charles I were desperate to increase Crown revenues, and the granting of monopolies and levying of impositions on luxury goods were both strategies to achieve this. The flourishing domestic and colonial economies in tobacco sparked debates, especially during the 1621 parliament, on how the enterprise should be managed. This parliament was marred by "constitutional fears," culminating in the arrest of key members of the Virginia Company, including Sir Edwin Sandys, the Earl of Southampton, and John Selden, at the end of the session.[89] Members debated their privileges and asserted their rights at a time when they felt that there had never before been greater "invasions of parliamentary liberties."[90] A key concern was their right to free speech in the House of Commons, not least their freedom to discuss the Crown's right to levy impositions (duties upon imports and exports), grant charters, monopolies, and patents without recourse to parliament.[91] Virginia Company members were important participants in these debates and had vested interests not just as MPs. Instead, the influence of the colony seeped into the house with investors shaping debates on commerce and free trade.[92] Sir Edwin Sandys articulated the free trade principle in 1604 when he stated, "All free subjects are born inhabitable as to their lands for also to the free exercise of their industry to those trades whereto they apply themselves." He went on, "It is against the natural right and liberty of the subjects of England to restrain it [trade] into the hands of some few as now it is."[93] Under James, impositions continued to be debated in constitutional terms. On 23 June 1610, for example, Nicholas Fuller, a lawyer who was closely connected to the London mercantile community, spoke against them, arguing that they would force men from their "lawful trade," and only parliament possessed the power to "lawfully lay any impositions upon the subjects" goods.[94]

Without doubt, contemporaries realized that the prosperity of the commonwealth relied upon trade: "Of all other trades . . . the merchant is most tenderly to be regarded . . . the merchants are as the two legs whereupon the commonwealth doth go and travel . . . the principal means to make the realm to abound in wealth."[95] Yet, monopolies persisted and by 1620 England was in the grip of an export crisis. The supposed "decay of trade" dominated parliamentary debate.[96] In 1621, Sandys was appointed to look into the matter, and on 26 February gave a speech on the economic depression, arguing that high unemployment among the poor had been caused both by a shortage of coin and by the restrictions imposed on free trade by grants of monopoly. He reported that there was "Some 200 looms decayed in one Town, so many men turned out of their inheritance, the inheritance of their hands."[97] Significantly, Sandys used the transatlantic tobacco trade as evidence to argue that each year £100,000 was lost in bullion because the Spanish bought goods not with coin, but with tobacco, which was then sold in England. To look into these matters further, a grand committee, with Sandys at its head, was established, and on 10 April Sandys reported to the House of Commons its findings, reiterating that £100,000 was lost annually in purchasing Spanish tobacco: "Free trade [is] hindered by taking of tobacco excessively, lost in bullion £100,000 a year . . . If the shopkeeper can gain £10 by £20 lost, they care not, by which they spoil the merchant. The tobacco man cares not how much he pay, for he can get such a gain for it here. (Here is the wound)."[98] The domestic market had been flooded with Spanish tobacco, and English tobacco merchants were unable to compete. Sandys's concern was borne out by the evidence. In 1620, 98,397 pounds of Spanish tobacco were imported, while 119,021 pounds were received from English colonies. Yet, in 1621, there were just 73,777 pounds of English colonial tobacco compared to 174,3939 pounds from the Spanish Empire.[99] Sandys's solution was the prohibition of Spanish tobacco in favor of that from the English colonies: "Now the cure . . . Tobacco is daily bettered by plantations . . . if cure be had in the plantation, it may be as beneficial as the Indies." But the main obstacle to Sandys's proposal was the 1604 peace treaty between England and Spain; many MPs did not want to antagonize their Continental neighbor. But Sandys reassured the house that Spain operated a protectionist policy on wine imports, "till their own be spent," and so England would reasonably follow Spain's example.[100]

Individuals who had vested interests in the success of the colonial tobacco trade shaped the debate that followed.[101] After the Easter recess Sir Lionel

Cranfield objected, "we must regard the treaty," but Sir Dudley Digges responded, "I think (speaking as an Englishman) no treaty can be so beneficial to us in England as £100,000 per annum."[102] On 3 May, the tobacco bill was entrusted to Sandys, his brother Sir Miles, and, among others, several more prominent figures in the Virginia Company, including Sir Nathaniel Rich, Sir Henry Mildmay, John Drake, Sir William Cavendish I, and Sir Henry Montagu.[103] As seven of the ten MPs were investors in the Virginia Company, it is no surprise that the committee decided in favor of colonial tobacco. Nevertheless, some members in the Virginia Company still had to be placated. A syndicate of Virginia Company merchants, led by Sir Thomas Roe, held a patent for the sole importation of tobacco, including that from the Spanish colonies, and they persuaded the committee to amend the bill in order to allow them to sell off their stock before Spanish tobacco was prohibited altogether. Finally, on 16 May, Sandys announced on behalf of the committee that from 1 October only tobacco from the English colonies was to be imported, but the bill never made it through the House of Lords. Nevertheless, when the tobacco patent was renewed in December 1621, Sandys won a significant victory for the Virginia colony: Spanish imports were limited to 60,000 pounds per annum, while colonial tobacco was left unrestricted.[104]

The idea that English subjects should have freedom in trade was dispersed across English societies and did not diminish. In 1622, a new tobacco contract was proposed that would grant the Virginia Company and Bermuda Company a monopoly on tobacco imports, including up to 40,000 pounds of Spanish tobacco. But some Virginia colonists complained that the "heavy charge laid upon Tobacco by this Contract" would discourage planters from exporting tobacco to England, who they said would be driven to "poverty and want," even "revolt." Investors and colonists alike emphasized that tobacco was essential to the subsistence of the colony. Moreover, they were discontented because the contract was an encroachment upon personal freedoms. They asserted "the Laws of England . . . do not allow the good Subject to be dispossessed of his goods without his Consent." The investors concluded that "It were a dangerous Precedent and never heard of that plurality of voices," meaning those assembled at the Virginia Company court meeting "should conclude the goods of other men without their Consent." Like tobacco pipe-makers before them, when faced with a monopoly, the planters invoked the property rights of English subjects and their rights to subsistence. The demands of pipe-makers to carry on in their trades freely were as inflected by constitutional debate, on custom, the common law, and royal proclamations as the appeal of Virginia investors to "the Laws of England." In opposition to patents and monopolies, subjects at all levels of English society reminded their superiors that they had freedom to practice in the trade of their choosing. Notably, their appeals did not fall on deaf ears, and the 1622 tobacco contract was abandoned.[105]

Tobacco Retail Licenses

In 1624, the English parliament passed the monopolies bill, and the following year Virginia tobacco planters were granted what they had long desired: free trade. With trade unhindered, the number of merchants operating in the tobacco trade grew exponentially, with 175 tobacco merchants trading in 1634, and as many as 300 by 1640.[106] The tobacco trade was open to every sort of "adventurer," including women with limited means. Hannah Snode traded one hogshead of tobacco, and Jane, "a poor woman," four hogsheads, from Virginia to England in 1631.[107] Yet, in the intervening years, and across different areas of the tobacco industry, individuals continued to face challenges. Projectors continued to suggest schemes to the Crown that would bring it greater revenue and control over the trade, affecting those in the business of pipe production and tobacco growth, as well as those who sold it. In August 1626, William Anys presented a plan to the Commission for the King's Revenue, which proposed making the Crown the sole receiver of tobacco imports from Virginia, then limited to 250,000 pounds per annum. Under this contract, the Crown's commissioners would sell the tobacco in England at fixed rates. On 7 August 1626, he also suggested that "licences may be granted to some certain trades, as Apothecaries, Druggists, Grocers, and the like to sell it . . . which licences with their rents will yield the King a great yearly Rent."[108] The movement to restrict tobacco retail was in some measure prompted by vendors themselves, including apothecaries and grocers. One group of petitioners argued in 1625 that only those in respected trades should be entitled to retail tobacco. "Lewd persons, under pretence of selling tobacco," they claimed, "keep unlicensed alehouses, and others barter with mariners for stolen and unaccustomed tobacco, to the disadvantage of the petitioners."[109] Not only was there a supposedly moral dimension to their concerns, the petitioners suggested that the Crown was losing revenue too.[110]

Following his accession to the throne in 1625, Charles I did not immediately act upon proposals to grant tobacco retail licenses. Yet, with the dissolution of parliament in 1629 and the beginning of his Personal Rule, the king was in greater need of extra revenue. In April 1632, the Privy Council wrote to civic aldermen and Justices of the Peace requesting the names of those who were deemed suitable to retail tobacco in their localities. Initially, then, the decision of who could retail tobacco was to be managed through local authority, with officeholders licensing retailers with little oversight from central government.[111] Some responses have survived, with Hampshire JPs writing that "we cannot find within the county where we intermeddle . . . that any quantity of Tobacco is usually vented nor where it may be vented and sold . . . saving only within the city of Winchester."[112] This system did not last long and in 1633 the Privy Council issued an act that restricted retail to individuals who were recommended by local officials and who had also purchased a license.[113] The introduction of licenses would generate income for the Crown in three ways: through payment for the licenses themselves, through rents paid twice a year by the licensees, and finally, through fines for retailing without license. According to Alexander Taylor, a total of 1,801 licenses were issued between March 1634 and September 1635 and they proved to be incredibly profitable too. Between March 1634 and June 1635, £9,459 was collected in rent on the licenses, an estimated 1¼ percent of Charles I's average annual revenue.[114] Between February 1635 and February 1636, a further £1,929 3s. 4d. was collected across several counties in one year, of which £1,750 went straight into the Crown's coffers.[115]

Central state power married with local authority in order to manage and put the scheme into effect. The Court of Exchequer commissions gave local gentlemen and officeholders authority to conduct investigations on its behalf into unlicensed retailing, a system that required Crown agents, local officeholders, and licensees to work together.[116] The commissioners' investigations left a rich archival footprint of depositions that can tell us much about the consumption of tobacco, as well as how ordinary people responded to government policy.[117] As the commissioners discovered, in spite of the requirement for licenses, many continued to retail without them. William Childes, a yeoman, was ordered to appear before the Worcestershire JPs on 20 October 1634 and "answer for selling tobacco by retail contrary to proclamation."[118] Judith Lyon, of Tavistock, Devon, confessed to dealing in tobacco several times without a license. She admitted to buying half a pound from Elizabeth Jewson "a month since," and "two months since several quarters" were purchased, she said, from Ann Tickell and her husband Robert: "of all which tobacco she saith she sold in her house in Tavistock some they used [for] their own drinking and part she saith she giveth away to her friends and more she cannot depose."[119] In Plymouth, Orenge Shepeard confessed that she had bought a number of "rolls" of tobacco since the "prohibited times" amounting to, she estimated, fifty pounds in weight; but whom she bought it from or sold it to, "she saith she knoweth not."[120] When questioned, individuals used various methods to frustrate their interrogators, including feigning ignorance or simply claiming that they believed they had legitimately purchased tobacco.

For those who ran alehouses, tobacco was tied up with their regular trade.[121] In York, alehouse-keepers and tipplers bought tobacco in order to "give [it] away" to their customers. Tipplers Elizabeth Cundell and Ann Clark both claimed to have bought tobacco that they then gave "unto those which doth vend her drink."[122] The proclamation issued in 1633 had prohibited alehouse-keepers, although not their wives, from selling tobacco. Moreover, the women claimed to give it away, not sell it.[123] Tipplers George and Mary Dickinson, in Killinghall, Yorkshire, received between twelve and sixteen pounds of tobacco from their son William, who lived in Wapping, London. George described how "some part of it he made use of it himself and some part of the best his wife Mary sold."[124] While the depositions often describe the local, even domestic, nature of the exchange and consumption of tobacco, the testimony of individuals like George and Mary Dickinson reminds us that they participated in a much larger transatlantic economy. The tobacco that they bought had already undergone a transatlantic voyage and process of exchange between planters and merchants in London before they sold it across the table to their customers.

Often the kinds of responses that the officers recorded suggest that there was a limited amount of cooperation from those who were examined. Even if individuals claimed to have forgotten the details of whom or from where they had bought their tobacco, they supplied the officers with an admission of guilt. However, in Worcester in October 1636, the officials were faced with some resistance, recording responses that were more charged. Under questioning about whether or not his master had sold tobacco without a license, Charles Davis, a twenty-two-year-old mercer, answered that "as far as that question doth touch Robert Bedford his new master, he sayeth that he conceiveth he is not bound to answer, or to discover his secret." Similarly, when Phillip Sillie, an apothecary, aged thirty-three, was asked whether he had sold any tobacco illicitly, "he sayeth and answereth that he the said examinant is not bound to accompt himself."[125] In York too, Robert Browne, a grocer's servant, "obstinately refused" to answer the officers, and in Durham Philip Sanderson, a mercer, "refuseth to be sworn for any more by him sold."[126] In Carmarthen, Suge Allington, the wife of Philip William, alongside another man, did both "utterly refuse to be sworn." An apprentice, John Hugh, refused to depose against his master, Thomas Lewis, a mercer, unless his examiners agreed to pay him bonds of £500 to release him and his friends from their apprenticeship to Lewis.[127] In Banbury, Oxfordshire, the people were also in an uncooperative mood, with many refusing to take an oath or be examined.[128]

It was not uncommon for government officials with legal warrants, but who were deemed to lack broader authority, to be met with suspicion.[129] The difference between the deponents in Worcester and those in York, Durham, and elsewhere, however, is that the latter "refused" to cooperate, even if the grounds on which they did so is not recorded.[130] In Worcester, rather, they articulated that they were "not bound" to cooperate. In both cases, the deponents were refusing to acknowledge the authority of their examiners, or the legitimacy of the tobacco licenses themselves. That they were met with such responses is perhaps unsurprising. The year 1637 was, more generally, a fractious time. The Caroline regime faced increasing opposition, including hostility to the ship money tax and prayer book crisis in Scotland.[131] It is telling, therefore, that in Worcester the clerk recorded responses that seem to have been more noticeably inflected by contemporary vernacular political discourse. Yet, the town of Worcester and the responses of its inhabitants, Charles Davis and Philip Sillie included, is perhaps significant for another reason too. Worcestershire was located next to Gloucestershire (England's tobacco heartland in the Severn Valley) and had its own reputation for tobacco cultivation. As discussed below, throughout the seventeenth century, planters in these areas refused to give up sowing tobacco.

These issues of locality are likely to have been relevant in 1636 too, as the deponents in the Severn Valley did not just have memories of earlier impositions upon tobacco cultivation, of more below, brought about by the influence of the Virginia Company and colonists, but they lived among families who strengthened these transatlantic networks. John Wyatt and Henry Tracy of Gloucestershire, for example, who hailed from families with long-established connections in Virginia, were identified as selling and receiving tobacco illicitly.[132] On the other hand, Sir John Tracy, the kinsman of Henry, was tasked with suppressing tobacco cultivation in Winchcombe, Gloucestershire.[133] The familial networks associated with Virginia were particularly germane in Worcestershire, as the interrogator who signed the depositions was Martin Sandys. Martin was the nephew of Sir Edwin Sandys, previously the Virginia Company treasurer, and his own father, Samuel Sandys, uncles Edwin and George Sandys, his cousins Thomas, Henry, and Richard Sandys, and another named Sir Thomas Wilford, had all invested in the Virginia Company. His sister Margaret married Francis Wyatt, who was governor of the colony, from 1621 to 1626 and 1639 to 1642.[134] George Sandys was still active in Virginia affairs throughout the 1630s, and actually tried to revive the Virginia Company (for the second time) in 1640.[135] Therefore, in 1636, Martin Sandys and his family were still very much connected to, and had interests in, Virginia and the tobacco trade. It was not in the interest of planters in Virginia (or those who were invested in colonial trade) for others—their rivals—to sell tobacco without paying the relevant fines. The tobacco sellers may also have been aware of Martin's family and Virginia connections, and this awareness may have shaped the nature of their response. Rather than denying knowledge of illicit trade in a more passive fashion, they harnessed the little power they had, responding in terms of their rights and consent. They refused and were "not bound," in their words, to cooperate, because of what they thought was the illegitimacy of Martin Sandys's authority and appointed task.

There was also agitation in parliament to have the licenses abolished. Whereas they had previously supported the introduction of licenses, in 1640, a group of grocers and Virginia planters petitioned the House of Lords to complain about the abuses that they had suffered since their implementation. They began by reminding the king that "freedom of trades is the life and one of the principal liberties of the subjects of this kingdom." However, they claimed that some individuals had "upon pretence of regulating that said commodity . . . set out to restrain the retailing of tobacco only to such as shall take licence off them." Through threats and terror some had been "enforced to such licences . . . rather than be utterly undone for want of their trades . . . upon which they and their lives are supported."[136] It is perhaps significant that in 1639 the restriction on alehouse-keepers selling tobacco had been lifted, so for other retailers the need for licenses was perhaps now much less attractive. There was also, as suggested above, growing dissatisfaction with monopolies more generally.[137] In 1641, another group of tobacco retailers similarly complained about the corruption associated with the licenses, including false imprisonment. They said that one Thomas Colton was "pretending and alleging unto your petitioners that he for the sum of £15 by him already paid to his majesty . . . was lawfully authorised, and had solely power by virtue of letters patents unto him granted . . . to vent and sell tobacco . . . within the several liberties of the clink, and Montague Close and in the County of Surrey."[138] As with earlier encroachments, tobacco retailers denied that their natural freedom in trade could be curtailed by a group of monopolists. Just as pipe-makers had done before them, they asked for relief because the monopolists were clearly corrupt and because this industry was their key means to subsistence: "upon which they and their lives . . . [were] supported." Examining the depositions of those who were implicated in the illicit retail of tobacco demonstrates how ordinary people became entangled in imperial politics. They responded, like others who petitioned parliament or gave speeches in the House of Commons, in language that appealed to their constitutional and customary rights as English subjects. Although no formal revocation of the tobacco licenses has survived, they appear to have discontinued around 1641.[139]

English Planting "Under Colour of Their Poverty"

The year after the licenses were introduced, Charles I wrote to the Council in Virginia lamenting that the colonies were entirely built on smoke. The foundations of the colonies would, in short time, "be far weaker if we did not restrain the planting of English tobacco."[140] As early as 1619, the Virginia Company had similarly identified English tobacco cultivation as a threat to the colonial trade. In a series of court meetings, investors indicated their worry that English tobacco would prove to be "prejudicial" to the colony.[141] A proclamation published in 1619 claimed that if English tobacco planting was left unchecked, both the colonies in Virginia and Bermuda would be "choked and overthrown." Moreover, the proclamation argued, English tobacco was inferior to that grown in America; its cultivation was ruining the landscape of England; it was more harmful to bodies; and, finally, English planters paid no dues to the Crown.[142] Therefore, the Crown reaped little or no benefit, financial or otherwise, from the cultivation of English tobacco. This point of view was advanced by the Virginia Company, who agreed on 12 January 1620 that they would pay higher custom duties to the Crown—one shilling for each pound of tobacco they exported to England—if English tobacco cultivation was suppressed.[143] In the years to come, the suppression of English tobacco cultivation helped to bring about conflict between the

Crown and royal prerogative versus parliament and statute. Yet, it also revealed the fractures in policies that, on the one hand, wanted to privilege England's colonial interests, while on the other, protect the rights of English subjects at home and avoid local provocation.

Shortly before the proclamation was issued, the Crown had tried to stem the proliferation of tobacco cultivation in England. The Privy Council sent letters to JPs in September 1619, ordering the suppression of tobacco "in any place near the cities of London or Westminster." The council complained that plots of land that should have been used to grow food were wasted producing the noxious weed.[144] But, like their counterparts in the tobacco pipe industry, tobacco planters proved difficult to subdue. In 1626 and 1627, the Privy Council wrote letters to JPs ordering them to be more vigilant. They were sent to Lincoln, York, Nottinghamshire, Buckinghamshire, Gloucestershire, and Wootton Bassett, Wiltshire, with the last two locations singled out as "especially guilty."[145] Joan Thirsk suggested that people in Gloucestershire proved to be particularly defiant because there was a unique type of "social egalitarianism" that pervaded the region, meaning that local gentry were largely unwilling to chastise their neighbors.[146] Indeed, there was a precedent for this kind of behavior. One generation before, in 1607, starch house licenses were introduced, followed by the prohibition of starch making altogether in 1610. What followed in Gloucestershire was an "uncooperative mood" among local officials; they claimed to have been granted discretion by the Lord Chancellor, who instructed "if there be anything in their letters seeming harsh either in law or otherwise, they should in their wisdom moderate the same."[147] It is impossible to determine all that happened when officers were ordered to stamp out English tobacco. But it seems likely that as well as being met with resistance, officers were also unwilling to exert too much pressure, especially when an industry from which local people profited was threatened by orders from London.[148]

Understanding why the suppression of English tobacco proved to be so controversial over several decades requires examining what happened on the ground as well as in parliament. In the House of Commons, broader constitutional debates on customary rights and the common law were at stake. Sir Edward Coke denounced the prohibition of English tobacco during a speech on 17 April 1621, arguing that the recent proclamation was "against the Freedom of a Subject," inciting his colleagues to "set down here, that we may plant upon our own Grounds, what we will." He reminded the commons that Elizabeth I had previously revoked a patent on woad, used to produce dyestuff, to allow subjects, "for their good," to "employ their grounds" for its cultivation.[149] Unlike other imported luxuries that the government tried to levy taxes upon (with intermittent success), tobacco was produced at home.[150] Therefore, this dynamic presented unique challenges. Many considered tobacco a domestic crop, part of the subsistence economy, and not a luxury. In Gloucestershire, for example, a local vicar, John Deanes, attempted to collect tithes on tobacco. Whether this was a unique example or not is unclear.[151] Coke himself explained the distinction on 27 February, arguing "As well I may be prohibited to sow wheat on my freehold as Tobacco, [w]oad, or the like, for it is my *liberum tentum*" or freehold.[152] Coke also argued that while the ban on English tobacco could be ordered by act of council "*pro tempore*," or for a time, it should continue no longer unless by an act of parliament. Instead, it had been prohibited by royal proclamation, the use of which was contested.[153] The royal prerogative was, in Coke's opinion, "ultimately subservient to, the practice of commonwealth as it was constituted by common law and parliament."[154] Therefore, in the commons and elsewhere, English subjects demonstrated an understanding of domestic tobacco cultivation, which had been practiced for generations, as protected by both custom and the common law.

In light of this, when tobacco growers protested, their actions were reinforced both by a collective, cultural memory in the Severn Valley region of tobacco cultivation, as well as understandings of their customary rights. In spite of the 1619 proclamation, tobacco cultivation continued and was viewed as a real threat to the survival of the plantations. One person claimed in 1631 that 300,000 pounds of tobacco was planted in England.[155] Constables in Worcestershire, however, returned reports in 1634 that they had not seen any tobacco planted.[156] Either estimations were wildly exaggerated, or local officeholders were concealing the extent of the problem. From 1634 to 1635, during continued efforts to suppress English tobacco, the Privy Council recorded how growers responded angrily to Justices of the Peace. In Winchcombe, JPs reported to the council that "divers inhabitants within the town," the apparent center of English tobacco cultivation, "threatened that they will not suffer their said tobacco to be destroyed," and others "by their poverty think to be excused."[157] Then in 1638, conflict between JPs and planters (again in Gloucestershire) broke out in a supposedly "riotous and tumultuous manner." The council reprimanded the justices and ordered them to "not again be remiss."[158] This was the same year that Crown agents reported that tenants in Winchcombe had converted pastures and orchards into arable land, probably, according to Thirsk, an "oblique reference" to continued tobacco cultivation.[159] The lack of force and willingness exhibited by officeholders in the region frustrated efforts to suppress tobacco cultivation for many decades.

There was, it seems, an ongoing dispute in the Winchcombe area of Gloucestershire over whether tithes could be gathered on tobacco, which may also be key to understanding its continued cultivation in this region. If the church could also profit from this local industry, perhaps its continued production was frequently overlooked. In 1638, when questioned by the curate, John Bestpitch, a local woman named Elizabeth Cowley demonstrated that she had knowledge of the proclamations forbidding tobacco cultivation. Any tobacco that was planted, she answered, should "by virtue of the said proclamation . . . [be] gathered and plucked up by the roots." Yet, Cowley challenged the curate's attempt to levy tithes on the crop, saying she "believeth that there is no tithe to be paid out of such tobacco." Any tobacco that was planted, she answered wryly, ought to be "burnt," and not "valued and prized." Neither did she believe that she was "bound by law to confess or acknowledge that she did set, sow or plant any tobacco within the parish of Winchcombe and tithable places thereof . . . because they are matters criminal and not to be answered in this court."[160] The following year, planters in Winchcombe, Tewkesbury, and Cheltenham again pleaded with the JPs, this time "under colour of their poverty," to be exempted from the continued prohibition of English tobacco.[161] Their appeals resonated with a shared understanding of the moral community, or even the "moral economy," not least customary rights to subsistence.[162] In doing so, tobacco growers demonstrated a tactic that John Walter has identified elsewhere as "manipulating" the "public transcript," or instances when the commoners confronted their superiors by appealing to a shared discourse and set of values.[163] The tobacco growers understood not just the principles they appealed to, but also the persuasive and sympathetic impact their words might have on those in higher authority. This is an illuminating example of English subjects invoking the moral economy in relation to a commodity, usually deemed a non-essential luxury, that was not traditionally associated with subsistence.[164]

Their words and actions are significant then, as they allow us to interpret how English citizens responded to an expanding colonial economy and its associated pressures. It is implausible to suggest that they were unaware of the earlier proclamations that had been issued to prohibit the cultivation of English tobacco, and the clear connection that was drawn between its suppression and English colonies in the Atlantic world. Indeed, Elizabeth Cowley demonstrated that she was familiar with "several proclamations" concerning tobacco.[165] Even if they could not read the proclamations that were pasted in towns, news would have traveled orally following the aural reception of the proclamation from the town crier.[166] Moreover, the significant connections between Gloucestershire and the colony, in trade and migration, have already been discussed. It presents the possibility that the tobacco growers' continued cultivation was a restatement of their customary rights. In the space of a few generations, tobacco had been subsumed into local economic practice and was deemed essential for their living.

The growers' emphasis on poverty suggests that tobacco was an important part of their subsistence economy, and they might really have relied upon peddling small amounts of tobacco to their neighbors, or even wider markets. According to Thomas Birke, one William Palmer of Tewkesbury managed to sell forty pounds of his English tobacco in Worcester.[167] This was perhaps an unusual example as Thirsk suggests it was largely a "peasant activity," employing hundreds of the poor in the 1640s and 1650s.[168] It is unclear how much tobacco individual planters in Gloucestershire were able to cultivate, but it was probably not enough to sustain a family all year round. In 1636, a pound of English tobacco was said to fetch 8d. in Worcester, which was not much less than the market value of colonial tobacco.[169] Yet, to equal the day wage of a skilled tradesman (2s.), a planter would have to sell three pounds of tobacco each day, and it is unlikely that English planters, like their colonial counterparts, were cultivating such large amounts.[170] Whether or not they were actually poor is perhaps less important than their own realization that appealing to their poverty might work to provide protection (remember, they "did think to be excused") from the economic and political pressures of what had developed, over time, into a formidable transatlantic industry.

"Refractory and Rebellious Persons"

The production of English tobacco was hindered, initially, because of the Virginia Company's influence, but even after the company was dissolved colonial planters continued to lobby the government, threatening that if English tobacco was not thwarted, the plantations would be ruined. Efforts to obliterate domestic tobacco growth were to no avail, and by mid-century it was grown in at least eighteen English counties.[171] On 1 April 1652, the Act Prohibiting the Planting of Tobacco in England was passed, succeeding by a marginal vote. Gloucestershire planters responded quickly, petitioning the Commonwealth government to be allowed to cultivate that year's crop, and on 6 May they were granted clemency, for one year only.[172] Between 1653 and 1655, the government received several petitions from Virginia merchants and planters calling for English tobacco to be immediately stamped out. In 1653, despite their earlier petitions and the 1652 act, merchants feared "that there will be more [English tobacco] made in several places of this common wealth this year then hath usually been in one year brought from Virginia which will tend much to the damage of this common wealth."[173] Those who tried to suppress its cultivation in Worcestershire, Gloucestershire, Herefordshire, and Somersetshire were met with "resistance," "cruel threats and meanness." The planters were said to be "utterly undeterred"; rather they were "encouraged with a high hand to proceed in contempt thereof."[174] The merchants presented several reasons why it had to be prohibited, aside from the economic hardship that Chesapeake planters would face. English tobacco was, they suggested, "very unwholesome the climate being unsuitable to it" and "much rich land is employed in the planting." Neither was any custom or excise paid on English tobacco.[175] This final complaint seems to have hit home, as, on 15 August 1653, parliament reached another compromise with Gloucestershire tobacco planters following their petitions, this time allowing the planters to enjoy their current crop if they agreed to pay 3d. in excise duty on every pound of tobacco.[176] It was a policy that, it was hoped, would deter some in England from planting tobacco, appease colonial interests, and also profit the government.

No doubt this rapprochement infuriated the Virginia planters and merchants. The regime of the 1650s was, as Bernard Capp suggests, trying to avoid provoking "popular resentment" at home, and the Severn Valley, in particular, was known for its obstinacy. The interests of Virginia planters, a stoutly Royalist colony throughout the English Revolution, were valued less than those who lived in the back garden of the regime.[177] Virginia merchants petitioned again in April 1654, calling for the earlier act of 1652 to be enforced.[178] Their plea was followed by an ordinance, or order, issued that month, to enforce the earlier act; but, even then, there was continued resistance.[179] In the following months, the conflicting interests of domestic and colonial commerce led to eruptions of violence in the tobacco-growing areas around Gloucestershire.[180] It is impossible to know exactly how much tobacco was being cultivated in England, but those that planted tobacco certainly felt that it was an industry worth protecting. One report sent to the

Council of State in June stated that there were still considerable quantities of tobacco planted in Gloucestershire. Moreover, it was said the planters of Winchcombe "make resistance, and have endeavoured about 300 horse and foot armed, some with guns, some with other weapons, resolving to fight the Troop that was in those parts if it came at them." The planters' "Resolution" was that "they were bred to the trade" and would not give it up: "when they lose it they will lose their lives."[181] Later, some Winchcombe planters apologized, "with sorrow," for the "rashness of those that did inadvisably assemble . . . to none other end but to preserve their Tobacco."[182] Henry Lawrence, Lord President of the council, wrote to the governor of Gloucester that news had reached London of the Winchcombe planters' continued opposition. Echoing the complaint of the Privy Council in 1638, he described how they had "assemble[d] together in a riotous and tumultuous manner." Lawrence called on the governor to "suppress all tumultuous meetings in your parts . . . find out the ringleaders of the said resistance, and upon their discovery, to cause them to be apprehended and secured."[183]

As well as sparking violent unrest, the continued pressing of colonial interests on local people also resulted in petitioning. One petition with 110 signatures, including those of many widowed women, was presented to parliament in June 1654. It told how, following earlier appeals, they had been allowed to keep their crop "as a means of preventing us perishing." In spite of the recent ordinance, the planters hoped they would be shown the same leniency once again. As with the much earlier written and oral petitions of tobacco pipe makers in 1621 and planters in the 1630s, they appealed to their customary rights and the moral economy, complaining that planting tobacco was "the Trade and Occupation wherein your petitioners have for well near forty years been trained up in and many have served apprenticeships in it."[184] This claim was echoed on the ground in Winchcombe too.

The following year, hundreds of merchants trading to America signed and submitted a petition, once again requesting the "total suppression of planting Tobacco in England."[185] This was followed by another list of the reasons why it should be inhibited. A new claim, which was added in a second hand, was that while Virginia was currently inhabited by Protestants, if the colonial tobacco trade collapsed, they would be forced to leave the region. If that happened, they would have abandoned their mission to convert the Virginia Algonquians to Christianity, "which will be highly to the honour of God."[186] Virginia merchants complained that even though no one in Gloucestershire could possibly "pretend ignorance" of the recent ordinance, which was displayed in marketplaces and parish churches, still "we find divers refractory and rebellious persons around Winchcombe, Cheltenham and the places adjacent who still continue their resolutions." It was April and the planters were preparing their ground to sow more tobacco. While some, adhering to the 1652 act and 1654 ordinance, had destroyed their beds of tobacco, apparently replacing it with more supposedly useful crops such as barley and flax, many others "would willingly destroy their Tobacco beds, but only their eyes are fixed upon the Rebellious Crew." Alluding to the state's previously flexible approach, the merchants claimed that the planters were deterred because they suspected, as in previous years, that they might be allowed to keep their crops of English tobacco after all.[187]

Local efforts to stamp out tobacco continued, with thirty-six horsemen traveling to Cheltenham in July 1658. However, they were met on the road by a "multitude . . . weaponed guarding the highway and their fields of tobacco." Some of the horsemen charged through the crowd and made their way into the center of the town, where they found the "street full of the rabble of men and women." Some two hundred more from Winchcombe joined the crowds, and the anonymous author of the report wrote they feared that there would have been blood spilt if violence had erupted. The tobacco planters were not at all fearful, apparently "saying they valued not our order nor 200 men in arms." The government's agent felt helpless to do more: there was such an "abundance of tobacco . . . that 10 men cannot destroy it in 4 days."[188] Yet, as was also the case in the decades before, it was unclear just how much local officeholders were willing to assist central authority in stamping out this domesticated, local industry. John Beaman reported that the local officeholders were of little use; rather they were a "hinderance," as many were themselves "dealers and planters in the vale."[189] In Worcestershire in 1659 too, JPs heard that land was let to tobacco growers.[190] In this part of the country, whose relationship with tobacco was at least forty years old, the weed had taken hold and would be difficult to uproot, in more ways than one.

The long-standing tradition of English tobacco planting could not be denied, and despite commercial competition and conflict, it had developed into an industry that clearly permitted some accommodation between colonial and domestic planters. For example, Chesapeake merchants claimed "some dealers in Tobacco in London trying English Tobacco for Wrappers . . . found to their great loss, that it did not only fall to dust and rottenness itself but [did] eat out the heart of the other Tobacco." By mid-century, then, retailers in London were experimenting with employing English tobacco as a "wrapper" for cigars. "If useful for anything," the merchants said, "it would be for that." However, to protect their own commercial interests, they disputed whether English tobacco was even fit for this particular purpose.[191] Following the Restoration in 1660, there was a further bill prohibiting the "planting, setting, or sowing of tobacco in England or Ireland." It included accommodations though, such as allowing tobacco to be grown in physic gardens if it was under one half of one pole.[192] Although this was meant to allow its cultivation for genuine medicinal purposes, it probably enabled some to circumvent the order. Even in 1663, there was evidence of continued tobacco growth. Sir Martin Noel wrote to Lord Ashley, Chancellor of the Exchequer, that "there is great quantities of tobacco planted in Worcestershire, Gloucestershire and other parts of England." He requested soldiers and seamen to be sent to assist him in pulling it up, as "unless some effectual stop be given to it . . . the foreign plantations will be destroyed."[193] Noel's claim was, perhaps, mere hyperbole. In the early 1660s, 7.4 million pounds of colonial tobacco was exported to England.[194] The colonial industry would only require such careful protection if, in fact, English tobacco planters could compete on this scale. There is no clear evidence that English planters could really match the scale of colonial production, but according to contemporaries, if the produce of English growers made its way into the marketplace, it could certainly have snuffed out a portion of colonial planters' profits.

Following the Restoration, the government periodically attempted to stamp out tobacco growing in Gloucestershire. The Privy Council regularly sent letters to JPs, reminding them of the ban on tobacco. Yet, in 1667, one Privy Council searcher reported the continued refractory attitude toward the government's orders. The council had found that tobacco was growing "upon the High Sheriff's land, the bishop's land, and scarce one of the justices but on their land tobacco is planted, possibly without their privity." This report highlighted the mutuality of interest between those with land and those who grew tobacco in this region: "The tenants set [let] their ground to planters who are poor people who plant and give half the crop for the use of the ground. So, if destroyed, the planter loseth, the tenant loseth his half of the crop, and thereby is disabled to pay his rent."[195] Another act was issued a decade later and troops of horses were sent to the area throughout the 1660s and 1670s, but the last Privy Council order to search the area was in 1690. Joan Thirsk suggests that it might have been the plummet in the price of Chesapeake tobacco that put an end to widespread English tobacco cultivation.[196] Perhaps it was no longer seen as a worthwhile occupation. In the 1680s, better-quality

Chesapeake tobacco could be had in England for as little as 4d. per pound, down from between 6d. and 8d. in the 1660s.[197] The price of English tobacco may also have fallen from the 8d. per pound fetched in 1636.[198] The retail price of tobacco obviously obscures significant differences in labor and resources that were available to planters, meaning that, in many ways, English and Chesapeake tobacco omits comparison. Since 1619, Chesapeake tobacco planters had used enslaved African labor to work their plantations, and the development of a plantation system that was reliant upon enslaved labor grew rapidly in the last third of the seventeenth century, enabling planters to grow larger crops at relatively little expense.[199] Plantation slavery was not replicated in England and, in this sense, English planters could not compete.

Commenting on tobacco, one early twentieth-century historian, Berthold Laufer, remarked, "Of all luxuries it is the most democratic and the most universal."[200] His statement rings true for the early seventeenth century too. Tobacco underwent a process of popularization in early modern England, as would be the case with other imperial consumables, including sugar, tea, and coffee. Yet, tobacco underwent a unique process of domestication too, showing how ordinary people in England had or, in some cases, had not, learned to accommodate colonial produce, practices, and interests. Its universality and production in the domestic context are key to understanding how the transatlantic tobacco industry shaped politics and social relations in early modern England. The impact of tobacco smoking on contemporary elite political discourse and sociability is well documented; what is not so well understood is how English pipe-makers, retailers, and growers responded to shifts in overlapping domestic and colonial policy. Using petitions and popular protest, individuals with interests in the tobacco industry appealed to their rights to subsistence and the moral economy, pitching their dependence on tobacco against older, established discourses of custom and consent. They could not have failed to appreciate how their livelihoods were tied to the fortunes of England's burgeoning empire, but if, like many tobacco growers, they had forgotten (or chose to ignore) the American antecedents of their trade, individuals with colonial interests were ready to remind them. Tobacco defined England's early relationship with Virginia, but it was not a simple case of demand and supply, as the flashpoints discussed above demonstrate. Tobacco threw into sharp relief the competition between both local English and colonial interests, even while they overlapped, and between parliament and the Crown. The debates taking place "on the ground" spoke to wider concerns in early Stuart England regarding political and moral economy.

It is not easy to clearly delineate the various strands that made up the larger domestic tobacco industry. As the above examples show, interests and alliances shifted across time and space, and because of the tightly woven personal connections between England's tobacco-growing areas and the colonies themselves, in the regions of Gloucestershire and Worcestershire especially, loyalties were split. Perhaps then, it is no surprise that transformations in English tobacco policies often accompanied regime change. The Cromwellian state of the 1650s made several accommodations to allow English growers to keep their crops, while at the same time introducing a new act and ordinance to suppress domestic tobacco planting altogether. It was, then, a somewhat hollow attempt to placate Chesapeake planters. Yet, under Charles II, the interests of the loyal, Royalist planters of Virginia were once again promoted, with no official concessions to English growers. With the Glorious Revolution of 1688 there was further change. As had been the case in the 1650s, the priority was to appease English citizens, and in 1689 the ban on English tobacco was reversed, exactly seventy years since it had first been prohibited.[201] Tobacco had transformed in the minds of English folk by mid-century, and arguably long before, from an Indigenous, American crop to an English one.[202] Neither the English colony in Virginia nor tobacco held the same appeal that they had once possessed—no longer so unfamiliar or strange—yet neither could be given up.

CONCLUSION

Taken together, Katherine Conway's letters bear the impressions of the impact that colonization made upon people's lives in seventeenth-century England. They speak to us of several experiences, such as that of the Scottish men recently returned from Newfoundland and the maidservant who was formerly employed in the Tracy household. The English Atlantic empire was still in its infancy, and the fate that befell the Tracy family reminds us of the individual lives and local settings that fulfilled colonial promise in America: the Gloucestershire wives, husbands, and children who drifted across the Atlantic Ocean to build a new commonwealth. Katherine's role as a Virginia Company investor and Irish planter, and her consideration of acquiring land in Newfoundland, embodies the very entangled nature of English citizens' imperial interests too. She is a reminder of the role of metropolitan women as investors in, and the beneficiaries of, this phase of English colonization in America. Focusing on women like Katherine broadens the scope of who we understand to have been the agents of early modern empire building and also sheds light on their motivations.

Katherine's church memorial, which survives to this day in St. Mary's, Acton, in West London, exemplifies the personal, quotidian impulse that underpinned her investment in the "New World." High on the wall of the church, the tablet serves as a material artifact of her "blessed charity," including the bequests she made in her will to the Dutch Church and Grocers' Company.[1] Round the corner, there is a further wall panel that details her alms to provide bread for the poor each Sunday.[2] The wealth that she imagined generating through colonization and enterprise in the Atlantic world would not only have furthered her social standing, it would have allowed her to gift even greater charitable bequests and bolster the riches she left to her heirs. Throughout the centuries, money from Katherine's philanthropy was used to apprentice and educate Acton children, and provide clothing and food for its poor. As late as 1980, contributions from various donors, including

Katherine, were still supplying funds for apprenticeships, nursing, and relief in the parish.[3] The tendrils and profits of colonialism reached even more deeply into English society in this era than we have fully appreciated, pervading the English countryside as well as ports and cities.[4] In the end, Virginia's riches and Newfoundland's silver may not have furnished Katherine's generous giving, but plantation in Ireland certainly did, and the source of her wealth, extracted through colonial violence and exploitation, would have deep and lasting implications.[5]

The practices associated with colonial enterprise in the period up to 1660, from the exchange of knowledge to the mobilization of formal and informal financial investment, labor, and trade, shaped, and was shaped by, the ideas and behaviors of individuals and institutions across society, many of whom were not directly connected to the Virginia Company. English women, children, and men actively engaged with empire building in the Atlantic world—they were not uninterested contributors to early modern colonization. Colonization was a much wider social enterprise, rather than a marginal concern, limited, at best, to educated elites.[6] People at the time understood the significance of using "poor men's hands and the rich men's purses" to colonize, but the contributions of ordinary English citizens were even more varied and extensive than this anonymous statement suggests.[7] A larger public of women and men, whose everyday anxieties were rooted in local, customary culture and communities, determined how colonization developed. Their ideas and the practices they deployed went to the heart of issues that English citizens cared about and encountered on an everyday basis. While the broader public approval of and participation in English colonial enterprise needs to be emphasized, this should not come at the expense of also examining the ways that colonial interests were frequently fettered by domestic concerns.

In this period, English people did not fail to recognize that colonial enterprise had transformed domestic society. It altered how they judged the world around them, affecting the ways in which they invested their wealth, what they consumed, and how they understood their communities, with colonization putting pressure upon debates concerning charity, poverty, and subsistence. Bringing these issues to light has required casting a much wider net for evidence, including examining the archives and fragmentary records that speak to the experiences of the obscure, as well as eminent, members of seventeenth-century English society. Parish records and court depositions, alongside elite letters and leftover receipts, reveal a rich tapestry of stories

Figure 5. Attributed to Daniel Lysons, *Memorial to Lady Katherine, Viscountess Conway*, between 1796–1811. Accession # B1977.14.20282. By permission of the Yale Center for British Art, Paul Mellon Collection.

about early modern English empire building, illuminating the extensive reach and impact of colonization on the domestic sphere. One of my aims in writing this book is to demonstrate the potential of mining the imperial margins of local archives, thus bringing imperial history to bear on English social history. When these records are brought into conversation with printed literature, parliamentary debate, and rich biographies, a different, more diverse, narrative unfolds that helps us to get at the discreet, harder-to-reach corners of early modern society. In myriad unexpected ways, empire building seeped into the everyday life, and the accompanying documentary record, of early modern English society.

Another story illustrates this point. In the summer of 1630, Justices of the Peace in Somerset heard and recorded many sets of testimony concerning local offenses. One of them related to a housebreaking and the theft of several items of clothing, by a wandering, vagrant man named Hughe Walker. Richard Evans was the victim and he claimed that Hughe was guilty, although the accused had another explanation. He denied committing the theft himself, instead alleging that he had unknowingly received the stolen goods from a pair he met walking through the country lanes. They had "desired him" to carry the goods, "for they were weary." The justices must have pressed Hughe about his origins and recent history, because they wrote down, that while he was a Devonshire man by birth, and was, in fact, on his way there to receive the hospitality of friends, he was "lately from Virginia." In the course of offering an account that would get himself off the hook, Hughe inspired the justices to imprint on the archive his own personal experience of American colonization. On his homeward voyage he had been robbed by the "Dunkerkes" and lost the whole of his stock of beaver skins, the only riches returned with him from Virginia. They would have fetched a good price too: the following year, Katherine Conway would pay £1 for a beaver hat. There is much about Hughe's account that is unsurprising: sea voyages were notoriously perilous and beaver pelts were emblematic of transatlantic trade in the 1630s. What is striking, however, is that the justices decided to record these details at all—which had absolutely no bearing on the case in hand. Hughe's statement is a strange glimpse into the storytelling of a poor man who had traveled to and safely returned from America. It was a tale—whether it was true or if they believed it—that captivated his audience.[8]

The Virginia Venture has explored some of the ways that colonial enterprise was experienced in England, and the contribution made to it by a diverse set of people such as Hughe Walker and Katherine Conway. Colonists transformed the places where they arrived and settled, but their departures also brought about transformations in the places from which they departed. English rural landscapes and local means of subsistence were permanently altered, while new practices and policies were introduced in parishes and more widely, that continued to shape communities. These transformations also included other, less perceptible changes that made colonization in America more tangible to people at home. Through the circulation of travelers like Hughe and material samples like tobacco seeds in the Atlantic world, greater familiarity with colonial ventures was established, adding texture and color to a burgeoning English imperial imaginary. The overall effect, as the domestication of tobacco neatly suggests, was that America permeated English society, from the humble hearthside of a rural laborer to the House of Commons. It is essential that we understand how overseas colonization and the origins of empire impacted early modern English society, in its broadest sense, as the everyday ties to empire that were first established then continue to reverberate with us today.

NOTES

Introduction

1. Henry Smyth to Katherine Conway, London, 3 April 1626, SP 16/523, f. 126, National Archives.

2. See Susan Myra Kingsbury, ed., *The Records of the Virginia Company of London,* 5 vols. (Washington, DC, 1906–1935), 1:535, 3:396, 405, 569. The original document provides evidence that next to Mary's name the words "slain dead" were crossed through by John Smyth, suggesting that she survived. See Dwight Tracy, *Recently Discovered Ancestry of Governor William Tracy of Virginia 1620* (New Haven, 1908), 18.

3. Paul Hunneyball, "Conway, Sir Edward (c. 1563–1631)," *The History of Parliament,* https://www.historyofparliamentonline.org/volume/1604-1629/member/conway-sir-edward-i-1563-1631. Also, Daniel Starza Smith, "John Donne and the Conway Papers: A Biographical and Bibliographical Study of Poetry and Patronage in the Seventeenth Century" (unpublished PhD thesis, University College London, 2011), 22, 41.

4. For example, in 1621, Edward Conway (1594–1655), Lady Conway's stepson, married Frances Popham, the granddaughter of Lord Chief Justice Popham, the chief patron of the Sagadahoc (or "Popham") colony. See James Knowles, "Conway, Edward, Second Viscount Conway and Second Viscount Killultagh," *Oxford Dictionary of National Biography,* https://doi.org/10.1093/ref:odnb/55441.

5. Details about Katherine Conway's life are discussed extensively in Misha Ewen, "Women Investors and the Virginia Company in the Early Seventeenth Century," *The Historical Journal* 62 (2019), esp. 16–17.

6. Original in the Smyth of Nibley Papers, New York Public Library. "Gatscomb" was probably the hamlet of Gatcombe in Gloucestershire. Kingsbury, *Records,* 3:183–84, 187.

7. I have borrowed the term "micro-narratives" from Linda Colley, *Captives: Britain, Empire and the World 1600–1850* (London, 2003), 17.

8. Nicholas Canny, "Introduction," in William Roger Louis, ed., *The Oxford History of the British Empire,* 5 vols. (Oxford, 1998), 1:5, 32. Other scholars are also skeptical about wider public engagement with colonial enterprise and the impact it had on English society. See Trevor Burnard, "Empire Matters? The Historiography of Imperialism in Early America, 1492–1830," *History of European Ideas* 33 (2007), 92; David Armitage, "Literature and Empire," in Louis, *Oxford History of the British Empire,* 1:110; Gavin Hollis, *The Absence of America: The London Stage, 1576–1642* (Oxford, 2015), 4; and Catherine Armstrong, *Writing North America in the Seventeenth Century: English Representations in Print and Manuscript* (Aldershot, 2007), 197.

9. Lauren Working, *The Making of an Imperial Polity: Civility and America in the Jacobean Metropolis* (Cambridge, 2020), 90–91, 200; and Ken MacMillan, *The Atlantic*

Imperial Constitution: Center and Periphery in the English Atlantic World (New York, 2011), esp. chapter 4.

10. James Horn, *A Kingdom Strange: The Brief and Tragic History of the Lost Colony of Roanoke* (New York, 2010), 189–90.

11. Kenneth R. Andrews, *Elizabethan Privateering: English Privateering During the Spanish War 1585–1603* (Cambridge, 1964); MacMillan, *Atlantic Imperial Constitution*, 32–34.

12. Peter C. Mancall, *Hakluyt's Promise: An Elizabethan's Obsession for an English America* (New Haven, 2010), 252–53, 260–69.

13. Christopher J. Bilodeau, "The Paradox of Sagadahoc: The Popham Colony, 1607–1608," *Early American Studies: An Interdisciplinary Journal* 12 (2014), 1–35.

14. See the essays in this recent volume, Paul Musselwhite, Peter C. Mancall, and James Horn, eds., *Virginia 1619: Slavery and Freedom in the Making of English America* (Chapel Hill, 2019).

15. For responses to the attack, see Karen Ordahl Kupperman, *Indians and English: Facing Off in Early America* (London, 2000), 223–26.

16. Alison Games, "Violence on the Fringes: The Virginia (1622) and Amboyna (1623) Massacres," *History* 99 (2014), 507.

17. Jack P. Greene, "From John Smith to Adam Smith: Virginia and the Founding Conventions of English Long-Distance Settler Colonization," in Musselwhite, Mancall, and Horn, *Virginia 1619*, 295–96.

18. "Examination of Ruthe Pittman," 20 October 1619, Q/SR/34/91, Somerset Archives and Local Studies.

19. Register of Prisoners Delivered for Trial, 17 April 1634, MJ/GB/R/004, ff. 152v, 155, London Metropolitan Archives.

20. Jo. Beaman, Gloucester, to Thomas Colclough or Mr. John Jeffries, 31 July 1658, SP 18/182, f. 87, National Archives.

21. Waters v. Dorling, 23 January 1623, C 2/JASI/W6/68/1, National Archives.

22. Susanah Shaw Romney, *New Netherland Connections: Intimate Networks and Atlantic Ties in Seventeenth-Century America* (Chapel Hill, 2014), 28–29.

23. Marisa J. Fuentes, *Dispossessed Lives: Enslaved Women, Violence, and the Archive* (Philadelphia, 2016), 7.

24. "The Lady Viscountess Conway, Her Accounts," April–September 1631, CR 114 A/768/1, Warwickshire County Record Office.

25. "The Lady Viscountess Conway, Her Accounts," April 1633, CR 114 A/769, Warwickshire County Record Office.

Chapter 1

1. Francis Walsingham to Richard Hakluyt, 11 March 1582; and Francis Walsingham to Thomas Aldworth, 11 March 1582, G.b.10, f. 9v, Folger Shakespeare Library. Walsingham backed Martin Frobisher's ventures to discover the Northwest Passage between 1576 and 1578 and later supported John Davis's adventures in the Arctic between 1585 and 1587. His connection with Hakluyt endured, with Hakluyt dedicating the first edition of *Principal Voyages* (1589) to Walsingham. See Simon Adams, Alan Bryson, and Mitchell Leimon, "Walsingham, Sir Francis (c. 1532–1590)," *Oxford Dictionary of National Biography*, https://doi.org/10.1093/ref:odnb/28624. Interestingly, the above episode and his interest in Virginia is not detailed in the above biography. Sir George Peckham had an interest in colonization since at least 1574 and fi-

nanced Gilbert's first attempts to establish a colony in North America. Peckham was also the author of *True Reporte, of the Late Discoveries . . . by That Valiant and Worthy Gentleman, Sir Humphrey Gilbert* (1583; STC 19523). See James McDermott, "Peckham, Sir George (*d.* 1608)," *Oxford Dictionary of National Biography*, https://doi.org/10.1093/ref:odnb/21743.

2. Aldworth to Walsingham, 27 March 1582, G.b.10, ff. 9v–10, Folger Shakespeare Library.

3. Italics in original quote. Mancall, *Hakluyt's Promise*, 238–43, 304.

4. Armstrong, *Writing North America*, 196.

5. On how experiences of colonization shaped a "widening English identity," see Working, *Imperial Polity*, 92.

6. David B. Quinn, *England and the Discovery of America, 1481–1620: From the Bristol Voyages of the Fifteenth Century to the Pilgrim Settlement at Plymouth; The Exploration, Exploitation, and Trial-and-Error Colonization of North America by the English* (London, 1974), 418.

7. Thomas Harriot, *A Briefe and True Report* (1590; STC 12786), ff. 7–12.

8. Coll Thrush, *Indigenous London: Native Travelers at the Heart of Empire* (New Haven, 2016) quote at 35, also 47–49, 58; Alden T. Vaughan, "Sir Walter Ralegh's Indian Interpreters, 1584–1618," *William and Mary Quarterly* 59 (2002), 342. Manteo and Wanchese left Croatan Island and Roanoke Island respectively in 1584 with Captains Philip Amadas and Arthur Barlowe. They may have intended to gather information about England in anticipation of a longer-term English presence in the region. Ibid., 346. For recent discussion of the importance of emphasizing Indigenous peoples' humanity and agency, rather than representations of Indigenous peoples, see Alyssa Mt. Pleasant, Caroline Wigginton, and Kelly Wisecup, "Materials and Methods in Native American and Indigenous Studies: Completing the Turn," *William and Mary Quarterly* 75 (2018), 215.

9. Christina Faraday, "Lively Limning: Presence in Portrait Miniatures and John White's Images of the New World," *British Art Studies* 17 (2020), 1–2, 32, 35. https://dx.doi.org/10.17658/issn.2058-5462/issue-17/cfaraday.

10. Rachel Winchcombe, *Encountering Early America* (Manchester, 2021), 132–34, quote at 133.

11. Andrew Fitzmaurice, *Humanism and America: An Intellectual History of English Colonisation, 1500–1625* (Cambridge, 2003), 25.

12. Armstrong, *Writing North America*, 38–39; Andrew Fitzmaurice, "'Every Man, That Prints, Adventures': The Rhetoric of the Virginia Company Sermon," in Lori Ann Ferrell and Peter McCullough, eds., *The English Sermon Revised: Religion, Literature and History, 1600–1750* (Manchester, 2000), 26.

13. Michael Drayton, "To the Virginian Voyage," 1613, Ig D799 605e, l. 67–70, Beinecke Rare Book and Manuscript Library.

14. Travel writing on America and the East gained a much wider readership in England by the 1630s. See Andrew Hadfield, *Amazons, Savages and Machiavels, Travel and Colonial Writing in English, 1550–1630: An Anthology* (Oxford, 2001), 9. There is a vast body of literature on representations of the East in European literature, including, Ros Ballaster, *Fabulous Orients: Fictions of the East in England 1662–1785*, (Oxford, 2005), 36. Two renowned English travelers to Mughal India, whose accounts were published, include Thomas Coryate and Thomas Roe. See Richmond Barbour, *Before Orientalism: London's Theatre of the East, 1576–1626* (Cambridge, 2003), 132, 158.

15. Samuel Purchas, *Purchas His Pilgrimage* (1613; STC 20505); Samuel Purchas, *Purchas His Pilgrimes* (1625; STC 20509). Also, Armstrong, *Writing North America*, 178, 191.

16. Clive Wilkins-Jones, ed., *Norwich City Library, 1608–1737* (Norwich, 2008), 34; Norwich City Library Donation Book, 1614, MS 4228, f. 6v, Norfolk Record Office; Armstrong, *Writing North America*, 191.

17. These texts all appeared between 1605 and 1611. David B. Quinn, "North America," in L. E. Pennington, ed., *The Purchas Handbook. Studies of the Life, Times and Writings of Samuel Purchas*, 2 vols. (Farnham, 1996), 1:312.

18. Quinn, "North America," 314–15.

19. See Chapter 3.

20. Jean Klene, ed., *The Southwell-Sibthorpe Commonplace Book: Folger MS. V.b.198* (Tempe, 1997), xiv–xix. For an inventory of her goods to be transported to Acton, see "Miscellany of Lady Anne Southwell," 1626–1636, V.b.198, ff. 59–61, Folger Shakespeare Library.

21. Diane K. Bolton, Patricia E. C. Croot, and M. A. Hicks, "Acton: Churches," in T. F. T. Baker and C. R. Elrington, eds., *A History of the County of Middlesex: Volume 7, Acton, Chiswick, Ealing and Brentford, West Twyford, Willesden* (London, 1982), 35–39.

22. "Miscellany of Lady Anne Southwell," 1626–1636, V.b.198, ff. 64v-66r, Folger Shakespeare Library. The publication dates given are those of first publication in England, as the editions that Southwell owned is unclear.

23. "Annual Accounts, Earl of Southampton," 1622–1623, no. 480, Ferrar Papers; Linda Levy Peck, *Consuming Splendor: Society and Culture in Seventeenth-Century England* (Cambridge, 2005), 100.

24. This could be Counseil of Virginia, *A Briefe Declaration of the Present State of things in Virginia* (1616; STC 24834); Counseil of Virginia, *A Declaration of the State of the Colonie and Affaires in Virginia* (1620; STC 24841.2); Patrick Copland, *Virginia's God Be Thanked* (1622; STC 5727); "Annual Accounts, Earl of Southampton," 1622–1623, no. 480, Ferrar Papers.

25. Ballads were distributed and consumed, and were also part of the "visual fabric" in alehouses. See Mark Hailwood, *Alehouses and Good Fellowship in Early Modern England* (Woodbridge, 2014), 121–34, quote at 127.

26. Armstrong, *Writing North America*, 177.

27. William Symonds, *Virginia. A Sermon Preached at White-Chappel* (1609; STC 23594), sigs. D1v–D2r.

28. William Symonds, *Virginia: A Sermon Preached at White-Chappel* (1609), in Joshua Eckhardt, ed., *Virginia Company Sermons 1.2* (Richmond, 2013), 9–11, 13.

29. Symonds, *A Sermon Preached at White-Chappel*, sigs. H3r-H3v.

30. Ibid., sig. H3v.

31. Anon., *Londons Lotterie* (1612; STC 16756.5); "Good Newes from Virginia, 1623," *William and Mary Quarterly* 5 (1948), 354–58.

32. Games, "Violence on the Fringes," 523.

33. "Good Newes from Virginia, 1623," 354–58.

34. For further discussion of ballads, see Armstrong, *Writing North America*, 181–83.

35. Dated 4 May 1623. Kingsbury, *Records*, 4:166. The letter, according to Kingsbury's transcription, was addressed to Harworth (there is a Harworth in Nottinghamshire), but it seems likely that it was actually addressed to Hurworth, close to Darlington.

36. Jason Peacey, *Print and Public Politics in the English Revolution* (Cambridge, 2013), 59–60.

37. He was not yet a member of the Virginia council, but his brother John was elected deputy to the new treasurer, Sir Edwin Sandys, in the spring of 1619.

38. "Copy of a Letter," 17 January 1619, no. 99, Ferrar Papers.

39. John Rolfe, *A True Relation of the State of Virginia Left by Sir Thomas Dale Knight in May Last 1616,* in "Interesting Account of Virginia, in 1617," *Southern Literary Messenger* 5 (1839): 401–6.

40. "Copy of a Letter," 17 January 1619, no. 99, Ferrar Papers.

41. John Smith, *The Generall History of Virginia* (1624; STC 22789), sig. A1v. See Karen Kupperman, *The Jamestown Project* (Cambridge, MA, 2007), 138–39.

42. For a statement on his status as eyewitness, see Ralph Hamor, *A True Discourse of the Present Estate of Virginia* (1615; STC 12736), f. 2.

43. Hamor, *A True Discourse,* ff. 25–26, 34.

44. Although a copy of one journal, kept in the winter of 1610, was sent to Samuel Purchas, he decided not to print it. See Gillian T. Cell, *English Enterprise in Newfoundland, 1577–1660* (Toronto, 1969), 61–62, 69.

45. Sir Ferdinando Gorges to Robert Cecil, Earl of Salisbury, 3 December 1607, CP 123/81b, Hatfield House.

46. William Ferrar is believed to have died either on the journey to Virginia or soon after arriving. Nicholas W. S. Cranfield, "Ferrar, Nicholas (1593–1637)," *Oxford Dictionary of National Biography,* https://doi.org/10.1093/ref:odnb/9356.

47. The annotation is under the title and before the opening paragraph. Robert Johnson, *The New Life of Virginea* (1612; STC 14700), sig B1r, Folger Shakespeare Library. Thank you to Sarah Powell, the paleographer on the Folger Shakespeare Library's EMMO project, for her help in both identifying the origins of and translating this quote.

48. C. John Sommerville, *The News Revolution in England: Cultural Dynamics of Daily Information* (Oxford, 1996), 18; Peacey, *Print and Public Politics,* 93.

49. Kingsbury, *Records,* 3:222.

50. Ian Atherton, "'The Itch Grown a Disease': Manuscript Transmission of News in the Seventeenth Century," in Joad Raymond, ed., *News, Newspapers, and Society in Early Modern Britain* (London, 1999), 42–43; David Coast, *News and Rumour in Jacobean England: Information, Court Politics and Diplomacy, 1618–25* (Manchester, 2014), 33–34.

51. Lindsay O'Neill, *The Opened Letter: Networking in the Early Modern British World* (Philadelphia, 2015), 55.

52. P. J. Finkelpearl, "Chamberlain, John (1553–1628)," *Oxford Dictionary of National Biography,* https://doi.org/10.1093/ref:odnb/5046. In the mid-seventeenth century, the Royal Exchange replaced St. Paul's "as a centre for the exchange of news." See Natasha Glaisyer, *The Culture of Commerce in England, 1660–1720* (Woodbridge, 2006), 35.

53. See M. Greengrass, "Winwood, Ralph (1562/3–1617)," *Oxford Dictionary of National Biography,* https://doi.org/10.1093/ref:odnb/29783; Michelle O'Callaghan, "Patrons of the Mermaid Tavern (act. 1611)," *Oxford Dictionary of National Biography,* https://doi.org/10.1093/ref:odnb/95279; and Sonia P. Anderson, "Trumbull, William (c.1576–1635)," *Oxford Dictionary of National Biography,* https://doi.org/10.1093/ref:odnb/27775.

54. Logan Pearsall Smith, ed., *The Life and Letters of Sir Henry Wotton,* 2 vols. (Oxford, 1907), 1:431–32.

55. Historical Manuscripts Commission, *Report on the Manuscripts of the Marquess of Downshire,* 6 vols. (London, 1924–1995), 2:258–59.

56. Historical Manuscripts Commission, *Downshire,* 2:251.

57. Kupperman, *Jamestown Project,* 259.

58. Historical Manuscripts Commission, *Downshire,* 2:126. John More was Sir Ralph Winwood's servant from 1598 to 1617. See Virginia C. D. Moseley and Rosemary Sgroi, "More, John II (1578–1638)," *The History of Parliament,* https://www.historyofparliamentonline.org/volume/1604-1629/member/more-john-ii-1578-1638.

59. Historical Manuscripts Commission, *Downshire,* 2:195.

60. Ibid., 2:197–98.

61. Italicizations my own. Historical Manuscripts Commission, *Downshire,* 2:197–98.

62. John Chamberlain to Dudley Carleton, 1 August 1613, SP 14/74, f. 100, National Archives.

63. Kingsbury, *Records,* 4:31.

64. Historical Manuscripts Commission, *Downshire,* 2:225.

65. Virginia Company of London, *For the Plantation in Virginia, or Nova Britannia* (1609; STC 24831).

66. Virginia Company in London, *Considering There Is No Publicke Action* (1609; STC 24830.9).

67. Coast, *News and Rumour,* 33–34.

68. John Chamberlain to Dudley Carleton, 8 July 1620, SP 14/116, f. 20, National Archives.

69. Kingsbury, *Records,* 3:79.

70. Walter Ralegh to Robert Cecil, 10 November 1595, CP 36/4, Hatfield House. On Cecil's patronage, see Joyce Lorimer, *English and Irish Settlement on the River Amazon, 1550–1646* (Farnham, 1989), 16–19.

71. Ralegh to Cecil, 13 November 1595, CP 36/9, Hatfield House. After Martin Frobisher's return from Baffin Island, ore was similarly tested by German specialists. See Stephen Alford, *London's Triumph: Merchants, Adventurers, and Money in Shakespeare's City* (London, 2017), 166. On colonial projectors and metallurgical expertise, see Karin A. Amundsen, "Thinking Metallurgically: Metals and Empire in the Projects of Edward Hayes," *Huntington Library Quarterly* 79 (2016), 570, 581.

72. Lady Ralegh to Robert Cecil, undated July 1596, CP 43/29, Hatfield House.

73. Working, *Imperial Polity,* 36, 167.

74. John Smith, *A True Relation of . . . Virginia* (1608; STC 22795.3), sig. A1v.

75. Glaisyer, *Culture of Commerce,* 35; and Hollis, *Absence of America,* 13.

76. Alford, *London's Triumph,* 45–46.

77. Macham published an important early text on Virginia, Robert Johnson's *Nova Britannia* (1609; STC 14699.5). Samuel Macham to Henry Hastings, 5th Earl of Huntingdon, 18 July 1611, mssHA, Box 6/8510, Huntington Library.

78. Mancall, *Hakluyt's Promise,* 236.

79. C. M. McInnes, *Ferdinando Gorges and New England* (Bristol, 1965), 4.

80. Ferdinando Gorges to Robert Cecil, Earl of Salisbury, 7 August 1607, CP 121/172, Hatfield House.

81. Gorges to Salisbury, 1 December 1607, CP 123/77, Hatfield House.

82. Gorges to Salisbury, 3 December 1607, CP 123/81, Hatfield House.

83. Gorges to Salisbury, 7 February 1608, CP 120/66a, Hatfield House.

84. Fitzmaurice, *Humanism and America,* chapter three; Armitage, "Literature and Empire," 106–7; David Armitage, *The Ideological Origins of the British Empire* (Cambridge, 2000), 72–73.

85. Working, *Imperial Polity,* 165.

86. Armstrong, *Writing North America,* 41.

87. For the issue of distinguishing between "elite" and "popular" culture, see Tim Harris, "The Problem of 'Popular Political Culture' in Seventeenth-Century London," *History of European Ideas* 10 (1989), 43–58. Multiple scholars have shown that ideas about civic humanism penetrated vernacular political discourse. See Fitzmaurice, *Humanism and America*, 16; Richard Cust, "Reading for Magistracy: The Mental World of Sir John Newdigate," in John F. McDiarmid, ed., *The Monarchical Republic of Early Modern England: Essays in Response to Patrick Collinson* (Aldershot, 2007), 198–99.

88. Fitzmaurice, "Rhetoric of the Virginia Company Sermon," 25; Early Modern Research Group (EMRG), "Commonwealth: The Social, Cultural, and Conceptual Contexts of an Early Modern Keyword," *Historical Journal* 54 (2011), 660.

89. Early Modern Research Group, "Commonwealth," 660–62, 671.

90. Phil Withington, *Society in Early Modern England: The Vernacular Origins of Some Powerful Ideas* (Cambridge, 2010), 137, 144–46. The term commonwealth was used in several publications: Counseil for Virginia, *Considering There Is No Publicke Action* (1609; STC 24830.9); Virginia Company in London, *For the Plantation in Virginia, or Nova Britannia* (1609; STC 24831); Counseil for Virginia, *A True and Sincere Declaration* (1610; STC 24832a), sig. D3r; and Counseil for Virginia, *A Brief Declaration of the Present State of Things in Virginia* (1616; STC 24834), sig. A1v. The term "public good" was used in only one company publication, Conseil for Virginia, *A Publication by the Counsell of Virginea, Touching the Plantation There* (1610; STC 24831.7).

91. Craig Muldrew, *The Economy of Obligation: The Culture of Credit and Social Relations in Early Modern England* (Basingstoke, 1998), 126.

92. Anon., *Londons Lotterie* (1612; STC 16756.5).

93. Gorges to Salisbury, 7 February 1608, CP 120/66a, Hatfield House.

94. For allegories of the commonwealth and body politic, see Early Modern Research Group, "Commonwealth," 674.

95. Chamberlain to Carleton, 9 July 1612, SP 14/70, f. 5, National Archives.

96. Counseil for Virginia, *A True and Sincere Declaration* (1610; STC 24832a), sig. D3r.

97. Counseil for Virginia, *A Publication by the Counsell of Virginea, Touching the Plantation There* (1610; STC 24831.7). Also, Catherine Armstrong, "'Boiled and Stewed with Roots and Herbs': Everyday Tales of Cannibalism in Early Modern Virginia," in Angela McShane and Garthine Walker, eds., *The Extraordinary and the Everyday in Early Modern England, Essays in Celebration of the Work of Bernard Capp* (Basingstoke, 2010), 167.

98. Counseil of Virginia, *A True Declaration of the Estate of the Colonie in Virginia* (1610; STC 24833), sig. A3r.

99. Robert Johnson, *The New Life of Virginea* (1612; STC 14700), sig. A3v.

100. Adam Fox, "Rumour, News and Popular Political Opinion in Elizabethan and Early Stuart England," *History Journal* 40 (1997), 599; Coast, *News and Rumor*, 82.

101. Conseil for Virginia, *A Publication by the Counsell of Virginea, Touching the Plantation There* (1610; STC 24831.7).

102. Noah Millstone, *Manuscript Circulation and the Invention of Politics in Early Stuart England* (Cambridge, 2016), 185; Coast, *News and Rumour*, 86.

103. See Counseil of Virginia, *A True and Sincere Declaration* (1610; STC 24832a); Counseil of Virginia, *A True Declaration of the Estate of the Colonie in Virginia* (1610; STC 24833). Also, Armstrong, *Writing North America*, 33; and Gaskill, *Between Two Worlds: How the English Became Americans* (Oxford, 2014), 18–19.

104. Chamberlain to Carleton, 9 July 1612, SP 14/70, f. 5, National Archives.

105. For further discussion of news gathering from multiple sources, see Peacey, *Print and Public Politics*, 111.

106. William Brewster to Dudley Carleton, undated 1607, CP 124/17, Hatfield House.

107. Walter Cope to Robert Cecil, Earl of Salisbury, undated 1607, CP 124/18, Hatfield House.

108. Deborah E. Harkness, *The Jewel House: Elizabethan London and the Scientific Revolution* (New Haven, 2007), quote at 22, also 26, 33, 37.

109. Macham to Earl of Huntington, 18 July 1611, mssHA, Box 6/8510, Huntington Library. Harkness also argues that naturalists wanted to verify reports by receiving specimens themselves. Harkness, *Jewel House*, 37.

110. Earl of Huntington to Captain Nicholas Martiau, 8 July 1624, mssHA, Box 10/5486, Huntington Library. The "Epitome" was probably *A Briefe Declaration of the Plantation of Virginia Duringe the First Twelve Years . . . by the Ancient Planters*. See Kate Langley Bosher, "The First House of Burgesses," *North American Review* 184 (1907), 733–39.

111. Martiau to Earl of Huntington, 12 December 1625, mssHA, Box 13/9170, Huntington Library. On the supposedly medicinal properties of sassafras, see Harriot, *Briefe and True Report*, f. 9.

112. See below, Chapter 2.

113. Captain Peter Wyn[ne] to Sir John Egerton, 26 November 1608, mssEL, Box 59/1683, Huntington Library.

114. Earl of Huntington to Martiau, 8 July 1624, mssHA, Box 10/5486, Huntington Library.

115. MacMillan, *Imperial Constitution*, 86–87, 122; April Lee Hatfield, *Atlantic Virginia: Intercolonial Relations in the Seventeenth Century* (Pennsylvania, 2004), 39.

116. Macham to Earl of Huntington, 18 July 1611, mssHA, Box 6/8510, Huntington Library.

117. Earl of Huntington to Nicholas Martiau, 8 July 1624, mssHA, Box 10/5486, Huntington Library.

118. Martiau to Earl of Huntington, 12 December 1625, mssHA, Box 13/9170, Huntington Library.

119. William Payne to James Meddus, 30 June 1628, SP 16/108, f. 126, National Archives.

120. Anthony Pagden, *European Encounters with the New World: From Renaissance to Romanticism* (New Haven, 1993), 51; and Rachel Winchcombe, "Authenticating El Dorado: Frustrated Knowledge Production in Walter Ralegh's *Discoverie of Guiana*," *Itinerario* 43 (2019), 445.

121. Thrush, *Indigenous London*, 47–49, 58; Vaughan, "Indian Interpreters," 342.

122. Rich, Dale, and De La Warr are discussed in Chapter 2. See Alden T. Vaughan, "Powhatan's Abroad: Virginia Indians in England," in Robert Appelbaum and John Wood Sweet, eds., *Envisioning an English Empire: Jamestown and the Making of the North Atlantic World* (Philadelphia, 2005), 51–52, 58–59; and Smith, *Generall History of Virginia*, f. 123.

123. Lady Ralegh to Robert Cecil, undated July 1596, CP 43/29, Hatfield House.

124. Millstone, *Manuscript Circulation*, 170.

125. The treatment of interest in American colonization has tended to focus on discrete areas like promotional literature or theatre. See Armstrong, *Writing North America*; and Hollis, *Absence of America*. More recently, Lauren Working has offered a fuller picture, examining these genres alongside epistolary networks and material culture. See Working, *Imperial Polity*, especially chapter 5.

Chapter 2

1. Cesellye Sherley West, Lady De La Warr (d. 1661/62), Circle of Cornelius Johnson, JYF2005.54, Jamestown Settlement, Williamsburg. On women's wearing of pearls in seventeenth-century portraiture and their association with virtue and worth, see Molly A. Warsh, *American Baroque: Pearls and the Nature of Empire, 1492–1700* (Chapel Hill, 2018), 219–21.

2. See below, and "Petition of Lady Cicely De La Warr," undated 1634–1635, CO 1/8:18, National Archives. She petitioned Charles II in 1661, shortly before her death, for her annuity of £500 to continue to her heirs. See E. M. Rose, "Lord Delaware, First Governor of Virginia, 'the Poorest Baron of this Kingdom,'" *Virginia Magazine of History and Biography* 128 (2020), 246.

3. Shannon Miller, *Invested with Meaning: The Raleigh Circle in the New World* (Philadelphia, 1998), 134.

4. On "women's centrality to the early modern economy," see Alexandra Shepard, "Crediting Women in the Early Modern English Economy," *History Workshop Journal* 79 (2015), 3.

5. Also, Ewen, "Women Investors," 855–57. There is some discussion of the aristocratic women in Queen Anna's circle who were Virginia Company investors in L. H. Roper, *The English Empire in America, 1602–1658: Beyond Jamestown* (London, 2009), 74, 77–78; and Working, *Imperial Polity*, 21.

6. Networks are especially revealing of the agency of women and non-Europeans. Aske Laursen Brock, "Networks," in William A. Pettigrew and David Veevers, *The Corporation as a Protagonist in Global History, c. 1550–1750* (Leiden, 2019), 98. On the significance of global kinship networks for state building in India, see David Veevers, "'Inhabitants of the Universe': Global Families, Kinship Networks, and the Formation of the Early Modern Colonial State in Asia," *Journal of Global History* 10 (2015), 103.

7. The East India Company (EIC), chartered in 1600, was the first English joint-stock company, but the Virginia Company was the first time that a joint-stock company was established for settlement as well as trade. See Edmond Smith, "The Global Interests of London's Commercial Community, 1599–1625: Investment in the East India Company," *The Economic History Review* 71 (2018)," 1123–24; and Andrews, *Trade, Plunder and Settlement*, 261–62.

8. See Theodore K. Rabb, *Enterprise and Empire: Merchant and Gentry Investment in the Expansion of England: 1575–1630* (Cambridge, 1967), 59–61, 104.

9. Ibid., 59–61, 104. Membership to the EIC, on the other hand, was £200.

10. Edmond Smith, "The Social Networks of Investment in Early Modern England," *The Historical Journal* (2020) 9.

11. Ewen, "Women Investors," 866; Smith, "Social Networks of Investment," 3; Working, *Imperial Polity*, chapter 5.

12. Kingsbury, *Records*, 1:211. Smythe was company treasurer until 1619. After then, meetings were held at the Ferrar household on St. Sythe's Lane. See below.

13. Virginia Company v. Ackland, 28 April 1613, C 8/19/94, f. 1, National Archives.

14. Virginia Company v. Townsend, undated December 1612, C 2/JasI/U2/27 f. 2, National Archives.

15. Virginia Company v. Townsend, 11 January 1612/13, C 2/JasI/U2/27 f. 4, National Archives.

16. Fifty-six livery companies invested in the Virginia Company in 1609. *The Second Charter of Virginia* (1609), in Alexander Brown, ed., *The Genesis of the United States*, 2 vols. (New York, 1964) 1:206–37.

17. Other companies that received the same letter and precept included the Fishmongers', Clothworkers', Merchant Taylors', Mercers', and Drapers. Fishmongers' Court Minute Book, MS05570/001, ff. 547, 549–50, Guildhall Library; Orders of Court, CL/B/1/4, f. 46, Clothworker Company's; Merchant Taylors' Court Minute Book, MS34010/004, f. 363, Guildhall Library; Acts of Court, 1595–1629, f. 96, Mercers' Company; Court of Assistants' Minutes, 7 April 1609, MB 13, Drapers' Company.

18. Grocers' Court Minute Book, MS11588/002, ff. 528, 574, Guildhall Library.

19. Leveson v. Smith, 5 February 1613, C 8/88/61, National Archives.

20. Grocers' Court Minute Book, MS11588/002, f. 582, Guildhall Library.

21. Vintners' Court Book, MS15201/002, ff. 26, 30, Guildhall Library.

22. Merchant Taylors' Court Minute Book, MS34010/004, f. 364, Guildhall Library.

23. Ibid.

24. "Papers Relating to Dover," 23 May 1610, Egerton MSS 2087, f. 3, British Library.

25. Common Council Proceedings, undated March 1606, M/BCC/CCP/1, Vol. 1, f. 4, Bristol Archives. Also, Alan Davidson, "James, Thomas (c. 1555–1619)," *The History of Parliament*, https://www.historyofparliamentonline.org/volume/1604-1629/member/james-thomas-1555-1619.

26. Common Council Proceedings, 1 April 1606, M/BCC/CCP/1, Vol. 1, f. 115, Bristol Archives. Thomas Aldworth (sometimes Aldsworth) was previously the mayor of Bristol.

27. Virginia Company v. Townsend, 11 January 1612/13, C 2/JasI/U2/27, f. 4, National Archives.

28. Virginia Company v. Townsend, undated December 1612, C 2/JasI/U2/27, f. 2, National Archives.

29. Virginia Company v. Townsend, 11 January 1612/13, C 2/JasI/U2/27, f. 4, National Archives.

30. Virginia Company v. Sammes, undated November 1613, C 2/JasI/U2/69, National Archives.

31. Smith, "Social Networks of Investment," 6.

32. See discussion in Working, *Imperial Polity*.

33. Amy Froide, *Silent Partners: Women as Public Investors during Britain's Financial Revolution, 1690–1750* (Oxford, 2017), 101, 106; Krista J. Kesselring and Tim Stretton, "Introduction: Coverture and Continuity," in Krista J. Kesselring and Tim Stretton, eds., *Married Women and the Law: Coverture in England and the Common Law World* (Montreal, 2013), 12.

34. Amy Louise Erickson, *Women and Property in Early Modern England* (London, 1993), 5, 24–25, 104–5. See also, Bernard Capp, *When Gossips Meet: Women, Family, and Neighbourhood in Early Modern England* (Oxford, 2003), 91–92.

35. Eleanor Hubbard, *City Women: Money, Sex, and the Social Order in Early Modern London* (Oxford, 2014), 189, 195.

36. Marjorie K. McIntosh, "The Benefits and Drawbacks of Femme Sole Status in England, 1300–1630," *Journal of British Studies* 44 (2005), 416–17.

37. Shepard, "Crediting Women," 3; Alexandra Shepard, "Making Their Own Business: Married Women and Credit in Early Eighteenth-Century London," *Transactions of the Royal Historical Society* 25 (2015), 55; and Amy M. Froide, *Never Married: Singlewomen in Early Modern England* (Oxford, 2005), 134–35. See also Richard Grassby, *The Business Community of Seventeenth-Century England* (Cambridge, 1995), 317–20; and Richard Grassby, *Kinship and Capitalism: Marriage, Family, and Business in the English-Speaking World, 1580–1740* (Cambridge, 2001), 92–93, 305.

38. Susan D. Amussen and Allyson M. Poska, "Shifting the Frame: Trans-Imperial Approaches to Gender in the Atlantic World," *Early Modern Women* 9 (2014) 5, 10.

39. For discussion of social capital in the context of early modern corporations see, Withington, *Society in Early Modern England*, 205; and Sheilagh Ogilvie, *Institutions and European Trade: Merchant Guilds, 1000–1800* (Cambridge, 2011), 7. When the Scots Company was launched, elite women gave it a similar boost. Gina G. Bennett, "Imperial Women of Darien: Scottish Migration and Gender in the Atlantic World, 1650–1740" (unpublished PhD thesis, University of Texas at Arlington, 2020), 29.

40. For the development of this argument elsewhere, see Ewen, "Women Investors," 873–74.

41. Several works that examine Virginia Company investment and investors have completely failed to address or engage with women's investment. Fitzmaurice, *Humanism and America*; Rabb, *Enterprise and Empire*; and Robert Brenner, *Merchants and Revolution: Commercial Change, Political Conflict, and London's Overseas Traders, 1550–1653* (Cambridge, 1993).

42. Froide, *Silent Partners*, 71.

43. The marriage was not actually solemnized until his return in 1616. See Aske Laursen Brock and Misha Ewen, "Women's Public Lives: Navigating the East India Company, Parliament and Courts in Early Modern England," *Gender & History* 33 (2020) fn. 19.

44. W. H. K. Wright, ed., *The Western Antiquary* (Plymouth, 1885), 4:85.

45. Froide, *Silent Partners*, 84–85.

46. In the context of corporations, I believe that "stranger" most likely designated someone who was not a shareholder, rather than a foreigner. Kingsbury, *Records*, 4:182.

47. For evidence of meetings on St. Sythe's Lane, see Kingsbury, *Records*, 1:261.

48. Kingsbury, *Records*, 1:497.

49. *The Second Charter of Virginia* (1609), in Brown, *Genesis of the United States*, 1:206–37; and Kupperman, *Jamestown Project*, 242–43.

50. Kingsbury, *Records*, 3:87, 89.

51. Will of John West, 10 September 1613, PROB 11/122/205, National Archives. See Froide, *Silent Partners*, 94.

52. Parish registers: St. Giles Cripplegate, City of London, 17 April 1593, P69/GIS/A/002/MS06419/001, London Metropolitan Archives; and Marriage Allegations, Diocese of London, 7 March 1603, DL/A/D/002/MS10091/002, London Metropolitan Archives.

53. Thomas Lappidge was a Freeman of the Silkweavers' Company, and William Parker a Freeman of the Brewers' Company. Will of Samuel Ramsden, Gent., 20 October 1606, MS 9172/23B, London Metropolitan Archives; Will of John Worsley, 26 August 1603, PROB 11/102, National Archives. Milicent Young had a daughter, Dorcas Worsley, indicating that these women were the kin of John Worsley. Will of Milicent St. John, Wiltshire, 11 May 1636, PROB 11/171/70, National Archives.

54. Kingsbury, *Records*, 1:235, 3:60. For her marriage to St. John in 1609: Act Book, 20 December 1609, D1/39/1/37, f. 130, Wiltshire and Swindon History Centre.

55. They included the countesses of Bedford, Pembroke, and Derby. Roper, *English Empire*, 74, 77–78.

56. *The Third Charter of Virginia* (1612) in Brown, *Genesis of the United States*, 2:540–53; "The Complete List of Shareholders in 1618, with Amount of Stock," in Kingsbury, ed., *Records*, 3:79–90. For Bedford's investment in the Bermuda or Somers Island Company, see Michael Jarvis, *In the Eye of All Trade: Bermuda, Bermudians, and the Maritime Atlantic World, 1680–1783* (Chapel Hill, 2010), 20.

57. For the exchange of shares in the Virginia Company between 1615 and 1623, and women's shareholding, see Kingsbury, *Records,* 3:58–66, 83. As before April 1619 the records of the Virginia Company are incomplete, it is impossible to capture all of women's involvement in company affairs.

58. Withington, *Society in Early Modern England*, 205.

59. Romney, *New Netherland Connections*, 18.

60. Roper, *English Empire*, 10.

61. Kingsbury, *Records,* 3:122. This web of family connections and investment was reconstructed through several *Oxford Dictionary of National Biography* entries: John Considine, "Grey, Elizabeth, countess of Kent (1582–1651)," https://doi.org/10.1093/ref:odnb/11530; Victor Stater, "Herbert, William, third earl of Pembroke (1580–1630)," https://doi.org/10.1093/ref:odnb/13058; David L. Smith, "Herbert, Philip, first earl of Montgomery and fourth earl of Pembroke (1584–1650)," https://doi.org/10.1093/ref:odnb/13042; Margaret Patterson Hannay, "Herbert [Sidney], Mary, countess of Pembroke (1561–1621)," https://doi.org/10.1093/ref:odnb/13040; Carole Levin, "Cavendish, William, first earl of Devonshire (1551–1626)," https://doi.org/10.1093/ref:odnb/4944; Sidney Lee, rev. by Victor Stater, "Cavendish, William, second earl of Devonshire (1590–1628)," https://doi.org/10.1093/ref:odnb/4945.

62. Kingsbury, *Records,* 3:86.

63. Froide, *Silent Partners*, 178–79.

64. Kingsbury, *Records,* 3:64. I have been unable to discover the first name of Lady Pell, making it difficult to know who her kin were and who she might have inherited shares from.

65. Ibid., 2:122.

66. "Petition of Lady Cicely De La Warr," undated 1634–1635, CO 1/8:18, National Archives.

67. Erickson, *Women and Property*, 24–26, 103.

68. Kingsbury, *Records,* 3:64.

69. Ibid., 3:62.

70. Ibid., 3:93.

71. Ibid., 3:60.

72. Ibid., 3:61, 62, 64, 66.

73. Ibid., 3:290.

74. It was common for more experienced investors to lead groups of less experienced investors; of course, this meant that trust between the partners was a necessity. See Smith, "Social Networks of Investment," 9.

75. Kingsbury, *Records,* 3:63–64. See also Elaine V. Beilin, "Carey [Carew], Elizabeth, Lady Hunsdon [née Elizabeth Spencer; other married name Elizabeth Eure, Lady Eure] (1552–1618)," *Oxford Dictionary of National Biography,* https://doi.org/10.1093/ref:odnb/4641; Jan Broadway, "John Smyth of Nibley: A Jacobean Man-of-Business and His Service to the Berkeley Family," *Midland History* 24 (1999), 86.

76. J. E. Gethyn-Jones, "Berkeley Plantation, Virginia," *Transactions of the Bristol and Gloucestershire Archaeological Society* 94 (1976), 7.

77. See Kingsbury, *Records,* 3:58. Mabel Collymore was the wife of London Mercer Sir John Collymore, originally of Canterbury. See Andrew Thrush, "Lovelace, Sir William (1561–1629)," *History of Parliament,* https://www.historyofparliamentonline.org/volume/1604-1629/member/lovelace-sir-william-1561–1629.

78. R. C. D. Baldwin, "Argall, Sir Samuel (*bap.* 1580, *d.* 1626)," *Oxford Dictionary of National Biography,* https://doi.org/10.1093/ref:odnb/640.

79. Lovelace of Bethersden (Kent), was married to Elizabeth, daughter of Edward Aucher of Bishopsbourne (Kent). Sir Anthony Aucher of Bishopsbourne (Kent) was the son of Margaret (née Sandys), Sir Edwin Sandys's sister. See Andrew Thrush, "Lovelace, Sir William (1561–1629)," *The History of Parliament*, https://www.historyofparliamentonline.org/volume/1604-1629/member/lovelace-sir-william-1561-1629; and Andrew Thrush, "Aucher (Agar, Archer), Sir Anthony (c. 1586–1637)," *The History of Parliament*, https://www.historyofparliamentonline.org/volume/1604-1629/member/aucher-sir-anthony-1586–1637. John Tradescant the Elder (d. 1638) married Elizabeth Day in Meopham (Kent), which may explain his connection to this group. See Arthur MacGregor, "Tradescant, John, the elder (*d.* 1638)," *Oxford Dictionary of National Biography*, https://doi.org/10.1093/ref:odnb/27654.

80. Familial and local connections in relation to early East India Company investors is discussed in Smith, "Social Networks of Investment," 12, 15–16. On the parish networks of merchant investors in the Company of Scotland Trading to Africa and the Indies, see Bennett, "Imperial Women," 48. Women's patronage in the Virginia Company is ignored altogether in Fitzmaurice, *Humanism and America*, 62–63.

81. Paul Hunneyball, "Selden, John (1584–1654)," *The History of Parliament*, https://www.historyofparliamentonline.org/volume/1604-1629/member/selden-john-1584-1654.

82. Paul Christianson, "Selden, John (1584–1654)," *Oxford Dictionary of National Biography*, https://doi.org/10.1093/ref:odnb/25052.

83. David Colclough, "Donne, John (1572–1631)," *Oxford Dictionary of National Biography*, https://doi.org/10.1093/ref:odnb/7819; and Helen Payne, "Russell [née Harrington], Lucy, countess of Bedford (*bap.* 1581, *d.* 1627)," *Oxford Dictionary of National Biography*, https://doi.org/10.1093/ref:odnb/24330. Stanley Johnson, "John Donne and the Virginia Company," *ELH* 14 (1947), 127, 130. Lauren Working also discusses Bedford's patronage of individuals with interest in colonization, in Working, *Imperial Polity*, 42.

84. See Ewen, "Women Investors," 862, 869; Brock and Ewen, "Women's Public Lives," 7–8.

85. Sir Samuel Argall v. William Browne and Ralph Wright, undated 1624–1625, C 2/ChasI/A48/53, National Archives.

86. Froide, *Silent Partners*, 106.

87. Sir Samuel Argall v. William Browne and Ralph Wright, undated 1624–1625, C 2/ChasI/A48/53, National Archives.

88. Sir George Yeardly was also included in this partnership, but soon withdrew; Throckmorton also withdrew at a later date and William Tracy took over his share. See Gethyn-Jones, "Berkeley Plantation," 7.

89. [Sir Edward Conway] to Navy Commissioners, 1 July 1623, SP 14/148, f. 10, National Archives.

90. Brock and Ewen, "Women's Public Lives," 9–13.

91. Kingsbury, *Records*, 1:483, 2:14.

92. Will of Robert Smallay, 15 November 1621, PROB 11/137/664, National Archives; Lady Dale v. Smalley, 27 May 1623, C 2/ChasI/D22/64, National Archives.

93. Kingsbury, *Records*, 3:291.

94. Ibid., 3:293.

95. "Annual Accounts of the Earl of Southampton and Nicholas Ferrar," 22 May 1622–22 May 1623, no. 480; "Certificate of Virginia Company," 12 May 1623, no. 476; and "Interest and Warrant," 23 December 1620–22 May 1622, no. 383, Ferrar Papers.

96. Ewen, "Women Investors," 862; Brock and Ewen, "Women's Public Lives," 3.

97. Leveson v. Smith, 5 February 1613, C 8/88/61, National Archives.

98. Smith, "Social Networks of Investment," 5.

99. Barbara Todd, "Property and a Woman's Place in Restoration London," *Women's History Review* 19 (2010), 182.

100. Richard Berkley to John Smyth, 3 August 1633, MSCol 2799/42, New York Public Library.

Chapter 3

1. Translated from the Latin, *Possibilia spes comitatur.* Historical Manuscripts Commission, *Fifth Report of the Royal Commission of Historical Manuscripts, Part 1, Report and Appendix* (London, 1876), 559. Quoted in Gaskill, *Between Two Worlds*, 50.

2. There is a second purse in the Victoria and Albert Museum, embroidered with the same phrase, dating from the 1630s and decorated with acorns. Bag, 1630–1639, T.56–1927, Victoria and Albert Museum.

3. Hannah Robb, "Purses and the Charitable Gift," *Journal of Social History* 49 (2015), 395–99.

4. William A. Pettigrew and Aske Laursen Brock, "Leadership and Social Agendas of the Seventeenth-Century English Trading Corporation," in William A. Pettigrew and David Chan Smith, eds., *A History of Socially Responsible Business, c. 1600–1950* (London, 2017), 5; and Edmond J. Smith, "Socially Responsible and Responsive Business in Seventeenth-Century England," in Pettigrew and Smith, eds., *A History of Socially Responsible Business, c. 1600–1950*, 67.

5. Counseil for Virginia, *By His Majesties Counsell of Virginea* (1612; STC 24833.4).

6. John Holles, 1st Earl of Clare, Commonplace and Letter Book, undated 1613, Add MS 70505, f. 37v, British Library.

7. For the proclamation "Suppressing the Lottery for Virginia, and All Others," dated 8 March 1621, see James F. Larkin and Paul L. Hughes, eds., *Stuart Royal Proclamations*, 2 vols. (Oxford, 1973–1983), 1:500–502.

8. On 17 May 1620, the company reported receiving £7,000 from the lotteries, and according to an audit made in June 1621 the sum total from the "running lotteries" was £29,000. It is unclear whether, as Scott suggests, the earlier estimated profit of £7,000 was included in the later total. If so, this could mean that the lotteries raised up to £38,000 by the time they were suspended. See Kingsbury, *Records*, 1:335, 556; and William Robert Scott, *The Constitution and Finance of English, Scottish and Irish Joint-Stock Companies to 1720*, 3 vols. (Cambridge, 1910–1912), 2:258. In 1620, Sir Edwin Sandys claimed that money from the lotteries had already helped to send eight hundred people to the colony. See Kingsbury, *Records*, 1:412.

9. David Dean, "Elizabeth's Lottery: Political Culture and State Formation in Early Modern England," *Journal of British Studies* 50 (2011), 590–91.

10. Anon., *The Great Frost* (1608; STC 11402), sig. C3v.

11. *The Third Charter of Virginia* (1612), in Brown, *Genesis of the United States*, 2:540–53.

12. Brown, *Genesis of the United States*, 2:571–72.

13. Historical Manuscripts Commission, *Downshire*, 3:307.

14. Edward Arber, ed., *A Transcript of the Registers of the Company of Stationers of London, 1554–1640*, 5 vols. (London, 1875–1894), 3:216v; John Stow, *Annales, or, A Generall Chronicle of England* (1632; STC 23340), f. 1002; Robert Johnson, "The Lotteries of the Virginia Company," *Virginia Magazine of History and Biography* 74 (1966), 261.

15. Johnson, "Lotteries of the Virginia Company," 265.

16. Kupperman, *Jamestown Project*, 255.

17. Fitzwilliam v. West, January 1615, STAC 8/144/6, f. 2, National Archives; Ewen, "Women Investors," 871–73.

18. The Candlemas term began on 2 February. Counseil for Virginia, *By His Majesties Counsell of Virginea* (1612; STC 24833.4).

19. Ibid.

20. Historical Manuscripts Commission, *Downshire*, 4:268.

21. R. W. Greaves, ed., *The First Ledger Book of High Wycombe* (Welwyn Garden City, 1947), 109.

22. On 15 July 1615, Richard Martin, a lawyer and Virginia Company investor, thanked the mayor for the citizens' contribution. Martin was native to Exeter, where both his father and grandfather were merchants. HMC Commission, *Report on the Records of the City of Exeter* (London, 1916), 99. See Virginia C. D. Moseley and Rosemary Sgroi, "Martin (Martyn), Richard (c. 1570–1618)," *The History of Parliament*, http://www.historyofparliamentonline.org/volume/1558-1603/member/martin-richard-1570-1618.

23. Great Yarmouth Assembly Book, 2 June 1615, YC/19/5, f. 150, Norfolk Record Office; Chris Kyle, "Hardware, George (1569–1635)," *The History of Parliament*, http://www.historyofparliamentonline.org/volume/1604-1629/member/hardware-george-1569-1635. For the lottery in Great Yarmouth, see "Photographs of Assembly Book, Entries Relating to the Virginia Lottery," 13 April 1615, Y/TC 69/25, Norfolk Record Office. Dover also contributed £5 toward the Second Great Standing Lottery. See Brown, *Genesis of the United States*, 2:768–69; and Johnson, "Lotteries of the Virginia Company," 280.

24. Virginia Company of London, *A Declaration for the Certaine Time of Drawing the Great Standing Lottery* (1615; STC 24833.8). Because it was printed 22 February Old Style, the year was actually 1616. Also, Johnson, "Lotteries of the Virginia Company," 272.

25. See Ian W. Archer, *The Pursuit of Stability: Social Relations in Elizabethan London* (Cambridge, 1991), chapter 4, esp. 119–24.

26. W. K. Jordan, *The Charities of London 1480–1660: The Aspirations and the Achievements of the Urban Society* (London, 1960), 106.

27. Vintners' Company Court Book, 18 May 1612, MS15201/002, f. 76, Guildhall Library. In 1614, the Vintners' agreed to use the £4 remaining from their investment in the lottery to contribute toward buying a share in the Virginia Company. Vintners' Company Court Book, 9 May 1614, MS15201/002, f. 138, Guildhall Library.

28. Book of Orders of Court, 20 April 1612, CL/B/1/4, f. 92, Clothworkers' Company. Sir Thomas (d. 1624), the son of William Hewett (d. 1599), Freeman of the Clothworker's Company and brother of Sir William Hewett (1572–1637), a merchant and MP for New Windsor, invested in the East India and Bermuda Companies too. See Alan Davidson and Andrew Thrush, "Hewett, Sir William (1572–1637)," *The History of Parliament*, http://www.historyofparliamentonline.org/volume/1604-1629/member/hewett-sir-william-1572-1637; and Rabb, *Enterprise and Empire*, 313.

29. Court of Assistants' Minutes, 15 June 1612, MB 13, Drapers' Company; and Court of Assistants' Minutes, 11 May 1614, MB 13, Drapers' Company.

30. Acts of Court, 20 May 1612, f. 124, Mercers' Company; and Acts of Court, 25 May 1614, f. 133, Mercers' Company.

31. Haberdashers' Company Court of Assistants' Minute Book, 2 September 1614, MS15842/001, f. 189, Guildhall Library.

32. See also, "Letter from the Privy Council, Whitehall, to the Deputy Lieutenants of Staffordshire," 22 February 1615, L.a.751, Folger Shakespeare Library. The text mentioned was likely Counseil for Virginia, *A True Declaration of the Estate of the Colonie in Virginia* (1610; STC 24833). Also, Terence H. O'Brien, "The London Livery Companies and the Virginia Company," *Virginia Magazine of History and Biography* 68 (1960), 149–51.

33. Grocers' Company Court Minute Book, 25 April 1614, MS11588/002, f. 809, Guildhall Library. The Grocers' Company had previously given £57 10s. to the lottery in 1612. Grocers' Company Court Minute Book, 29 April 1612, MS11588/002, f. 681, Guildhall Library. See Charles Welch, revised by Trevor Dickie, "Myddelton [Middleton], Sir Thomas (1549×56–1631)," *Oxford Dictionary of National Biography*, https://doi.org/10.1093/ref:odnb/19685.

34. Fishmongers' Company Court Minute Book, 15 June 1612, MS05570/002, f. 52, Guildhall Library; and Fishmongers' Company Court Minute Book, 11 April 1614, MS05570/002, ff. 105–6, Guildhall Library.

35. "Draft of Open Letter," undated 1619, no. 134, Ferrar Papers; and Anon., *Londons Lotterie.*

36. Muldrew, *Economy of Obligation*, 151; and Evelyn Welch, "Lotteries in Early Modern Italy," *Past & Present* 199 (2008), 81.

37. Anon., *Londons Lotterie.*

38. Ibid.; Hollis, *Absence of America*, 170, 212.

39. Virginia Company of London, *A Declaration for the Certaine Time of Drawing the Great Standing Lottery* (1615; STC 24833.8). For further discussion, see Hollis, *Absence of America*, 121; and Thrush, *Indigenous London*, 49–50. Eiakintomino was depicted a second time, standing in St. James Park, surrounded by flora and fauna, dated around 1615–1616. See Alden T. Vaughan, *Transatlantic Encounters: American Indians in Britain, 1500–1776* (Cambridge, 2006), 53. The original watercolor is in the Edinburgh University Library. Anon., *Londons Lotterie.*

40. "Draft of Open Letter," undated 1619, no. 134, Ferrar Papers.

41. For Chester, "Letter from the Council of the Virginia Company," 15 June 1616, ZM/L/6/107, Cheshire Archives and Local Studies; Norwich, "Virginia Company to the Mayor and City of Norwich," 4 December 1617, NCR/17/B/7, ff. 17–18, Norfolk Record Office; and Leicester, "Letter RE: Lottery for Plantation of Virginia," 2 May 1618, BRII/18/12, no. 289, Record Office for Leicestershire, Leicester and Rutland.

42. "Letter from the Council of the Virginia Company," 15 June 1616, ZM/L/6/107, Cheshire Archives and Local Studies.

43. Kupperman, *Jamestown Project*, 267; Jordan Goodman, *Tobacco in History: The Cultures of Dependence* (London, 1993), 134–35.

44. Kingsbury, *Records*, 3:49–57.

45. Fitzwilliam v. West, January 1615, STAC 8/144/6, f. 2, National Archives.

46. "Letter from the Council of the Virginia Company," 15 June 1616, ZM/L/6/107, Cheshire Archives and Local Studies.

47. Ibid. Also, Welch, "Lotteries in Early Modern Italy," 86.

48. Anon., *The Great Frost*, sig. C4r.

49. "Letter RE: Lottery for Plantation of Virginia," 2 May 1618, BRII/18/12, no. 289, Record Office for Leicestershire, Leicester and Rutland.

50. "Account of the Lottery in Leicester," 12 June 1618, BRII/18/12, no. 296, Record Office for Leicestershire, Leicester and Rutland.

51. "Examination of Walter Cole," 20 October 1619, Q/SR/34/110, Somerset Archives and Local Studies.

52. Johnson, "Lotteries of the Virginia Company," 285; Peter Walne, "The 'Running Lottery' of the Virginia Company: In Reading, 1619, and in Chester, 1616," *Virginia Magazine of History and Biography* 70 (1962), 31.

53. For example, "Expenses Hiring Men in Sussex," before 9 March 1621, no. 232, Ferrar Papers; "Letter," 5 December 1619, no. 132, Ferrar Papers; and Kingsbury, *Records*, 3:187.

54. Norwich City Library Donation Book, 1614, MS 4228, f.5v, Norfolk Record Office; Wilkins-Jones, *Norwich City Library*, 1, 3, 7.

55. *Records of Maidstone: Being Selections from Documents in the Possession of the Corporation* (Maidstone, 1926), 56, 73.

56. For Leicester, see Helen Stocks, ed., *Records of the Borough of Leicester: Being a Series of Extracts from the Archives of the Corporation of Leicester*, 7 vols. (London, 1923), 4:204, 208, 288; for Maidstone, see *Records of Maidstone*, 55–56, 73; for Dorchester, see Charles Herbert Mayo, ed., *The Municipal Records of the Borough of Dorchester, Dorset* (Exeter, 1908), 559; for Devizes, see Howard Cunnington, ed., *Some Annals of the Borough of Devizes: Being a Series of Extracts from the Corporation Records, 1555 to 1791*, 2 vols. (Devizes, 1925), 2:57–59; for Reading, see Rev. J. M. Guilding, ed., *Reading Records: Diary of the Corporation*, 4 vols. (London, 1895), 2:65–66, 291; for Manchester, see Court Leet of Manchester, 20 October 1620, M621/1/2, f. 115, Manchester Central Library; for Tiverton and Cirencester, see Johnson, "Lotteries of the Virginia Company," 285–86; and for Warwick, see Warwick Corporation Minute Book, 1610–1662, 20 June 1627, CR 1618/W21/6, f. 86, Warwickshire County Record Office.

57. St. Ewen's: Churchwardens' Accounts, 8 May 1617, P.St E/ChW/2, f. 194r, Bristol Archives; City of Gloucester Corporation Minutes, 20 September 1617, GBR/B3/1, f. 448v, Gloucestershire Archives. No further record of Virginia Company lotteries in either Bristol or Gloucester has been found, but as the Virginia Company wrote to the mayor of Salisbury in December 1616, requesting that a lottery be held there, the lottery managers could have traveled to the neighboring towns soon afterward. Kingsbury, *Records*, 3:67–68. Moreover, the recording of money for the poor, out of lottery funds, fits with what we know about other Virginia Company lotteries.

58. Charity Papers, 1 April 1620, D/B/BW/186, Somerset Archives and Local Studies. The records in Warwick suggest that civic loans of £5 were also dispersed. See Warwick Corporation Minute Book, 1610–1662, 20 June 1627, CR 1618/W21/6, f. 86, Warwickshire County Record Office.

59. The common council of an incorporated town was usually responsible for dispensing civic loans. See Phil Withington, *The Politics of Commonwealth: Citizens and Freemen in Early Modern England* (Cambridge, 2005), 181; Jordan, *Charities of London*, 27; Steve Hindle, *On the Parish? The Micro-Politics of Poor Relief in Rural England c. 1550–1700* (Oxford, 2004), 182.

60. Wells Convocation Act Book, 15 November 1619, WCC/242, f. 697, Wells Cathedral Library and Archives.

61. Wells Convocation Act Book, 7 December 1619, WCC/242, f. 697, Wells Cathedral Library and Archives.

62. Cunnington, *Some Annals of the Borough of Devizes*, 2:57–58.

63. Stow, *Annales*, f. 1002; Kingsbury, *Records*, 3:52–56.

64. Fitzwilliam v. West, January 1615, STAC 8/144/6, f. 2, National Archives.

65. See Janette Dillon, "Clerkenwell and Smithfield as a Neglected Home of London Theatre," *Huntington Library Quarterly* 71 (2008), 115, 119–21; "The Bankside Playhouses and Bear Gardens," in Howard Roberts and Walter H. Godfrey, eds., *Survey of London: Volume 22, Bankside (The Parishes of St. Saviour and Christchurch Southwark)* (London, 1950) 66–77; Andreas Höfele, *Stage, Stake and Scaffold: Humans and Animals in Shakespeare's Theatre* (Oxford, 2011), 3–12; Peck, *Consuming Splendor*, 46–47; and Julia Merritt, *The Social World of Early Modern Westminster: Abbey, Court and Community, 1525–1640* (Manchester, 2018), 6.

66. Anon., *Londons Lotterie*; and Welch, "Lotteries in Early Modern Italy," 71, 102. On the contemporary ballad genre more broadly, see Angela McShane, "Recruiting Citizens for Soldiers in Seventeenth-Century English Ballads," *Journal of Early Modern History* 15 (2011), 108; and Tessa Watt, *Cheap Print and Popular Piety, 1550–1640* (Cambridge, 1991), 11–13.

67. Armstrong, *Writing North America*, 183; Margaret Aston, "Bibles to Ballads: Some Pictorial Migrations in the Reformation," in Simon Ditchfield, ed., *Christianity and Community in the West: Essays for John Bossy* (Aldershot, 2001), 117–18, 122.

68. Anon., *Londons Lotterie*.

69. Anon., *The Great Frost*, sig. C3v–C4r.

70. The author has identified new Virginia Company running lotteries that were not identified by previous scholars. In Bristol, St. Ewen's, see Churchwardens' Accounts, 8 May 1617, P.St E/ChW/2, f. 194r, Bristol Archives; in Gloucester, see City of Gloucester Corporation Minutes, 20 September 1617, GBR/B3/1, f. 448v, Gloucestershire Archives; and in Warwick, see Warwick Corporation Minute Book, 1610–1662, 20 June 1627, CR 1618/W21/6, f. 86, Warwickshire County Record Office. For other locations, see E. M. Rose, "The 'Bewitching Lotteries for Virginia,' 1616–21: A List of Sites and Charitable Donations," *Huntington Library Quarterly* 81 (2018), 112–13; Johnson, "Lotteries of the Virginia Company," 282; Johnson, "'Running Lotteries,'" 156–57; T. Bruce Dilks, "A Lottery in Jacobean Bridgwater," in *Proceedings Somerset Archaeology and Natural History*, 79 (1943), 79–81; and Walne, "'Running Lottery,'" 30–34.

71. Kingsbury, *Records*, 3:223.

72. "Account of the Lottery in Leicester," 12 June 1618, BRII/18/12, no. 296, Record Office for Leicestershire, Leicester and Rutland.

73. Johnson, "'Running Lotteries,'" 163; Norwich Mayor's Court Book, 27 December 1617, NCR Case 16a, no. 15, f. 164, Norfolk Record Office.

74. "Examination of Richard Cokley," 29 June 1616, ZQSE/13/25, Cheshire Archives and Local Studies; and S. Barrow, J. D. Herson, A. H. Lawes, P. J. Riden, and M. V. J. Seaborne, "Local Government and Public Services: Municipal Buildings," in A. T. Thacker and C. P. Lewis, eds., *A History of the County of Chester: the City of Chester: Culture, Buildings, Institutions*, 5 vols., (London, 2005) 5:15–20.

75. Private correspondence with Julia Wood, 9 January 2018, Wells Cathedral Library and Archives.

76. Dave Postles, "The Market Place as Space in Early Modern England," *Social History* 29 (2004), 41.

77. "Letter from the Council of the Virginia Company," 15 June 1616, ZM/L/6/107, Cheshire Archives and Local Studies.

78. Using hired post horses during the summer months, with overnight rest, an experienced rider could have arrived within two or three days. See Mark Brayshay, "Knowledge, Nationhood and Governance: The Speed of the Royal Post in Early Modern England," *Journal of Historical Geography* 24 (1998), 276.

79. Barrow, Herson, Lawes, Riden, and Seaborne, "Leisure and Culture: Plays, Sports and Customs before 1700," in Thacker and Lewis, eds., *A History of the County of Chester*, 5.2:247–55.

80. "Examination of Richard Cokley," 29 June 1616, ZQSE/13/25, Cheshire Archives and Local Studies.

81. Ibid.

82. Charity Papers, 1 April 1620, D/B/BW/1890, Somerset Archives and Local Studies.

83. "Examination of Ruthe Pittman," 20 October 1619, Q/SR/34/91, Somerset Archives and Local Studies; and "Examination of Walter Cole," 20 October 1619, SRO, Q/SR/34/110, Somerset Archives and Local Studies.

84. Kingsbury, *Records*, 3:51.

85. Wallace Notestein, Frances Helen Relf, and Hartley Simpson, eds., *Commons Debates, 1621*, 7 vols. (London, 1935) 6:8; and Emily Rose, "The End of the Gamble: The Termination of the Virginia Lotteries in March 1621," *Parliamentary History* 27 (2008), 178.

86. Larkin and Hughes, *Stuart Royal Proclamations*, 2:500–502, at 501.

87. Kingsbury, *Records*, 1:451.

88. "Examination of Ruthe Pittman," 20 October 1619, Q/SR/34/91, Somerset Archives and Local Studies; and "Examination of Walter Cole," 20 October 1619, Q/SR/34/110, Somerset Archives and Local Studies.

89. "Petition of John Bargrave to the Privy Council," April 1622, CO 1/2:4, National Archives.

90. Quoted in Cell, *English Enterprise*, 57.

91. Their concern was that the proposed contract would economically cripple the colony. "Sundry Reasons Against the Contract and Joint Stock for the Virginia and Summer Islands Tobacco," 20 March 1623, CO 1/3:10, National Archives.

92. "A Project for the Advancing of the Intended Plantation by a Means, from Which Shall Accrue a Present Profit to His Majesty," undated, CO 1/5:70, National Archives.

93. Claire S. Schen, "Constructing the Poor in Early Seventeenth-Century London," *Albion* 32 (2000), 462; Ian W. Archer, "The Charity of Early Modern Londoners," *Transactions of the Royal Historical Society* 12 (2002), 241.

94. Colley, *Captives*, 76; Wyndham Anstis Bewes, *Church Briefs: or, Royal Warrants for Collections for Charitable Objects* (London, 1896), 96; and St. Thomas the Martyr: Churchwardens' Accounts, 1 March 1619/20, P.St. T/ChW, Vol. 62, f. 9, Bristol Archives. There is a broad literature on early modern charitable giving, including Ilana Krausman Ben-Amos, *The Culture of Giving: Informal Support and Gift-Exchange in Early Modern England* (Cambridge, 2008), chapter 4. For the use of charity or church briefs more specifically, see Mark Harris, "'Inky Blots and Rotten Parchment Bonds': London, Charity Briefs and the Guildhall Library," *Historical Research* 66 (1993), 99; Mark Harris, "The Finding and Use of Brief Records," *Archives* 21 (1994), 130; and R. A. Houston, "Church Briefs in England and Wales from Elizabethan Times to 1828," *Huntington Library Quarterly* 78 (2015), 494.

95. Crashaw penned the dedicatory in the printed edition of Alexander Whitaker's 1613 sermon. See Alexander Whitaker, *Good Newes from Virginia* (1613; STC 25354), sig. B3v.

96. *Brief for Collections to Convert the Indians in Virginia* (1616; STC 4587.7).

97. The dish could of course have originated from either the Americas or the Indian subcontinent. Yet, it is intriguing to think that the collection levied for the colony could have passed through this Virginia "Indian" ware. See St. Alphage: Churchwardens' Accounts, 1580–1631, P69/ALP/B/006/MS01432/003, ff. 117, 127v, London Metropolitan Archives. For

discussion of the ambiguity of "Indian" objects, and the "early modern generalization of otherness," see Christian Feest, "The Collecting of American Indian Artifacts in Europe, 1493–1750," in Karen Ordahl Kupperman, ed., *America in European Consciousness, 1493–1750* (London, 1995), 335.

98. "Copy of Project," undated 1620, no. 206, Ferrar Papers.

99. Houston, "Church Briefs," 497.

100. This figure is likely to be much higher. By comparison, Ireland received £610 5s., the Channel Islands £431, Wales £20,281, Scotland £36, 911 13s., and foreign nations £2,089 17s.. In total, donors in London made benefactions totaling £62,265 15s. toward causes outside of England. See Jordan, *Charities of London*, 426–27.

101. "Captain Baily's Project," 21 July 1623, CO 1/2:51, National Archives.

102. Kingsbury, *Records*, 3:540.

103. William Crashaw, *A Sermon Preached in London Before the Right Honourable the Lord Lawarre* (1610; STC 6029), sigs. Ir-Iv.

104. Kingsbury, *Records*, 3:540.

105. "Copy of Project," undated 1620, no. 206, Ferrar Papers.

106. Withington, *Society in Early Modern England*, 139.

107. Francisco J. Borge, "Prayers for Purses: The Rhetoric of Compensation in the Virginia Company Sermons," *Prose Studies* 32 (2010), 208. Also, Fitzmaurice, *Humanism and America*, 111.

108. Daniel Price, *Sauls Prohibition Staide* (1609; STC 20302), sig. F2v; William Crashaw, *A Sermon Preached in London Before the Lord Lawarre* (1610; STC 6029), sig. D1r.

109. As suggested in Borge, "Prayers for Purses," 215; Crashaw, *A Sermon Preached in London Before the Right Honourable the Lord Lawarre* (1610; STC 6029), sigs. B3v-B4r.

110. Crashaw, *A Sermon Preached in London Before the Right Honourable the Lord Lawarre* (1610; STC 6029) sigs. D1v, D2r.

111. See Houston, "Church Briefs," 494, 519; Archer, "The Charity of Early Modern Londoners," 241; and Colley, *Captives*, 76.

112. Kingsbury, *Records*, 1:354.

113. "Warrant of 10 March 1616/17 to Pay John Rolfe and the Lady Rebecca £100," 10 March 1617, no. 72, Ferrar Papers.

114. Kingsbury, *Records*, 1:220, 355.

115. *Brief for Collections to Convert the Indians in Virginia* (1616; STC 4587.7). Also, Peter Walne, "The Collections for Henrico College 1616–1618," *Virginia Magazine of History and Biography* 80 (1972), 262. A copy of the brief was published in the front matter of this issue. For the original draft of the brief, see "Draught of a Letter to the Two Archbishops Concerning Virginia," undated, CO 1/2:37, National Archives.

116. Harris, "'Inky Blots,'" 103.

117. *Brief for Collections to Convert the Indians in Virginia* (1616; STC 4587.7). See also, Ian Archer, "The Arts and Acts of Memorialization in Early Modern London," in J. F. Merritt, ed., *Imagining Early Modern London: Perceptions and Portrayals of the City from Stow to Strype 1598–1720* (Cambridge, 2001), 90; Colley, *Captives*, 77; and Merritt, *Social World of Early Modern Westminster*, 268.

118. "Sundry Reasons Against the Contract and Joint Stock for the Virginia and Summer Islands Tobacco," 23 March 1623, CO 1/3:10, National Archives.

119. This manuscript survived in the Ferrar Papers and has not previously been identified as a royal letter patent. See "Copy of Project," undated 1620, no. 206, Ferrar Papers. Although by the mid-seventeenth century charity briefs were much more standardized, at this time the form and terms of such letters patent were still undefined. Therefore, we can assume that this is a version of what scholars would now recognize as a brief.

120. See below and Chapter 4. Also, St. Thomas the Martyr: Churchwardens' Accounts, 30 August–27 September 1634, P.St T/ChW, Vol. 67, f. 10, Bristol Archives; and "Annual Accounts of the Earl of Southampton," 1622–1623, no. 480, Ferrar Papers.

121. "Copy of Receipt," 2 March 1617, no. 71, Ferrar Papers.

122. For collections for Virginia, see also Bewes, *Church Briefs*, 96; Paul Griffiths, *Lost Londons: Change, Crime and Control in the Capital* (Cambridge, 2008), 284–85; and Claire S. Schen, *Charity and Lay Piety in Reformation London, 1500–1620* (Aldershot, 2002), 194–95.

123. Court of Common Council: Journals, undated September 1618, COL/CC/01/01/031, f. 396, London Metropolitan Archives.

124. All Hallows, Staining: Churchwardens' Accounts, 1618–1619, P69/ALH6/B/008/MS04956/002, ff. 261v, 271, 292v, London Metropolitan Archives.

125. St. Alphage: Churchwardens' Accounts, 1618, P69/ALP/B/006/MS01432/003, f. 127v, London Metropolitan Archives.

126. St. Christopher-le-Stocks: Churchwardens' Accounts, 1619–1623, P69/CRI/B/007/MS04423/001, ff. 91, 93v, 94, 98v, London Metropolitan Archives.

127. St. James Garlickhythe: Churchwardens' Accounts, 1618–1619, P69/JS2/B/005/MS04810/001, ff. 196, 197v, 199v, London Metropolitan Archives.

128. Edwin Freshfield, ed., *The Account Books of the Parish of St. Bartholomew's Exchange in the City of London 1596–1698* (London, 1895), 57, 63.

129. St. Helen Bishopsgate: Churchwardens' Accounts, 1618–1619, P69/HEL/B/004/MS06836, f. 95v, London Metropolitan Archives.

130. Schen, *Charity and Lay Piety*, xx (n. 95), 194–95.

131. Kingsbury, *Records*, 1:355.

132. St. Helen Bishopsgate: Churchwardens' Accounts, 1618–1619, P69/HEL/B/004/MS06836, f. 95v, London Metropolitan Archives.

133. St. Michael Cornhill: Churchwardens' Accounts, 1619–1620, P69/MIC2/B/006/MS04071/002, f. 48, London Metropolitan Archives.

134. St. Botolph Bishopsgate: Churchwardens' Accounts, 1622, P69/BOT4/B/008/MS04524/001, ff. 182, 190v, London Metropolitan Archives.

135. "Annual Accounts of the Earl of Southampton," 1622–1623, no. 480, Ferrar Papers; Walne, "Collections for Henrico College," 264–66.

136. Cambourne Parish Church: Churchwardens' Accounts, 1581–1628, P27/5/2/2, f. 164r, Kresen Kernow; and Liskeard Parish Church: Churchwardens' Accounts, 1598–1666, P126/4/1, ff. 117v, 119v, Kresen Kernow.

137. Kingsbury, *Records*, 3:117.

138. Ibid. Mary Robinson was the daughter of William Ramsay, a Freeman of the Grocers' Company, and wife of John Robinson who was a Virginia Company shareholder. She also bequeathed £500, for the use of scholarships, to the Grocers' Company. Nicholas Ferrar (junior) was an executor of her will, which, as well as her husband's connection, suggests why she might have donated to the Virginia Company. Grocers' Company Court

Minute Book, 1616–1639, MS11588/003, ff. 95, 127, Guildhall Library; Jordan, *Charities of London*, 400.

139. Kingsbury, *Records*, 3:117.

140. The titles are St. Augustine, *The City of God* and *The Works of William Perkins*. See Kingsbury, *Records*, 1:421, 3:576; Shona MacLean Vance, "Copland, Patrick (c. 1572–c. 1651)," *Oxford Dictionary of National Biography*, https://doi.org/10.1093/ref:odnb/66917; and William S. Powell, "Books in the Virginia Colony before 1624," *William and Mary Quarterly* 5 (1948), 180–81.

141. Jordan, *Charities of London*, 106.

142. *National Archives Currency Converter*, http://www.nationalarchives.gov.uk/currency-converter/.

143. Alison Games, *The Web of Empire: English Cosmopolitans in an Age of Expansion 1560–1660* (Oxford, 2008), 3–4; Jordan, *Charities of London*, 426–27; Kingsbury, *Records*, 3:537–39.

144. A purser was an officer aboard ships who was responsible for provisions and keeping accounts. Kingsbury, *Records*, 3:537–39. For some discussion of the charity of sailors, see Jordan, *Charities of London*, 44.

145. Games, *Web of Empire*, 4–6.

146. Kingsbury, *Records*, 3:89, 577.

147. The money was presented to the company at their Quarter Court on 21 November 1621. Ibid., 3:539.

148. Jordan, *Charities of London*, 106.

149. Games, *Web of Empire*, 219.

150. One document in the state papers suggests that a collection was gathered in 1627 by Christopher Levett "for their relief" in Virginia, but there is no further evidence of this. It seems more likely that this collection was for York (Maine), Levett's colonial project that never got off the ground. See Grants of Plantation, 11 February 1628, CO 1/4:38, National Archives.

151. St. Christopher-le-Stocks: Churchwardens' Accounts, 1619–1623, P69/CRI/B/007/MS04423/001, ff. 98v, 170v, London Metropolitan Archives. Also, "Annual accounts of the Earl of Southampton," 1622–1623, no. 480, Ferrar Papers; All Hallows, Staining: Churchwardens' Accounts, 1618–1619, P69/ALH6/B/008/MS04956/002, f. 292v, London Metropolitan Archives.

152. Richard Whitbourne, *A Discourse and Discovery of New-Found-Land* (1612; STC 25373).

153. Dated 30 June 1621. W. L. Grant and James Munro, eds., *Acts of the Privy Council of England, Colonial Series*, 6 vols. (Hereford, 1908), 1:37, 419; Peter E. Pope, *Fish into Wine: The Newfoundland Plantation in the Seventeenth Century* (Chapel Hill, 2004), 52; Cell, *English Enterprise in Newfoundland*, 84. There is no discussion of this scheme in either Pope or Cell.

154. St. Thomas the Martyr: Churchwardens' Accounts, 30 August–27 September 1634, P.St T/ChW, vol. 67, f. 10, Bristol Archives.

155. Richard Grosvenor, *Papers of Sir Richard Grosvenor, 1st Bart (1585–1645)*, ed. Richard Cust (Manchester, 1996), 76; Ben-Amos, *Culture of Giving*, 129.

156. His father Sir Anthony Abdy, a Virginia Company investor, and his brother Roger made identical bequests in their wills. Will of Nicholas Abdy of London, Merchant, 1642, D/DAy F4, Essex Record Office; Abbot Emerson Smith, *Colonists in Bondage: White Servitude and Convict Labor in America, 1607–1776* (Chapel Hill, 1947), 150.

157. "Petition of P. D. L. to the King," 26 June 1634, CO 1/8:19, National Archives.

158. "Project for Settling a Colony in Carolina," undated >1625, CO 1/4:37, National Archives.

159. "A Project for the Advancing of the Intended Plantation by a Means, from Which Shall Accrue a Present Profit to His Majesty," undated 1629–1630, CO 1/5:70, National Archives.

160. "Copy of Project," undated 1620, FP, no. 206.

161. "Project Concerning Virginia," CO 1/2:53, National Archives.

162. "Project by Captain Baily," 21 July 1623, CO 1/2:51, National Archives.

163. Games, *Web of Empire*, 219.

164. "Copy of Project," undated 1620, FP, no. 206; "Project Concerning Virginia," CO 1/2:53, National Archives.

Chapter 4

1. Minutes of the Court of Governors, 24 August 1618, CLC/275/MS33011/006, f. 65; Court of Common Council: Journals, undated July 1618, COL/CC/01/01/031, f. 382; and Court of Common Council: Journals, September 1618, COL/CC/01/01/031, f. 396, London Metropolitan Archives.

2. See Robert C. Johnson, "The Transportation of Vagrant Children from London to Virginia, 1618–1622," in Howard S. Reinmuth Jr., ed., *Early Stuart Studies: Essays in Honor of David Harris Willson* (Minneapolis, 1970), 137–51. Children from Christ's Hospital were also sent to the colonies. See Peter W. Coldham, *Child Apprentices in America from Christ's Hospital, London 1617–1778* (Baltimore, 1990), 11–12. Sir Nathaniel Rich and Captain John Smith estimated that 8,500 poor children were sent to Virginia between 1619 and 1625, see Sandra L. Dahlberg, "'Doe Not Forget Me': Richard Frethorne, Indentured Servitude, and the English Poor Law of 1601," *Early American Literature* 47 (2012), 22, fn. 21.

3. Grant and Munro, *Acts of the Privy Council*, 1:11. Also, Ben-Amos, *Culture of Giving*, 125.

4. Thomas Festa, "The Metaphysics of Labor in John Donne's Sermon to the Virginia Company," *Studies in Philology* 106 (2009), 94.

5. Jack P. Greene, *Pursuits of Happiness: The Social Development of Early Modern British Colonies and the Foundation of American Culture* (London, 1988), 26; Edmund Morgan, *American Slavery, American Freedom: The Ordeal of Colonial Virginia* (New York, 1975), 21.

6. For discussion of the connection between forced transportation and colonization in Virginia, see: Gaskill, *Between Two Worlds*, 98; Nicholas Canny, "The Permissive Frontier: The Problem of Social Control in English Settlements in Ireland and Virginia 1550–1650," in K. R. Andrews, N. P. Canny and P. E. H. Hair, eds., *The Westward Enterprise: English Activities in Ireland, the Atlantic, and America, 1480–1650* (Liverpool, 1978), 26; and Steve Hindle, *The State and Social Change in Early Modern England, c. 1550–1640* (Basingstoke, 2000), 164. On the forced transportation of criminals and the poor in the context of English welfare reform, see: Griffiths, *Lost Londons*, 473; A. L. Beier, *Masterless Men: The Vagrancy Problem in England 1560–1640* (London, 1985); and Paul Slack, *Poverty and Policy in Tudor and Stuart England* (London, 1988), 167; Patricia Crawford, *Parents of Poor Children in England, 1580–1800* (Oxford, 2010), 235.

7. Christopher Tomlins, *Freedom Bound: Law, Labor, and Civic Identity in Colonizing English America, 1580–1865* (Cambridge, 2010), 78–80.

8. Peter Wilson Coldham, *Complete Book of Emigrants, 1607–1660* (Baltimore, 1987), 1.

9. Canny, "The Permissive Frontier," 25.

10. Horning writes that "extreme hardships . . . characterized the first few years of James Fort's existence." See Audrey J. Horning, *Ireland in the Virginian Sea: Colonialism in the British Atlantic* (Chapel Hill, 2013), 296–97.

11. Thomas Dale to Robert Cecil, Earl of Salisbury, undated 1611, CO 1/1:26, National Archives.

12. "Copy of Letter [c. March 1611]," 1616, no. 30, Ferrar Papers.

13. Grant and Munro, *Acts of the Privy Council*, 1:10.

14. Griffiths, *Lost Londons*, 284–85.

15. Coldham, *Complete Book of Emigrants*, 12.

16. Ibid.; and "Middlesex Sessions Rolls: 1619," in John Cordy Jeaffreson, ed., *Middlesex County Records*, 4 vols. (London, 1887), 2:142–50, available at *British History Online*, http://www.british-history.ac.uk/middx-county-records/vol2/pp142-150.

17. Paget was an active member of the Virginia Company, attending five court meetings in 1619. See Kingsbury, *Records*, 1:211, 224, 261, 265, 280.

18. Clapham's transportation order contradicts the Middlesex Sessions Rolls and says he was guilty of "housebreaking" and not burglary, thus not a felony. See, "Middlesex Sessions Rolls: 1619," in Jeaffreson, ed., *Middlesex County Records*, 2:142–50, available at *British History Online*, http://www.british-history.ac.uk/middx-county-records/vol2/pp142-150; and Coldham, *Complete Book of Emigrants*, 12.

19. Coldham, *Complete Book of Emigrants*, 12.

20. Larkin and Hughes, *Stuart Royal Proclamations*, 1:378.

21. Acts of the Court of High Commission, 18 June 1635, SP 16/261 f. 189, National Archives. See also, Matthew Reynolds, *Godly Reformers and Their Opponents in Early Modern England: Religion in Norwich, c. 1560–1643* (Woodbridge, 2005), 154–55.

22. "Middlesex Sessions Rolls: 1634," in Jeaffreson, ed., *Middlesex County Records*, 3:55–57, available at *British History Online*, http://www.british-history.ac.uk/middx-county-records/vol3/pp55-57.

23. Larkin and Hughes, *Stuart Royal Proclamations*, 1:378.

24. Quoted in Alison Games, *Migration and the Origins of the English Atlantic World* (London, 1999), 82.

25. "Middlesex Sessions Rolls: 1634," in Jeaffreson, ed., *Middlesex County Records*, 3:55–57, available at *British History Online*, http://www.british-history.ac.uk/middx-county-records/vol3/pp55-57.

26. Alexandra Shepard, *Accounting for Oneself: Worth, Status, and the Social Order in Early Modern England* (Oxford, 2015), 245.

27. "Middlesex Sessions Rolls: 1634," in Jeaffreson, ed., *Middlesex County Records*, 3:55–57, available *British History Online*, http://www.british-history.ac.uk/middx-county-records/vol3/pp55-57.

28. George Sandys was convicted of highway robbery and assault in 1616 and was hanged in 1618. Roger Burrow Manning, *Swordsmen: The Martial Ethos in the Three Kingdoms* (Oxford, 2003), 158.

29. His execution at Tyburn in 1626 was so infamous that a ballad was written about it. See *The Life and Death of Mr George Sandys* (1626), reprinted in Hyder E. Rollins, ed., *A Pepysian Garland: Black-Letter Broadside Ballads of the Years 1595–1639 Chiefly from the Collection of Samuel Pepys* (Cambridge, 2012), 248–55.

30. Coldham, *Complete Book of Emigrants*, 182.

31. Griffiths, *Lost Londons*, 285, 473.

32. John Bruce, ed., *Calendar of State Papers, Domestic Series, of the Reign of Charles I: 1625–1649*, 23 vols. (London, 1858–1897), 8:262.

33. Register of Prisoners Delivered for Trial, 25 June 1635, MJ/GB/R/004, f. 200v; and Sessions Roll: Goal Delivery, undated May–June 1635, MJ/SR/795/14, London Metropolitan Archives.

34. Register of Prisoners Delivered for Trial, 2 September 1635, MJ/GB/R/004, f. 206; and Sessions Roll: Goal Delivery, undated September 1635, MJ/SR/797/13, London Metropolitan Archives.

35. Not all records have survived, and some of the Newgate records in the London Metropolitan Archives are in bad condition or missing.

36. See Garthine Walker, "Women, Theft and the World of Stolen Goods," in Garthine Walker and Jenny Kermode, eds., *Women, Crime and the Courts in Early Modern England* (London, 1994), 91.

37. "Petition of Elizabeth Cotterell," 6 August 1638, CO 1/9:125, National Archives.

38. "Petition of John Carter, a Poor Distressed Prisoner, to the Privy Council," undated 1622, CO 1/2:12, National Archives.

39. Robinson's petition was successful, and he received a certificate from the judge, Henry Marten. "Petition of Henry Robinson, a Prisoner in the Marshalsea, to the King," undated 1634–1635, CO 1/8:93, National Archives.

40. Register of Prisoners Delivered for Trial, 17 April 1634, MJ/GB/R/004, ff. 152v, 155, London Metropolitan Archives. When the womb "quickened," this meant that movement of the fetus was perceptible.

41. There is no surviving record of her crime in 1635.

42. Register of Prisoners Delivered for Trial, 20 February 1637, MJ/GB/R/004, f. 239; and Sessions Roll: Goal Delivery, January 1636/37, MJ/SR/815/91, London Metropolitan Archives.

43. Women convicted of felonies were only supposed to receive the benefit of "pleading the belly" once; in the majority of cases they were found not pregnant by matrons. See Walker, *Crime, Gender and Social Order in Early Modern England* (Cambridge, 2003), 198.

44. The same warrant as above; see Bruce, *Calendar of State Papers*, 8:262.

45. Coldham, *Complete Book of Emigrants*, 157.

46. Variant spelling Ellin Sutton. Coldham, *Complete Book of Emigrants*, 158.

47. Register of Prisoners Delivered for Trial, 10 April 1635, MJ/GB/R/004, f. 189v, London Metropolitan Archives.

48. Variant spelling Mary Burbeck. Coldham, *Complete Book of Emigrants*, 160.

49. Variant spelling Jane Prymme. Register of Prisoners Delivered for Trial, 10 April 1635, MJ/GB/R/004, f. 190v; and Sessions Roll: Goal Delivery, undated April 1635, MJ/SR/778/23–24, London Metropolitan Archives.

50. Coldham, *Complete Book of Emigrants*, 158.

51. "Items from the Gaol Delivery Register: Temp. James I," in Jeaffreson, *Middlesex County Records*, 2:210–29, available at *British History Online*, http://www.british-history.ac.uk/middx-county-records/vol2/pp210-229.

52. Schen, *Charity and Lay Piety*, 178–79.

53. Masters were responsible for the conduct and punishment of their apprentices, and others who could not be disciplined were also transported. See Grassby, *Business Community*, 43; Withington, *Politics of Commonwealth*, 215.

54. Coldham, *Complete Book of Emigrants*, 72.

55. See Griffiths, *Lost Londons*, 226, 286. See also Faramerz Dabhoiwala, "Summary Justice in Early Modern London," *English Historical Review* 121 (2006), 797.

56. Tomlins, *Freedom Bound*, 79, 237, 243.

57. If an apprentice had served with his master for a number of years, the master was more invested in him: "in the last year or two of the term . . . such apprentices were, at this stage, useful and even profitable workers, apprised of the master's trade skills or secrets." See Joan Lane, *Apprenticeship in England, 1600–1914* (London, 1996), 203.

58. Griffiths, *Lost Londons*, 287.

59. Sonia Tycko, "Consent in Apprenticeship Indentures" (paper presented at the University of Oxford Early Modern Britain Seminar, 28 January 2021).

60. Minutes of the Court of Governors, 7 August 1619, CLC/275/MS33011/006, f. 62, London Metropolitan Archives.

61. Coldham, *Complete Book of Emigrants*, 84.

62. Ibid., 84.

63. Games, *Web of Empire*, 127.

64. Coldham, *Complete Book of Emigrants*, 78.

65. Minutes of the Court of Governors, 18 October 1617, CLC/275/MS33011/006, f. 14, London Metropolitan Archives.

66. Smith, *Colonists in Bondage*, 141.

67. "Testimony," 28 April 1637, Q/SR/76/48, Somerset Archives and Local Studies.

68. Mancall, *Hakluyt's Promise*, 143–45; Winchcombe, *Encountering Early America*, 130.

69. Robert Johnson, *Nova Britannia* (1609; STC 14699), sigs. D1r-v. See also Paul Slack, "'Plenty of People': Perceptions of Population in Early Modern England" (paper presented at the University of Reading, 18 November 2010), 3–4; Griffiths, *Lost Londons*, 36–37.

70. Hindle, *State and Social Change*, 51.

71. Robert Gray, *A Good Speed to Virginia* (1609; STC 12204), sig. B4r.

72. Eburne, *A Plaine Path-Way to Plantations* (1624; STC 7471), sig. A2r.

73. Johnson, *Nova Britannia*, sig. C4r.

74. Hindle, *State and Social Change*, 55.

75. Johnson, *Nova Britannia*, sig. D1v.

76. Eburne, *A Plaine Path-Way to Plantations*, sig. K2r.

77. "Petition of Richard Eburne, a Poor Minister in County of Somerset, to Parliament," undated 1624, DD\PH/212/45, f. 50, Somerset Archives and Local Studies.

78. See Karen Ordahl Kupperman, "The Beehive as a Model for Colonial Design," in Karen Ordahl Kupperman, ed., *America in European Consciousness, 1493–1750* (London, 1995), 272–73.

79. Richard Eburne, *A Plaine Path-Way to Plantations*, sig. D1r.

80. Gray, *A Good Speed to Virginia*, sig. B4r.

81. Eburne, *A Plaine Path-Way to Plantations*, sig. K2r.

82. Larkin and Hughes, *Stuart Royal Proclamations*, 1:378.

83. Notestein, Relf, and Simpson, *Commons Debates, 1621*, 4:274–75. On the shift toward towns in search of work, see Hindle, *State and Social Change*, 41.

84. Keith Wrightson, *Earthly Necessities: Economic Lives in Early Modern Britain* (London, 2000), 148. For a recent challenge to this argument, see Robb, "Purses and the Charitable Gift."

85. Notestein, Relf, and Simpson, *Commons Debates, 1621*, 5:113–14.

86. Counseil of Virginia, *A True and Sincere Declaration of the Purpose and Ends of the Plantation in Virginia* (1610; STC 24832a), sig. A4r.

87. Sir Walter Cope to the Earl of Salisbury, undated March 1606, CP 191/120, Hatfield House.

88. "Expenses Hiring Men in Sussex," 9 March 1621, no. 232, Ferrar Papers.

89. Games, *Migration and the Origins of the English Atlantic World*, 72.

90. "Expenses Hiring Men in Sussex," 9 March 1621, no. 232, Ferrar Papers.

91. "Receipt," 2 August 1619, no. 122, Ferrar Papers.

92. Kingsbury, *Records*, 3:187.

93. "Expenses Hiring Men in Sussex," 9 March 1621, no. 232, Ferrar Papers. As the daughter of a poor man, most likely she was bound to an artisan. See Grassby, *Business Community*, 153.

94. It is difficult to know how significant these sums were to the recipients. The average wage for a day laborer between c. 1580 and c. 1630 remained fairly constant at 8d. per day, or 12d. for a craftsman. Therefore, these sums would amount to between nine and ten days' wages for the families. See Joan Thirsk, *Economic Policy and Projects: The Development of a Consumer Society in Early Modern England* (Oxford, 1978), 79; Christopher M. Burlinson, "Jonson's Money," in *The Cambridge Works of Ben Jonson Online*, http://universitypublishingonline.org/cambridge/benjonson/k/essays/jonsons_money_essay/1/.

95. "Captain Baily's Project," undated 1623, CO 1/2:53, National Archives.

96. Hindle, *State and Social Change*, 51

97. "Petition of Richard Eburne, a Poor Minister in County of Somerset, to Parliament," undated 1624, DD\PH/212/45, f. 50; Richard Eburne to Sir Robert Phelips, 21 April 1625, DD\PH/219/63, f. 121; and "Note by Richard Eburne, Vicar of Henstridge," undated 1625, DD\PH/225/15, f. 30, Somerset Archives and Local Studies. Inmates were not the tenants of properties, but those who had been taken in. An act of 1589 sought to restrict the taking in of inmates and lodgers. See Hindle, *On the Parish*, chapter 5.

98. "Minutes from the Council of New England," 31 May 1622, CO 1/2:6, National Archives.

99. "Project for Settling a Colony in Carolina," undated (after 1625), CO 1/4:37, National Archives.

100. Counterarguments were made to the petition, some of which were in turn responded to. See, "Petition of P. D. L. to the King," 26 June 1634, CO 1/8:19, National Archives.

101. Paul Slack, *Poverty and Policy in Tudor and Stuart England* (London, 1988), 127; Wrightson, *Earthly Necessities*, 216; Hindle, *State and Social Change*, 58.

102. Slack, *Poverty and Policy*, 30.

103. Hindle, *State and Social Change*, 58, 163; Paul Slack, *Poverty and Policy*, 8–9, 30, 127; Wrightson, *Earthly Necessities*, 167, 216; Griffiths, *Lost Londons*, 7; Hindle, *On the Parish*, 173, 177–79; Pamela Sharpe, "Poor Children as Apprentices in Colyton, 1598–1830," *Continuity and Change* 6 (1991), 253–54.

104. C. S. L. Davies, "Slavery and Protector Somerset; the Vagrancy Act of 1547," *Economic History Review* 19 (1966), 536; Simon P. Newman, A *New World of Labor: The Development of Plantation Slavery in the British Atlantic* (Philadelphia, 2013), 31–32; Tomlins, *Freedom Bound*, 79.

105. For an overview, see Steve Hindle and Ruth Wallis Herndon, "Recreating Proper Families in England and North America: Pauper Apprenticeship in Transatlantic Context," in Ruth Wilson Herndon and James E. Murray, eds., *Children Bound to Labor: The Pauper Apprenticeship System in Early America* (Ithaca, 2009), 28–29. Recent research by James Fisher suggests that they did usually receive some training. James Fisher, "Inventing a New Form of Labour:

Early Indentures for Parish Apprentices, 1598–1630," University of Exeter (January 2021), https://humanities.exeter.ac.uk/history/research/economicandsocialhistory/inventinganewformoflabourearlyindenturesforparishapprentices1598-1630/.

106. Hindle and Herndon, "Recreating Proper Families," 29.

107. Hindle, *On the Parish,* 205, 253.

108. Dahlberg, "'Doe Not Forget Me,'" 1, 7.

109. Counseil of Virginia, *A True and Sincere Declaration*, sig. A4r; Smith, *Colonists in Bondage*, 147.

110. Kristen Grace Lashua, "Children at the Birth of Empire, c. 1600–1760," (unpublished PhD thesis, University of Virginia, 2015), 163–64.

111. Dahlberg, "'Doe Not Forget Me,'" 6, 9–10. This bill was mentioned at a company meeting on 11 June 1621, again on 13 June 1621, and finally on 21 November 1621, but there is no evidence that the bill was ever drawn up by Edwin Sandys, Dudley Digges, and John Danvers as planned. See Kingsbury, *Records*, 1:479, 489, 555.

112. See also the company's plan, dated 4 November 1620, to produce a publication in order to solicit JPs to send youths, above the age of fifteen, as apprentices to company tenants. Kingsbury, *Records*, 1:411.

113. Court of Common Council: Journals, undated July 1618, COL/CC/01/01/031, f. 374v, London Metropolitan Archives; and Dahlberg, "'Doe Not Forget Me,'" 5. Also, "Project of the Intended Voyage to Virginia . . . Addressed to Lord Zouch," undated 1618, CO 1/1:38, National Archives.

114. Court of Common Council: Journals, 15 September 1618, COL/CC/01/01/031, f. 382, London Metropolitan Archives.

115. Court of Common Council: Journals, undated September 1618, COL/CC/01/01/031, f. 396, London Metropolitan Archives.

116. "Draft of Decree, Quarter Court," 2 February 1619/20, no. 153, Ferrar Papers; Grant and Munro, *Acts of the Privy Council*, 1:28. See also, Court of Common Council: Journals, undated September 1618, COL/CC/01/01/031, f. 396.

117. Court of Common Council: Journals, 18 December 1619, COL/ CC/01/01/032, ff. 125–26, London Metropolitan Archives; Johnson, "Transportation of Vagrant Children," 138, 140–44.

118. Sir Edwin Sandys to Sir Robert Naunton, 28 January 1620, SP 14/112, f. 86, National Archives.

119. Grant and Munro, *Acts of the Privy Council,* 1:29.

120. Court of Common Council: Journals, 18 December 18, 1619, COL/CC/01/01/032, f. 125; and Court of Common Council: Journals, 10 January 1619/20, COL/CC/01/01/032, f. 128, London Metropolitan Archives; Crawford, *Parents of Poor Children*, 235. See also Dahlberg, '"Doe Not Forget Me,"' 10; and Griffiths, *Lost Londons,* 284–86.

121. Michael J. Braddick, *State Formation in Early Modern England, c. 1550–1700* (Cambridge, 2000), 34.

122. While constables and watchmen were unpaid householders, being a beadle was a full-time paid position. See "Policing," in *London Lives 1690–1800,* https://www.londonlives.org/static/Policing.jsp.

123. Dahlberg, '"Doe Not Forget Me,"' 24–25.

124. Rachel Winchcombe, "'If You Love Me You Will Redeeme Me': Strategies of Childhood in Richard Frethorne's Letters Home," *Cultural and Social History*, 5–7. DOI: 10.1080/14780038.2020.1753286.

125. "Letter," undated April 1621, no. 239, Ferrar Papers. See also Kupperman, *Jamestown Project*, 294.

126. Court of Common Council: Journals, 19 July 1622, COL/CC/01/01/033, f. 66v, London Metropolitan Archives.

127. Lord Mayor and Court of Aldermen of London to the Council, undated October 1632, SP, 16/224, f. 157, National Archives.

128. Otherwise known as "Act for Relief of the Poor 1601" (43 Eliz 1 c 2). See Eburne, *A Plaine Path-Way to Plantations*, sig. K3v.

129. "Minutes from the Council of New England," 31 May 1622, CO 1/2:6, National Archives.

130. "Minutes from the Council of New England," 5 July–15 November 1622, CO 1/2:6, National Archives.

131. Henry Spelman was a translator for the Jamestown colonists and lived, for a time, with Powhatan. Karen Ordahl Kupperman, *Pocahontas and the English Boys: Caught Between Cultures in Early Virginia* (New York, 2019), 43.

132. "Minutes from the Council of New England," 18 February 1622/23, CO 1/2:6, National Archives. There was also a fund to transport vagrant children to Massachusetts, organized by agents Thomas Weld and Hugh Peter. See discussion in Susan Hardman Moore, *Pilgrims: New World Settlers and the Call of Home* (New Haven, 2007), 108; and Carla Pestana, *The English Atlantic in an Age of Revolution, 1640–1661* (Cambridge, MA, 2007), 187.

133. Italics mine. "Captain Harvey His Proposition Touching Virginia," undated 1629–1630, CO 1/5:22, National Archives.

134. "Certain Answers to Captain Harvey's Propositions Touching Virginia," undated 1629–1630, CO 1/5:23, National Archives.

135. Lashua, "Children at the Birth of Empire," especially chapters 5 and 6.

136. Griffiths, *Lost Londons*, 473.

137. Myddelton was president of Bridewell and Bethlem from 1613 until his death in 1631. Simon Healy, "Sir Thomas Myddelton I (c. 1556–1631)," *The History of Parliament*, https://www.historyofparliamentonline.org/volume/1604-1629/member/myddelton-sir-thomas-i-1556-1631.

138. Minutes of the Court of Governors, undated June 1619, CLC/275/MS33011/006, f. 127, London Metropolitan Archives.

139. Minutes of the Court of Governors, 25 September 1618, CLC/275/MS33011/006, ff. 72; Minutes of the Court of Governors, 3 October 1618, CLC/275/MS33011/006, f. 74, London Metropolitan Archives.

140. Minutes of the Court of Governors, 24 August 1618, CLC/275/MS33011/006, f. 63, London Metropolitan Archives.

141. Coldham, *Complete Book of Emigrants*, 18.

142. The "deputy" was a paid deputy to the watch, so that householders could avoid service. Minutes of the Court of Governors, 10 October 1618, CLC/275/MS33011/006, f. 75, London Metropolitan Archives; Coldham, *Complete Book of Emigrants*, 18, 39.

143. Beier, *Masterless Men*, 167.

144. Minutes of the Court of Governors, 26 February 1619, CLC/275/MS33011/006, f. 101; Minutes of the Court of Governors, 3 July 1619, CLC/275/MS33011/006, f. 130v, London Metropolitan Archives.

145. Schen, *Charity and Lay Piety*, 191.

146. Braddick, *State Formation,* 113.

147. Minutes of the Court of Governors, undated July 1627, CLC/275/MS33011/006, f. illegible, London Metropolitan Archives.

148. Minutes of the Court of Governors, undated September 1627, CLC/275/MS33011/006, f. illegible, London Metropolitan Archives.

149. It is possible that Robinson was kept for another relation with the same name. Truelove donated £400 to the colony in July 1623 for the colony's relief. See Minutes of the Court of Governors, undated July 1627, CLC/275/MS33011/006, f. illegible, London Metropolitan Archives; Kingsbury, *Records*, 4:246.

150. Samuel Hartlib, *Londons Charity Inlarged, Stilling the Orphans Cry* (1650; Wing H993). Quoted in Paul Slack, *From Reformation to Improvement: Public Welfare in Early Modern England* (Oxford, 1999), 82. Note that Slack gives the date as 1649, which is suggested by a marginal note on one copy of the text according to the *English Short Title Catalogue*.

151. Charles Webster, *Samuel Hartlib and the Advancement of Learning* (Cambridge, 1970), 91, 98. For details of their collaboration, see "Title Page, in Hartlib's Hand," 1642, 15/1/13A-B; "Ms Title Page," 1642, 15/1/12A-B: 12B BLANK; "List of Recipients of New Comenian Book," undated, 23/13/1A-2B: 2B BLANK; and "Ephemerides 1639, Part 2," 1639, 30/4/9B-18A, Hartlib Papers, University of Sheffield. For the printed texts, see: Samuel Hartlib, *England's Thankfulness* (1642; Wing E3057); John Drury, *A Motion Tending to the Public Good of This Age and Posteritie* (1642; Wing D2874); and Johann Amos Comenius, *A Reformation of Schooles* (1642; Wing C5529).

152. S. A. Baron, "Sparke, Michael (*b.* in or before 1586, *d.* 1653)," *Oxford Dictionary of National Biography,* https://doi.org/10.1093/ref:odnb/37997; and "Minutes," 1634, Fa/AC4, Kent History and Library Centre.

153. Michael Sparke, *Greevous Grones for the Poore* (1621; STC 12391), sigs. A3v, C1r–v.

154. Michael Sparke, *The Poore Orphans Court, or Orphans Cry* (1636; STC 21509), sig. A3v. By "kept in a cage," Sparke was referring to a real form of punishment for vagrancy. See Schen, *Charity and Lay Piety,* 10.

155. Sparke, *Poore Orphans Court*, sig. B1v.

156. Ibid., sigs. A3v, B2r. For parochial funds spent on convivial meals, see Schen, *Charity and Lay Piety,* 149–50.

157. James Horn, *Adapting to a New World: English Society in the Seventeenth-Century Chesapeake* (London, 1994), 25; Newman, *New World of Labor,* 63.

Chapter 5

1. James VI and I, *A Counterblaste to Tobacco* (1604; STC 14363), sig. A3v.

2. See Sarah Augusta Dickson, *Panacea or Precious Bane: Tobacco in Sixteenth Century Literature* (New York, 1954), 105–6; Marcy Norton and Daviken Studnicki-Gizbert, "The Multinational Commodification of Tobacco, 1492–1650: An Iberian Perspective," in Mancall, ed., *The Atlantic World and Virginia*, 254–57; Marcy Norton, *Sacred Gifts, Profane Pleasures: A History of Tobacco and Chocolate in the Atlantic World* (Ithaca, 2008), 48–50; Goodman, *Tobacco in History,* 147.

3. Norton, *Sacred Gifts*, 183–84; Dickson, *Panacea or Precious Bane*, 53–54, 57–80; Ivan Gaskell, "Tobacco, Social Deviance, and Dutch Art in the Seventeenth Century," in Wayne E. Franits, ed., *Looking at Seventeenth-Century Dutch Art: Realism Reconsidered* (Cambridge,

1997), 68–77. The text in question is John Gerard, *The Herball or Generall Historie of Plantes* (1633; STC 11751), ff. 356–61.

4. Hollis, *Absence of America*, 66. For the proliferation of tobacco houses, see Working, *Imperial Polity*, 148–50.

5. Beverly Lemire, *Global Trade and the Transformation of Consumer Cultures: The Material World Remade, c. 1500–1820* (Cambridge, 2017), 191.

6. Carole Shammas, "Changes in English and Anglo-American Consumption from 1550 to 1800," in John Brewer and Roy Porter, eds., *Consumption and the World of Goods* (London, 2003), 179.

7. Lauren Working, "Locating Colonization at the Jacobean Inns of Court," *Historical Journal* 61 (2017), 14.

8. Michael Ziser, "Sovereign Remedies: Natural Authority and the 'Counterblaste to Tobacco,'" *William and Mary Quarterly* 62 (2005), 739–40.

9. See MacMillan, *Atlantic Imperial Constitution*, chapter 4.

10. As the attention of historians has turned toward the consumption of tobacco and other intoxicants, they have shown that not only were these products integrative to early modern empires and corporations, but political culture too. See Phil Withington, "Introduction: Cultures of Intoxication," *Past & Present* 222 (2014), 27; Phil Withington, "Intoxicants and Society in Early Modern England," *Historical Journal* 54 (2011), 631–57; and Steve Pincus, "'Coffee Politicians Does Create': Coffeehouses and Restoration Political Culture," *Journal of Modern History* 67 (1995), 807–34.

11. For discussion of patents and monopolies in the Jacobean era, see John Cramsie, "Commercial Projects and the Fiscal Policy of James VI and I," *Historical Journal* 43 (2000), 345–64; and Thirsk, *Economic Policy and Projects*, 99–100. On the Levant Company currant monopoly, see Brenner, *Merchants and Revolution*, 65–66; and Pauline Croft, "Parliamentary Preparations, September 1605: Robert Cecil, Earl of Salisbury on Free Trade and Monopolies," *Parliamentary History* 6 (1987), 127–32.

12. Horning, *Ireland in the Virginian Sea*, 298; William M. Kelso, Beverly Straube, and Daniel Schmidt, eds., *2007–2010 Interim Report on the Preservation Virginia Excavations at Jamestown, Virginia* (Richmond, 2012), 10, 36–37.

13. Melissa N. Morris, "Cultivating Colonies: Tobacco and the Upstart Empires, 1580–1640" (unpublished PhD thesis, Columbia University, 2017), 81–82.

14. See "Lord Sackville's Papers Respecting Virginia, 1613–31, I," *American Historical Review* 27, no. 3 (April 1922): 493–538, at 526. For discussion of impositions on Spanish tobacco and the revenue generated for the Crown, see Anthony R. Rowley, "How England Learned to Smoke: The Introduction, Spread and Establishment in England before 1640" (unpublished PhD thesis, University of York, 2003), 222–31.

15. Rolfe was one of the passengers with the "Third Supply," who, following a shipwreck, landed at Bermuda. Goodman, *Tobacco in History*, 134–35; Morris, "Cultivating Colonies," 209–10.

16. See Table 1.

17. Kingsbury, *Records*, 3:221.

18. For the figure in 1631, see C. G. A. Clay, *Economic Expansion and Social Change: England 1500–1700*, 2 vols. (Cambridge, 1984), 2:168; John Harvey to the Privy Council, 20 February 1633, CO 1/6:73, National Archives.

19. Withington, "Intoxicants and Society," 637; Carole Shammas, *The Pre-Industrial Consumer in England and America* (Oxford, 1990), 79.

20. Horn, *Adapting to a New World*, 140; Shammas, *Pre-Industrial Consumer*, 267–68.

21. Horn, *Adapting to a New World*, 142–44, 186, 291.

22. Ibid., 24–25; Morgan, *American Slavery*, 297.

23. Melissa Morris has suggested several reasons why the Virginia colonists were less successful. They were further from the Spanish Empire, so the advances made in techniques were slower to reach them; they were also slower to acquire enslaved laborers, with the desired skills; and the local Virginia Indians were practiced in the cultivation of *N. rustica*, not *N. tabacum*. Morris, "Cultivating Colonies," 99–100.

24. European botanists first thought tobacco was a type of henbane, hence its name. See Gerard, *Herball*, f. 356; and Morris, "Cultivating Colonies," 76.

25. MacMillan, *Atlantic Imperial Constitution*, 86.

26. Lemire, *Global Trade*, 199.

27. Susan Campbell Anderson, "A Matter of Authority: James I and the Tobacco War," *Comitatus: A Journal of Medieval and Renaissance Studies* 29 (1998), 143. For a seventeenth-century attribution to Ralegh, see John Josselyn, *An Account of Two Voyages to New-England* (1674; Wing J1091), f. 75.

28. Nancy Cox and Karin Dannehl, *Perceptions of Retailing in Early Modern England* (Woodbridge, 2007), 157.

29. Goodman, *Tobacco in History*, 37.

30. Ibid., 141; Ziser, "Sovereign Remedies," 724.

31. Neville Williams, "England's Tobacco Trade in the Reign of Charles I," *Virginia Magazine of History and Biography* 65 (1957), 406.

32. Kingsbury, *Records*, 3:392.

33. Ibid., 3:195.

34. C.T., *An Advice How to Plant Tobacco in England* (1615; STC 23612).

35. "Account for Our Tobacco Garden," 16 February 1619, no. 101, Ferrar Papers.

36. Henry Bluett, London, to Richard Weeks, Wiveliscombe, 19 March 1613, DD\SF/10/3/15, Somerset Archives and Local Studies. For discussion of the processes of tobacco cultivation in England, see Joan Thirsk, *The Agrarian History of England and Wales*, 8 vols. (Cambridge, 1967–2000), 5.1:168.

37. "Memorandum [of Items for Virginia]," undated 1621, no. 348, Ferrar Papers; Kingsbury, *Records*, 3:92.

38. Larkin and Hughes, *Stuart Royal Proclamations*, 1:457–60. Tobacco was also banned in Ireland. See Thirsk, *Agrarian History*, 5.2:527.

39. Thirsk, *Agrarian History*, 5.2:342.

40. MssCol 2799, f. 39, Smyth of Nibley Papers, New York Public Library.

41. 17 August 1626, Grant and Munro, *Acts of the Privy Council*, 1:107.

42. John Josselyn mentions "horse tobacco" as one of three varieties of merchantable tobacco, "having a broad long leaf piked at the end." The others were "round pointed Tobacco" and "sweet scented Tobacco." The variety of Peru tobacco described in John Gerard's *Herball* appears to match this description. See Francis South, Kelstern (Lincolnshire) to the Privy Council, 27 August 1626, SP 16/34, f. 68, National Archives; John Josselyn, *An Account of Two Voyages to New England* (1674; Wing J1091), f. 75; and Gerard, *Herball*, f. 357.

43. Gerard, *Herball*, f. 358.

44. For the early development of tobacco shops and the accompanying advertising imagery in England, see Catherine Molineux, "Pleasures of the Smoke: 'Black Virginians' in Georgian London's Tobacco Shops," *William and Mary Quarterly* 64 (2007), 338–39.

45. Cox and Dannehl, *Perceptions of Retailing*, 157. On the emergence of specialized tobacco shops, see Working, *Imperial Polity*, 148.

46. Examples in E178, National Archives. For the introduction of the licenses, see Grant and Munro, *Acts of the Privy Council*, 1:191–92; Larkin and Hughes, *Stuart Royal Proclamations*, 2:387–89. The proclamation stated that as of February 1634, "none but men of sufficiency, and such as shall bring certificate of their meetness" would be allowed to retail tobacco. See further discussion below.

47. John Taylor, *The Works of John Taylor the Water Poet* (1630), Ih D718 626, f. 70, Beinecke Library.

48. Kingsbury, *Records*, 4:233. Whether Marshall was principally a tobacco seller, or whether he used this imagery to entice customers, is unclear. In the Museum of London there are dozens of trade tokens from the mid- and late seventeenth century that use the device of the tobacco roll. See, for example, The Tobacco Roll, 1648–1673, 96.66/1050 (issued for John Nelson in Southwark); and The Tobacco Roll, 1648–1673, NN17484 (issued for a shop in Fore Street), Museum of London.

49. Molineux, "Pleasures of the Smoke," 344.

50. Ibid., 347.

51. The New Virginia, 1648–1673, N2090 (inscription: "At the New Virginne/ In Pankcrose Lane"); The Black Boy, 1653, 96.66/621; The Black Boy, 1648–1673, 96.66/276, Museum of London.

52. Molineux, "Pleasures of the Smoke," 348. While Molineux is talking here about a later period, I think her findings are still relevant.

53. Tanya Pollard, "The Pleasures and Perils of Smoking in Early Modern England," in Sander L. Gilman and Zhou Xun, eds., *Smoke: A Global History of Smoking* (London, 2004), 43.

54. Thomas Allen, *The History and Antiquities of London, Westminster, Southwark and Parts Adjacent*, 5 vols. (London, 1839), 2:423.

55. "Northamptonshire and Warwickshire," undated 1636, E178/5557; "Camarthen," 16 September 1638, E178/5933, National Archives.

56. Kingsbury, *Records*, 4:120.

57. "Examination," undated 1621, Q/SR/38/27, Somerset Archives and Local Studies.

58. Letter dated 30 August 1605. J. Rutherford, ed., *The Miscellaneous Papers of Captain Thomas Stockwell, 1590–1611*, 2 vols. (Southampton, 1632), 1:48.

59. Emphasis my own. "Book of Examinations," 2 April 1627, SC9/3/11, ff. 139–41, Southampton Archives.

60. Anon., *English Customs* (1628; STC 10408.6).

61. "Sussex," 23 September 1639, E 178/5685, National Archives.

62. Gerard, *Herball*, f. 358.

63. Withington, "Intoxicants and Society," 636.

64. Pollard, "Pleasures and Perils of Smoking," 39; Goodman, *Tobacco in History*, 61; Sander L. Gilman & Zhou Xun, "Introduction" in Gilman & Xun, *Smoke: A Global History of Smoking*, 11–13.

65. Goodman, *Tobacco in History*, 43.

66. "Book of Examinations," 2 April 1627, SC9/3/11, f. 139, Southampton Archives.

67. "Recipe Book by Mrs Corlyon," 1606, MS 213, f. 156, Wellcome Library.

68. "Recipe Book by Johanna St John," 1680, MS 4338, f. 209, Wellcome Library; Gerard, *Herball*, ff. 360–61.

69. James VI and I, *A Counterblaste to Tobacco*, sig. A3r–v.

70. Notestein, Relf, and Simpson, *Commons Debates 1621*, 3:148.

71. Rabb, *Enterprise and Empire*, 294; *Third Charter of Virginia* (1612) in Brown, ed., *Genesis of the United States*, 2:540–53.

72. John Walter, "Public Transcripts, Popular Agency and the Politics of Subsistence in Early Modern England," in Michael J. Braddick and John Walter, eds., *Negotiating Power in Early Modern Society: Order, Hierarchy, and Subordination in Britain and Ireland* (Cambridge, 2001), 146–47.

73. Goodman, *Tobacco in History*, 47, 64.

74. Withington, *Politics of Commonwealth*, 175.

75. James VI and I, *A Charter to Tobacco Pipe Makers* (30 July 1619); and *A Proclamation Commanding Conformity to His Majesty's Pleasure, Expressed in His Late Charter to the Tobacco-Pipe-Makers* (27 May 1620), in Larkin and Hughes, *Stuart Royal Proclamations*, 1:478–80. On 24 July 1618 Philip Foote, who was also named in the pipe company charter, received a patent for tobacco pipe clay for a term of twenty-one years at a rent of £6 3s. 4d. In 1621, it was cited as a monopoly and Foote apparently gave it up, citing that "'it hath undone him.'" See Notestein, Relf, and Simpson, *Commons Debates 1621*, 7:460.

76. James VI and I, *Charter to Tobacco Pipe Makers* (1619), in Larkin and Hughes, *Stuart Royal Proclamations*, 1:478–80.

77. See Table 1, above.

78. Jeremy Boulton, "London 1540–1700," in Peter Clark, ed., *The Cambridge Urban History of Britain, Vol. 2: 1540–1840* (Cambridge, 2000), 325–26.

79. Alice Clark, *The Working Life of Women in the Seventeenth Century* (London, 1992), 192.

80. James VI and I, *A Proclamation . . . to the Tobacco-Pipe-Makers* (1620), in Larkin and Hughes, eds., *Stuart Royal Proclamations*, 1:478–80.

81. "Petition of Samuel Twiford and a Multitude of Others," undated 1621, HL/PO/JO/10/13/9, Parliamentary Archives. This petition has been incorrectly dated as 1624–1625 in the Parliamentary Archives, but the records of the House of Commons date it to 1621. See Notestein, Relf, and Simpson, *Commons Debates 1621*, 2:461. On 20 August 1620, the king declared that it was lawful to break into houses in order to enforce the patent. Notestein, Relf, and Simpson, *Commons Debates 1621*, 7:461.

82. For a discussion of paternalism in petitions, see Brodie Waddell, *God, Duty and Community in English Economic Life, 1660–1720* (Woodbridge, 2012), 132–33.

83. Conrad Russell, *Parliament and English Politics, 1621–1629* (Oxford, 2003), 61.

84. Ian Archer, "The London Lobbies in the Later Sixteenth Century," *Historical Journal* 31 (1988), 43.

85. C. Dent, "'Generally Inconvenient': The 1624 *Statute of Monopolies* as Political Compromise," *Melbourne University Law Review* 33 (2009), 441.

86. Peacey, *Print and Public Politics*, 270–73. For the revocation of the patent, see Larkin and Hughes, *Stuart Royal Proclamations*, 1:514. The company was given a new charter

in 1634 and a second company was incorporated in 1663. See David Atkinson and Adrian Oswald, "London Clay Tobacco Pipes," *Journal of the British Archaeological Association* 32 (1969), 2–3.

87. See Waddell, *God, Duty and Community*, 127; and Peacey, *Print and Public Politics*, 8.

88. J. P. Sommerville, "Ideology, Property and the Constitution," in Richard Cust and Ann Hughes, eds., *Conflict in Early Stuart England: Studies in Religion and Politics, 1603–1642* (London, 1989), 57; and Russell, *English Politics*, 61.

89. Russell, *English Politics*, 57–58, 123.

90. David Underdown, *A Freeborn People: Politics and the Nation in Seventeenth-Century England* (Oxford, 1996), 32.

91. Williams, "England's Tobacco Trade," 404; Underdown, *Politics and the Nation*, 26; Russell, *English Politics*, 93–94.

92. MacMillan, *Atlantic Imperial Constitution*, 103. At this time, free trade was understood as unrestricted trading, meaning no monopolies or patents, and not the absence of tariffs, such as custom and impost. For background on earlier debates during Jacobean parliaments on free trade, see Theodore K. Rabb, "Free Trade and the Gentry in the Parliament of 1604," *Past & Present* 40 (1968), 165–73; Robert Ashton, "The Parliamentary Agitation for Free Trade in the Opening Years of the Reign of James I," *Past & Present* 38 (1976), 40–55; and Pauline Croft, "Free Trade and the House of Commons, 1605–6," *Economic History Review* 28 (1975), 17–27.

93. "Sandys, Sir Edwin," undated 1604, MS22, f. 5, Senate House Library.

94. Elizabeth Foster, ed., *Proceedings in Parliament, 1610*, 2 vols. (New Haven, 1966), 2:159.

95. Foster, *Proceedings in Parliament*, 2:152–53, 160.

96. Wrightson, *Earthly Necessities*, 199–200.

97. Notestein, Relf, and Simpson, *Commons Debates 1621*, 5:514; Rabb, "Free Trade and the Gentry," 172.

98. Notestein, Relf, and Simpson, *Commons Debates 1621*, 2:286–87.

99. See Tables 1 and 2.

100. Notestein, Relf, and Simpson, *Commons Debates 1621*, 2:286–87.

101. For discussions of corporate interests and competition in parliament, see David L. Smith, *The Stuart Parliaments, 1603–1689* (London, 1999), 112.

102. Notestein, Relf, and Simpson, *Commons Debates 1621*, 3:7–11. Cranfield joined the company in 1612 and Digges in 1609.

103. 3 May 1621, HMSO, *Journal of the House of Commons*, 1:605. Rich joined the Virginia Company in 1619, Mildmay in 1622, Drake in 1612, Cavendish in 1612, and Montagu in 1607.

104. Ibid., 1:622. In a proclamation issued in 1625, shortly after he acceded to the throne, Charles I restricted all tobacco imports from the English colonies. However, another proclamation issued in 1627 allowed small quantities of Spanish tobacco to be imported, up to 50,000 pounds per year. *A Proclamation Touching Tobacco* (9 April 1625) and *A Proclamation Touching Tobacco* (17 February 1627), in Larkin and Hughes, *Stuart Royal Proclamations*, 2:11–12, 131–36.

105. Kingsbury, *Records*, 4:53–55. For a detailed discussion of the contract, see MacMillan, *Atlantic Imperial Constitution*, 95–100.

106. Brenner, *Merchants and Revolution*, 105.

107. In 1631, there were at least 31 women in the trade. Dated 15 July 1631, Grant and Munro, *Acts of the Privy Council*, 1:164–65.

108. "Commissioners of the King's Revenue," 1626–1627, MS195, vol. 1, f. 11r, Senate House Library. For the most in-depth analysis of this project and its implications, see Tom Cogswell, "'In the Power of the State': Mr Anys's Project and the Tobacco Colonies, 1626–1628," *English Historical Review* 123 (2008), 35–64. Similar schemes were proposed in 1613, 1630, and 1631. See M. W. Beresford, *Time and Place: Collected Essays* (London, 1985), 228.

109. "Petition of apothecaries, grocers, and other retailers . . . to the king," undated 1625, SP 16/14, f. 16, National Archives. On 19 January 1619, James VI and I issued a proclamation that ordered that alehouse-keepers "shall not utter nor willingly suffer to be uttered, drunk, taken, and tippled any Tobacco within his said House, Shop, Cellar, or other place thereunto belonging." See Larkin and Hughes, *Stuart Royal Proclamations,* 1:411.

110. From 1632 onward, the duties on tobacco (subsidy and impost) were 4d. and 6d. per pound of tobacco from Virginia and the West Indies respectively. Alexander G. Taylor, "Tobacco Retail Licences and State Formation in Early Modern England," *Economic History Review* 72 (2019), 18.

111. Taylor, "Tobacco Retail Licences," 5–6.

112. "A Letter Intended for the Lords in Answer of the Tobacco Letter but Not Sent," 4 July 1632, 44M69/G3/1114/1–2, Hampshire Archives and Local Studies.

113. 14 August 1633, Grant and Munro, *Acts of the Privy Council*, 1:191–92.

114. Taylor, "Tobacco Retail Licences," 8, 14–16. The first registered licensee was Henry Shelley, who paid £6 13s. 4d. for the privilege. See Beresford, *Time and Place*, 229–30. Unfortunately, the original of this document has been missing in the National Archives since 1993.

115. The collectors of the rents, Thomas Mewtie, sometimes spelled Meautys, received £179 3s. 4d.. "Book of Accounts of Thomas Mewtie for Fines Received upon Licences," 12 February 1635–10 February 1636, E 122/218/26, f. 10v, National Archives.

116. Taylor notes that not only did this scheme demand cooperation, it had the effect of "deepening the presence of the state" in localities. Taylor, "Tobacco Retail Licences," 13–14.

117. Depositions were taken in several English and Welsh counties, including Carmarthenshire, Cornwall, Devon, Durham, Gloucestershire, Norfolk, Northamptonshire, Oxfordshire, Pembrokeshire, Sussex, Worcester City, and Yorkshire. See E 178, National Archives.

118. J. Willis Bund, *Worcestershire County Records: Quarter Sessions Rolls,* 3 vols. (Worcestershire County Council: Worcester, 1899), 1.2:549.

119. "Devonshire," undated September 1637, E 178/5239, National Archives.

120. Ibid.

121. Withington, "Intoxicants and the Early Modern City," in Steve Hindle, Alexandra Shepard, and John Walter, eds., *Remaking English Society: Social Relations and Social Change in Early Modern England* (Woodbridge, 2013), 151–52.

122. "Yorkshire," 3 November 1638, E 178/5793, National Archives.

123. *A Proclamation for Preventing of the Abuses Growing by the Unordered Retailing of Tobacco* (13 October 1633), in Larkin and Hughes, *Stuart Royal Proclamations,* 2:387–89; Rowley, "How England Learned to Smoke," 378.

124. "Yorkshire," 3 November 1638, E 178/5793, National Archives. See discussion in Rowley, "How England Learned to Smoke," 375.

125. "Commission . . . in Worcestershire," 6 October 1636, E 178/296, National Archives.

126. "Yorkshire," 25 October 1638, E 178/5793, National Archives; 10 March 1638, E/178/5284, National Archives.

127. "Carmarthenshire," 16 September 1638, E 178/5933, National Archives.

128. "Oxfordshire," 20 January 1640, E 178/5594, National Archives.

129. Braddick, *State Formation*, 87.

130. These are the only examples of these kinds of responses that I have found in depositions taken in Devon, Durham, Gloucestershire, Norfolk, Worcester and York.

131. Todd Butler, "Power in Smoke: The Language of Tobacco and Authority in Caroline England," *Studies in Philology* 106 (2009) 109–10. In 1637, there were also outbreaks of opposition in Helston (Cornwall) and Stepney (London). See Taylor, "Tobacco Retail Licences," 20.

132. "Gloucestershire: Tewkesbury," 30 January 1636, E 178/5315, National Archives. For the Wyatts, see below, and for the Tracys, see Gethyn-Jones, "Berkeley Plantation."

133. Local bailiffs investigated whether one John Ayres was growing tobacco in Winchcombe and reported back to Tracy, who informed the government. John Barkesdale and John Cowell to Sir John Tracy, Winchcombe, 29 August 1626, SP 16/34, f. 82; Sir John Tracy to Sec. Conway, Todington, 29 August 1626, SP 16/34, f. 81, National Archives. See Thirsk, *The Rural Economy of England: Collected Essays* (London, 1984), 282.

134. Martin, the second son of Sir Samuel, was named after his maternal grandfather, Martin Culpepper of Worcestershire. Martin had close ties to this region through his mother, Mercy Culpepper, and his father, who was JP in 1600, sheriff from 1618 to 1619, and MP for Worcestershire in 1604, 1614, and 1621. See Glyn Redworth and Ben Coates, "Sandys, Samuel (1560–1623)," *The History of Parliament*, http://www.historyofparliamentonline.org/volume/1558-1603/member/sandys-samuel-1560-1623. For their investments see Rabb, *Enterprise and Empire*, 372. For the outline of this family tree see Rabb, "Sandys, Sir Edwin (1561–1629)," *The History of Parliament*, http://www.historyofparliamentonline.org/volume/1604-1629/member/sandys-sir-edwin-1561-1629. The website *Tudor Place* also has useful genealogical research for the Sandys family: http://www.tudorplace.com.ar/SANDYS.htm.

135. James Ellison, "Sandys, George (1578–1644)," *Oxford Dictionary of National Biography*, http://oxforddnb.com/view/article/24651?docPos=2; and Warren M. Billings, *A Little Parliament: The Virginia General Assembly in the Seventeenth Century* (Richmond, 2004), 126.

136. "Petition of the Grocers and Others," 23 November 1640, HL/PO/JO/10/1/43, Parliamentary Archives.

137. Rowley, "How England Learned to Smoke," 326.

138. "Petition of William George and Others," 25 January 1641, HL/PO/JO/10/1/49, Parliamentary Archives. Taylor discusses the arguments made in terms of rights. Taylor, "Tobacco Retail Licences," 21.

139. Although Taylor suggests 1640, the above petition indicates a slightly later date. Taylor, "Tobacco Retail Licences," 20.

140. King James to the Council in Virginia, 28 September 1634, CO 1/8:28, National Archives.

141. Kingsbury, *Records*, 1:218–19, 258.

142. It came into effect on 2 February 1620. See James VI and I, *A Proclamation to Restrain the Planting of Tobacco in England and Wales* (30 December 1619), in Larkin and Hughes, *Stuart Royal Proclamations*, 1:457–60.

143. Kingsbury, *Records*, 1:290–93.

144. 28 September 1619, Grant and Munro, *Acts of the Privy Council*, 1:27.

145. 3 September 1626, Grant and Munro, *Acts of the Privy Council*, 1:09; 10 July 1627, Grant and Munro, *Acts of the Privy Council*, 1:115.

146. Thirsk, *Rural Economy*, 279. This local resistance persisted for decades. An act issued in 1660 gave local officers only ten days to destroy any discovered English tobacco. "Act Prohibiting the Planting, Setting or Sowing of Tobacco in England or Ireland," 29 December 1660, SP 29/24, f. 215, National Archives.

147. Thirsk, *Economic Policy and Projects*, 90.

148. For the friction between state authority and local office holding, see Braddick, *State Formation*, 39–40.

149. 17 April 1621, HMSO, *Journal of the House of Commons*, 1:579. For discussion of Coke's attitude toward property, see David Chan Smith, *Sir Edward Coke and the Reformation of the Laws: Religion, Politics and Jurisprudence, 1578–1616* (Cambridge, 2014), 260–61. For the patent on woad, see Thirsk, *Economic Policy and Projects*, 98.

150. For the levy on tobacco as well as currants in 1604, see Pauline Croft, "Fresh Light on Bate's Case," *Historical Journal* 30 (1987), 531.

151. "John Deanes, Vicar v. Hen. Somerscale: Tithe," 1619, GDR/B4/3/1342; and "John Deanes, Vicar v. John Stratford: Tithe," 1619, GDR/B4/3/1343, Gloucestershire Archives. Vicars were usually entitled to collect "small tithes" on livestock, wool, and usually non-cereal crops. However, Joan Thirsk notes that "custom provided many exceptions to these general rules." See Thirsk, *Agrarian History*, 5.2:390–402.

152. Notestein, Relf, and Simpson, *Commons Debates 1621*, 5:263.

153. 17 April 1621, HMSO, *Journal of the House of Commons*, 1:579. For Coke's attitude toward the use of proclamations, see Smith, *Sir Edward Coke*, 274.

154. Withington, *Politics of Commonwealth*, 56.

155. "Petition of Richard Quyney, William Allen, and Others, Merchants and Planters Trading to Virginia," 18 September 1641, CO 1/5:84, National Archives. If 300,000 pounds of English tobacco really was planted in 1630, at the cost of 8d. per lb., it could have fetched more than £1.2 million in the marketplace, according to contemporary prices. For the retail price, see deposition of Thomas Birke in "Gloucestershire: Tewkesbury," 30 January 1636, E 178/5315, National Archives.

156. Bund, *Worcestershire County Records*, 1.2:563–64.

157. Dated 24 July 1634, Grant and Munro, *Acts of the Privy Council*, 1:204; dated 10 July 1635, Grant and Munro, *Acts of the Privy Council*, 1:208.

158. Dated 27 June 1638, Grant and Munro, *Acts of the Privy Council*, 1:232.

159. Thirsk, *Rural Economy*, 277.

160. "John Bestpitch, Curate v. Giles Ridler: Tithe," 1638, GDR/B4/3/1349, Gloucestershire Archives.

161. Dated 13 July 1639, Grant and Munro, *Acts of the Privy Council*, 1:261.

162. John Walter and Keith Wrightson, "Dearth and the Social Order," *Past & Present* 71 (1976), 24. For traditional interpretations of the "moral economy," see Andy Wood, *Riot, Rebellion and Popular Politics in Early Modern England* (Basingstoke, 2002), esp. 95–99; E. P. Thompson, "The Moral Economy of the English Crowd in the Eighteenth Century," *Past & Present* 50 (1971), 76–136.

163. Walter, "Public Transcripts," 139.

164. Scholars have usually associated the moral economy with food riots in times of dearth and the English domestic economy. See note 162, above. A further exception is the discussion of imported calico in Waddell, *God, Duty and Community*, 215–16.

165. "John Bestpitch, Curate v. Giles Ridler: Tithe," 1638, GDR/B4/3/1349, Gloucestershire Archives.

166. Wood, *Riot, Rebellion and Popular Politics*, 177.

167. "Gloucestershire: Tewkesbury," 30 January 1636, E 178/5315, National Archives.

168. Thirsk, *Rural Economy*, 271–72; Thirsk, *Economic Policy and Projects*, 136, 141.

169. "Gloucestershire: Tewkesbury," 30 January 1636, E 178/5315, National Archives; and Table 2, above.

170. National Archives, "Currency Converter, 1270–2017," https://www.nationalarchives.gov.uk/currency-converter/

171. Williams, "Gloucestershire Tobacco Trade," 145; Waddell, *God, Duty and Community*, 208.

172. HMSO, *Journal of the House of Commons*, 7:112, 130. For the act, see C. H. Firth and R. S. Rait, eds., *Acts and Ordinances of the Interregnum, 1642–1660*, 3 vols. (London, 1911), 2:580.

173. "Petition of Merchants and Others Trading to Virginia," 28 May 1653, CO 1/12:5, National Archives.

174. "Petition of Merchants, Adventurers of London, Trading to Virginia," 20 July 1653, CO 1/12:8, National Archives.

175. "Reasons Why the English Plantations Abroad Ought to Be Encouraged . . . ," 28 May 1653, CO 1/12:5.1, National Archives.

176. HMSO, *Journal of the House of Commons*, 7:301. Also, "Petition of Divers Poor People in and Near Winchcombe," 30 June 1654, SP 18/72, f. 161, National Archives.

177. Bernard Capp, "Deference, Defiance, and Tobacco" (paper presented at Plebeian Cultures in Early Modern England: Thirty-Five Years after E. P. Thompson Conference, University of Warwick, 21 February 2009).

178. "Report of 'the Assistants to the Committee of the Council for the Treasuries,'" 6 April 1654, CO 1/12:18, National Archives.

179. "Ordinance Empowering Commissioners to Put into Execution the Act Forbidding the Planting of English Tobacco (1 April 1652)," 11 April 1654, SP 18/98, f. 265, National Archives.

180. In the 1650s, there was also localized violence in opposition to the excise duty. See Caroline Boswell, *Disaffection and Everyday Life in Interregnum England* (Woodbridge, 2017), 167–68.

181. "The State of the Business in Gloucestershire," 11 June 1654, SP 18/72, f. 76, National Archives.

182. "Petition of Divers Poor People in and Near Winchcombe," 30 June 1654, SP 18/72, f. 161, National Archives.

183. Henry Lawrence to the governor of the city of Gloucester, 14 June 1654, SP 25/75, ff. 374–75, National Archives. The "governor" was probably Thomas Pury, MP and mayor. Lawrence followed this up with further orders in 1655 for local officeholders to use their powers against those who "did obstinately persist in planting Tobacco." See, Lawrence to the officers in the counties, 7 June 1655, SP 25/76A, f. 65, National Archives. Also, Lawrence to Gloucestershire JPs, 27 March 1655, SP 25/76A, f. 22, National Archives.

184. Almost forty years before, in 1619, there was the first-recorded instance of commercial-scale tobacco cultivation in Gloucestershire, as discussed above. "Petition of Divers Poor People in and Near Winchcombe," 30 June 1654, SP 18/72, f. 161, National Archives.

185. "Petition of Merchants and Mariners, Trading to the English Plantation in America," 6 March 1655 CO 1/12:37, National Archives.

186. "Reasons by the Petitioners . . . for Suppressing the Planting of Tobacco in England," 24 March 1655, CO 1/12:40, National Archives.

187. "Representation of the Merchants and Traders to Virginia to the Council of the Lord Protector," 27 April 1655, CO 1/12:43, National Archives.

188. Jo. Beaman, Gloucester, to Thomas Colclough or Mr. John Jeffries, 31 July 1658, SP 18/182, f. 87, National Archives. Capp notes that unlike participants in "anti-improvement" riots, those who protested in Gloucestershire during 1658 were actually "pro-improvement." Capp rightly notes that the planters drew upon ideas of custom, but he does not discuss the prevalence of similar claims at the beginning of the century, or the much longer history of tobacco cultivation prior to 1619. See Capp, "Deference, Defiance, and Tobacco," 1.

189. Jo. Beaman, Gloucester, to Thomas Colclough or Mr. John Jeffries, 31 July 1658, SP 18/182, f. 87, National Archives.

190. Thirsk, *Agrarian History,* 5.1:169.

191. "Adding to Reasons Laid Out in the Merchants' Petitions," 7 June 1655, SP 18/98, f. 29, National Archives.

192. A pole was equivalent to 5 1/2 yards. *Manuscripts and Special Collections: Measurements*, https://www.nottingham.ac.uk/manuscriptsandspecialcollections/researchguidance/weightsandmeasures/measurements.aspx. HMSO, *Journal of the House of Commons*, 8:199, 212; "Act," 29 December 1660, SP 29/24, f. 215, National Archives.

193. Sir Martin Noel to Lord Ashley, 1 July 1663, SP 29/76, f. 8, National Archives.

194. George Louis Beer, *The Old Colonial System, 1660–1754,* 2 vols. (New York, 1912), 1:40.

195. Quoted in Thirsk, *Agrarian History,* 5.1:170.

196. Thirsk, *Agrarian History,* 5.1:170, 5.2:343.

197. See Table 2, above.

198. "Gloucestershire: Tewkesbury," 30 January 1636, E 178/5315, National Archives.

199. John C. Coombs, "The Phases of Conversion: A New Chronology for the Rise of Slavery in Early Virginia," *William and Mary Quarterly* 68 (2011), 334.

200. Berthold Laufer, *Introduction of Tobacco into Europe* (Chicago, 1924), 65.

201. Waddell, *God, Duty and Community*, 208.

202. Working suggests that in the Jacobean period tobacco transformed from a "'pagan' plant" to "'Virginia leaf' grown by enterprising Protestant planters." Working, *Imperial Polity*, 157.

Conclusion

1. Bolton, Croot, and Hicks, "Acton: Churches," 7:35–39, *British History Online,* http://www.british-history.ac.uk/vch/middx/vol7/pp35-39.

2. The wall panel reads, "On the above shelf is placed every Sunday bread for the sick and poor to be distributed after the service according to the will of Viscountess Conway in the year 1637; and Mrs Sarah Crayle in the year 1730."

3. See Diane K. Bolton, Patricia E. C. Croot, and M. A. Hicks, "Acton: Charities for the Poor," 7:49–50, *British History Online,* http://www.british-history.ac.uk/vch/middx/vol7/pp49-50.

4. Corinne Fowler, *Green Unpleasant Land: Creative Responses to Rural England's Colonial Connections* (Leeds, 2020), 28.

5. "The Lady Viscountess Conway, Her Accounts," April 1633, CR 114 A/769, Warwickshire County Record Office; Smith, "John Donne and the Conway Papers," 39–40.

6. Armstrong, *Writing North America*, 197; Burnard, "Empire Matters," 92; Canny, "Introduction," in Louis, ed., *Oxford History of the British Empire*, 1:5, 32.

7. "Petition of P. D. L. to the king," 26 June 1634, CO 1/8:19, National Archives.

8. "Examination," 4 August 1630, Q/SR/62/12, Somerset Archives and Local Studies. For Katherine Conway's beaver hat, see the Introduction.

SOURCES

Archive and Library Collections

BEINECKE RARE BOOKS, YALE UNIVERSITY, NEW HAVEN

Ig D799 605e	*Poems* by Michael Drayton (1613)
Ih D718 626	*Works of John Taylor the Water Poet* (1630)

BRISTOL ARCHIVES

Common Council
St. Ewen's: Churchwardens' Accounts
St. Thomas the Martyr: Churchwardens' Accounts

BRITISH LIBRARY, LONDON

Add. 70505	Portland Papers
Eg. MSS 2087	Dover Miscellaneous Papers

CHESHIRE ARCHIVES AND LOCAL STUDIES, CHESTER

Mayor of Chester
Quarter Sessions

CLOTHWORKERS' COMPANY, LONDON

Book of Orders of Court

DRAPERS' COMPANY, LONDON

Court of Assistants' Minutes

ESSEX RECORD OFFICE, CHELMSFORD

Records of Abdy Family

FOLGER SHAKESPEARE LIBRARY, WASHINGTON D. C.

G.b.10	Drue Burton Collection of State Papers
	Papers of the Bagot Family
V.b.198	"Miscellany of Lady Anne Southwell"

GLOUCESTERSHIRE ARCHIVES, GLOUCESTER

City of Gloucester Corporation Minutes
Gloucester Diocesan Records

GUILDHALL LIBRARY, LONDON

Fishmongers' Company
Grocers' Company
Haberdashers' Company
Merchant Taylors' Company
Vintners' Company

HAMPSHIRE ARCHIVES AND LOCAL STUDIES, WINCHESTER

Justices of the Peace: Hampshire

HATFIELD HOUSE LIBRARY AND ARCHIVES, HATFIELD

Cecil Papers

HUNTINGTON LIBRARY, SAN MARINO

Ellesmere Papers
Hastings Papers

KENT LIBRARY AND HISTORY CENTRE, MAIDSTONE

Faversham Borough Records

KRESEN KERNOW ("CORNWALL CENTRE"), REDRUTH

Cambourne Parish Church: Churchwardens' Accounts
Liskeard Parish Church: Churchwardens' Accounts

LONDON METROPOLITAN ARCHIVES

All Hallows, Staining: Churchwardens' Accounts
Corporation of London
Diocese of London
Middlesex Sessions of the Peace
Royal Hospitals of Bridewell and Bethlem
St. Alphage: Churchwardens' Accounts
St. Botolph Bishopsgate: Churchwardens' Accounts
St. Christopher-le-Stocks: Churchwardens' Accounts
St. Giles Cripplegate: Parish Records
St. Helen Bishopsgate: Churchwardens' Accounts
St. James Garlickhythe: Churchwardens' Accounts
St. Michael Cornhill: Churchwardens' Accounts

MAGDALENE COLLEGE, UNIVERSITY OF CAMBRIDGE

Ferrar Papers

MANCHESTER CENTRAL LIBRARY

Court Leet of Manchester

MERCERS' COMPANY, LONDON

Acts of Court

NATIONAL ARCHIVES, KEW

CO 1	America and the West Indies, Colonial Papers
C 2	Court of Chancery: Series I
C 8	Court of Chancery: Pleadings before 1714, Mitford
E 122	Exchequer: Kings Remembrancer: Particulars of Customs Accounts
E 178	Exchequer: Kings Remembrancer: Special Commissions of Enquiry
PROB 11	Prerogative Court of Canterbury Wills
SP 14	State Papers Domestic, James I
SP 16	State Papers Domestic, Charles I
SP 18	Council of State, Navy Commission and Related Bodies: Orders and Papers
SP 25	Council of State: Books and Accounts
SP 29	Secretaries of State: State Papers Domestic, Charles II
STAC 8	Court of Star Chamber: Proceedings, James I

NEW YORK PUBLIC LIBRARY

Smyth of Nibley Papers

NORFOLK RECORD OFFICE, NORWICH

Norwich City Library Donation Book
City of Norwich Records
Great Yarmouth Borough: Town Clerk

PARLIAMENTARY ARCHIVES, WESTMINSTER

Records of the House of Lords

RECORD OFFICE FOR LEICESTERSHIRE, LEICESTER AND RUTLAND, WIGSTON

Records of the Corporation of Leicester

SENATE HOUSE LIBRARY, UNIVERSITY OF LONDON

MS 22	Sandys, Sir Edwin
MS 195	"Commissioners of the King's Revenue, 1626–1627"

SHEFFIELD UNIVERSITY LIBRARY

Hartlib Papers

SOMERSET ARCHIVES AND LOCAL STUDIES, TAUNTON

Charity Papers
Sanford Family of Nynehead

Phelips Manuscripts
Quarter Sessions: Sessions Rolls

SOUTHAMPTON ARCHIVES

Quarter Sessions

WARWICKSHIRE COUNTY RECORD OFFICE, WARWICK

Seymour Family of Ragley Hall Papers
Warwick Corporation Minute Book

WELLCOME TRUST, LONDON

MS 213 "Recipe Book by Mrs Corlyon, 1606"
MS 4338 "Recipe Book by Johanna St John, 1680"

WELLS CATHEDRAL LIBRARY AND ARCHIVES

Wells Convocation Act Book

WILTSHIRE AND SWINDON HISTORY CENTRE, CHIPPENHAM

Act Book

Museum Collections

Jamestown Settlement, Williamsburg
Museum of London
Victoria and Albert Museum, London

INDEX

ACKNOWLEDGMENTS

Now that this book is completed, it's truly a pleasure to be able to thank all of the people who have supported me along the way. I am indebted to Jason Peacey for his kindness and encouragement. This project has morphed into something quite different from the PhD dissertation I first embarked on under his supervision at University College London. I hope that Jason will see in this book the great influence that he has had, and continues to have, on my work. Stephen Conway also guided me through unfamiliar historical territory and provided valuable support and feedback. I am very grateful for the friendship and generosity of the wider community of scholars in the Department of History at UCL, including Alessandro de Arcangelis, Marjolein van Bavel, Catherine Beck, Alys Beverton, Margot Finn, Shane Horwell, Edward Legon, Eleanor Robson, and Adam Smith. My PhD examiners Brodie Waddell and Malcolm Gaskill helped to clarify my thoughts about how I would develop the thesis into a book. I would like to thank them both for their continued support since that day.

This book has traveled with me between institutions and I am very grateful for the encouragement and collegiality of all my colleagues. My time on the Leverhulme Trust funded PEIC project at the University of Kent greatly influenced my analysis. I would like to thank Aske L. Brock, Peter Good, Liam Haydon, William Pettigrew, Edmond Smith, and David Veevers for their continued support and friendship. Two and a half years as a Hallsworth Research Fellow at the University of Manchester has also left its mark on this book. Rachel Winchcombe is an excellent editor, while Sasha Handley supported and mentored me through a tricky stage of postdoc life and offered sound advice on the book. Embarking on an academic career can be an isolating experience, so I'd like to thank Rachel and Sasha for their friendship too. I'm also grateful to Natalie Zacek, who offered advice on framing the manuscript at a crucial stage of its development.

During the time that I completed my PhD and since then, I have felt lucky to be part of a warm community of scholars. I would like to thank the many friends and colleagues who have helped to make the journey bringing this book to completion much more enjoyable. Susan Dwyer Amussen, Gina Bennett, Eilish Gregory, Jack Sargeant, and Sonia Tycko very kindly read and commented on drafts of chapters. The following people generously shared their expertise: Mark Brayshay, Bernard Capp, Marjorie K. McIntosh, Michael Scott, Bly Straube, Alexander Taylor, and Lauren Working. My appreciation also to Alex Craven for assisting me with Latin translations.

I would like to extend my heartfelt gratitude to the many archivists and librarians who patiently assisted me on my search through archives in England and the United States, including during my time as a fellow at the Huntington Library and Folger Shakespeare Library. I would especially like to thank Sarah Whale at Hatfield House for providing copies of documents when the coronavirus pandemic made visiting the archive impossible; Julia Wood at Wells Cathedral Library and Archives, who shared her office and expertise with me on a wintry day in 2018; and Sarah Powell at the Folger for helping me solve a Latin riddle. I visited Historic Jamestowne twice, in 2015 and 2017, and I would like to thank all of the staff, James Horn, Merry Outlaw, and David Givens in particular, for welcoming me to the site and allowing me to explore the collections.

At the University of Pennsylvania Press, I am indebted to Jill Twist and Noreen O'Connor-Abel for their careful copyediting, and Bob Lockhart, Peter Mancall, and the two anonymous reviewers for providing supportive and incisive feedback. The completion of this book was made possible by the generous support of the Society of Colonial Wars Fellowship in Memory of Kenneth R. LaVoy Jr., established by the Society of Colonial Wars in the State of Florida and administered by Florida Atlantic University.

A section of Chapter 2 uses material from my article "Women Investors and the Virginia Company in the Early Seventeenth Century," *Historical Journal* 62 (2019), 853–74, published by Cambridge University Press. Chapter 4 draws on some material from "'Poore Soules': Migration, Labor, and Visions for Commonwealth in Virginia," my contribution to Paul Musselwhite, Peter C. Mancall, and James Horn, eds., *Virginia 1619: Slavery and Freedom in the Making of English America* (Chapel Hill, 2019), 133–49. Both are reproduced here with permission.

Over the last eight years, I've spent several months abroad and many weeks working away from home. Henry has been by my side throughout this journey. His love, good humor, and the home we built together has helped to make the completion of this book a pleasure rather than a chore. My family, Deborah, Andrew, Naomi, and Isaac, are just as loving and supportive. For all my hard work, I wouldn't be where I am without him or them. I have no doubt that conversations with my great-grandmother, Alfreda, led to me becoming a historian. She has always indulged my interest in the past, and I dedicate this book to her.

CPSIA information can be obtained
at www.ICGtesting.com
Printed in the USA
LVHW101157300622
722323LV00001B/1/J

9 781512 822991